COMPUTERS OUR LIFELINE

6

Based on NEP

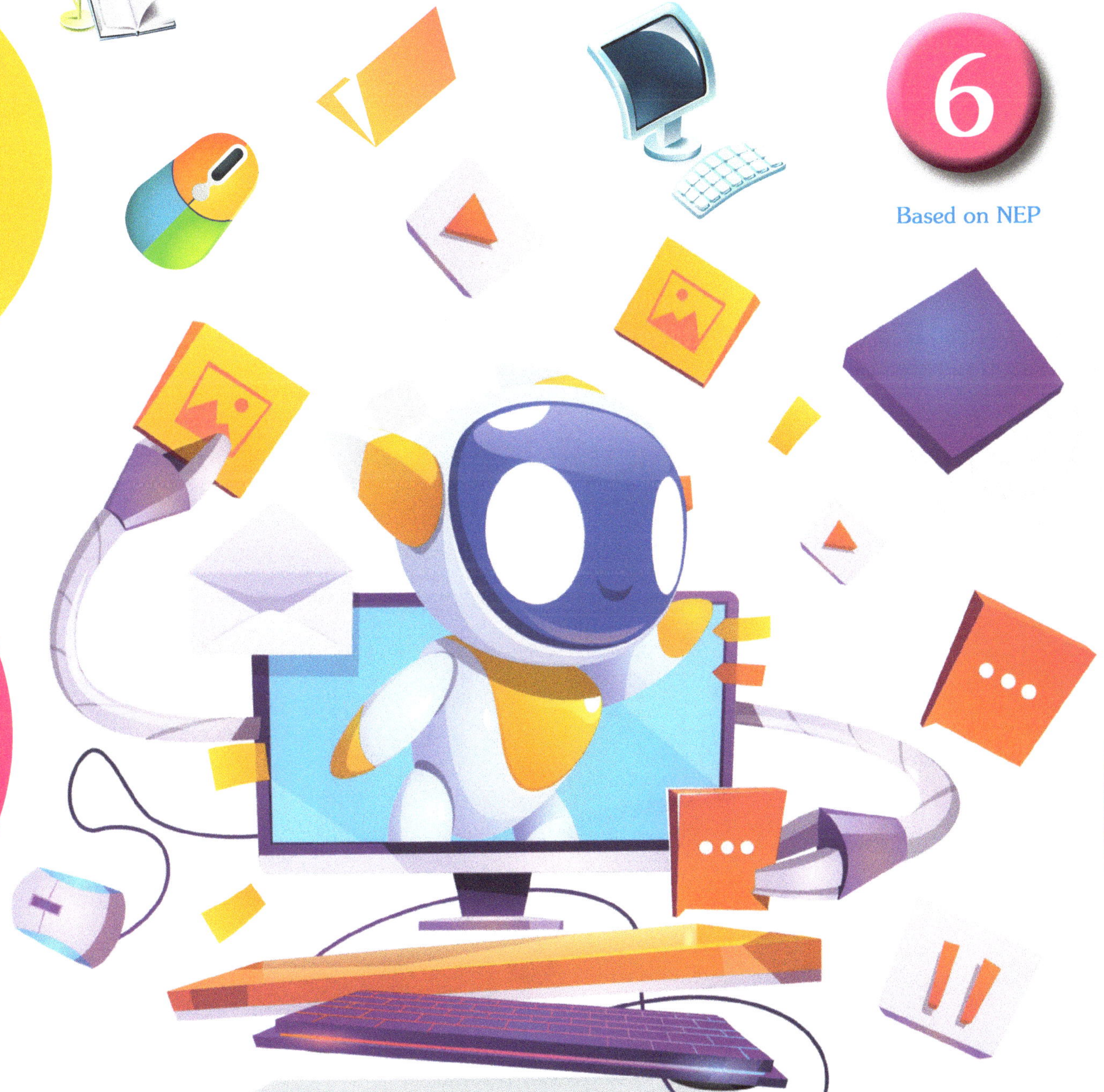

MANOJ PUBLICATIONS

COMPUTERS
Our Lifeline - 6

Publisher:
MANOJ PUBLICATIONS
761, Main Road, Burari, Delhi-110084 (INDIA)
Mobile : 09999476076, 09868112194,
08178823569, 08178854810
Email : info@manojpublications.com

For online shopping visit our website :
Website : www.sawanonlinebookstore.com

ISBN : 978-81-310-1644-2

Concept:
Puneet Gupta
M.B.A. (William & Mary, U.S.A.)

Edited by:
Davinder Singh Minhas
Rohan Kumar

PREFACE

This is the Age of Computers. In every nook and corner of the globe, computers have made their presence felt, be it school, office, post office, bank, shop, mall, hotel, restaurant, airport, railway station, Metro station and so on. Needless to say, they have become our lifeline as we can't do anything without them. In order to keep pace with the modern world, it is important to familiarise our children with computer applications right from the start. They ought to be taught the uses of computer in a lucid, interesting and enjoyable style: from basic to intermediate to advanced level.

Keeping in view the requirements of students, all the books in the series—Computers : Our Lifeline—have been designed to meet the purpose of acquiring a sound in-depth knowledge on computers with their uses. The contents of the books are based entirely on recently approved NEP (National Educational Policy).

The chapters in all the books contain a fairly good amount of illustrations which make the text very easy to understand. There are many computer books flooding the market. Our books are the books with a difference in order that they are well equipped with exhaustive exercises which test a student's mental horizon by making him take Formative Assessment as well as Summative Assessment. The knowledge of the latest software with their applications and types of computer language have been made available. Nay, students have been introduced to coding, the process of designing computer apps. The main goal of books in the series is to make a student computerate, *i.e.* computer literate.

We sincerely hope that all the books in this series will prove fruitful both to students and teachers. We shall be highly pleased to receive constructive suggestions in order to make the series more qualitative in the forthcoming editions.

– Author

CONTENTS

1 Fundamentals of Computer

In this chapter, we will learn:

⇒ About computer
⇒ Terms related to computer
⇒ Working of computer
⇒ Various hardware devices like Input, Output, Processing and Storage devices

INTRODUCTION

In today's world, computers have reshaped our life almost everywhere. Today for every activity whether personal, e.g., operating personal savings bank account or business-related, e.g., selling any product or services; in some or the other way, we rely on the computer system.

Due to the growing dependency on computers, every small and big organizations and other business companies have started offering computer-based service. Furthermore, the advancement of communications, electronic service networks, and multimedia have opened a new door for companies by providing an effective way of business processing, payment transfer, and service delivery.

Hence, we can say that there has been an enormous increase in the use of computers. Let us review the term computer and terms related to computer.

What is a Computer?

In simple terms, a computer is an electronic device that processes data, converting it into information that is useful to people.

Hence, we can formally define a computer as:

An electronic device that performs diverse operations with the help of instructions to process the data in order to achieve desired results.

Computer

Terms Related To Computer

There are some common terms related to the computer system.

Data : Data is an individual unit that contains raw materials which do not carry any specific meaning. It is the input given to the computer. The data may contain facts, numbers, images and sounds.

Processing : Data processing is the collection and manipulation of items of data to produce meaningful information.

Information : Information is organized or classified data, which has some meaningful values for the receiver. Information is the processed data on which decisions and actions are based.

User : The person who uses the computer and the information generated by it is called a user.

Hardware : Hardware is the term given to all the physical and mechanical equipment attached together to make a computer system. Examples of hardware in a computer are the Processor, Memory Devices, Monitor, Printer, Keyboard, Mouse, and the Central Processing Unit.

Software : Software is a program that performs different commands given by a user. The hardware components can function only when software components are added to the computer system. Software is an intangible part of hardware and controls the sequence of operations.

THE WORKING OF A COMPUTER

A computer is an electronic device that (1) accepts data, (2) processes data, (3) generates output and (4) stores data. The concept of generating output (information) from the input (data) is also referred to as input-process-output concept.

Input : The computer accepts input (data) from the user via an input device, like a keyboard. The data can be characters, word, text, sound, images, document, etc.

Process : The computer processes the input data. For this, it performs some actions on the data by using the instructions or program given by the user. The action could be an arithmetic or logic calculation, editing, modifying a document, etc. During processing, the data, instructions and the output are stored temporarily in the main memory of the computer.

Output : The output is the result generated after the processing of data. The output is in the form of text, sound, image, document, etc. The computer displays the output on a monitor, sends output to the printer for printing, sends the output on speakers for sound, etc.

Storage : The input data, instructions and output are stored permanently in the secondary storage devices like a disc or drive. The stored data can be retrieved later, whenever needed.

The input-process-output-storage concept of the computer is explained as follows:

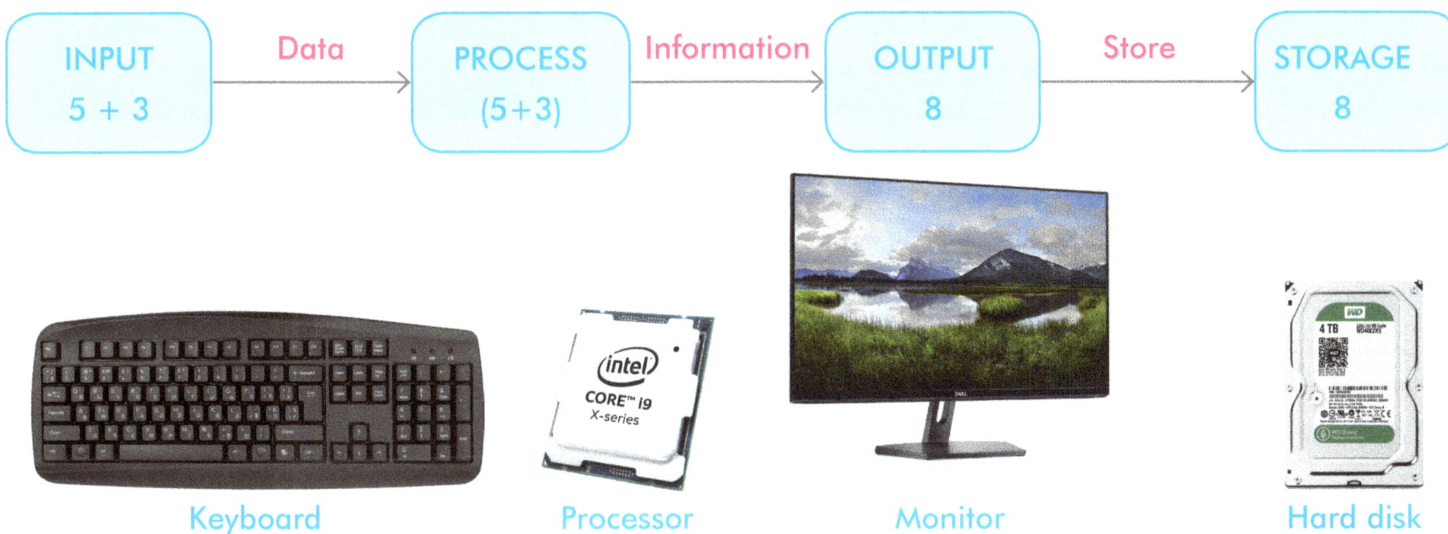

INPUT DEVICES

The devices which are used to input the data and the programs in the computer are known as Input Devices. Input devices read data and convert them into a form recognisable by the computer. They are mainly the external devices connected from outside to the computer system.

Users can enter data and instructions into a computer through a variety of input devices.

Let us read about these input devices in detail.

Keyboard

A keyboard is a common input device. It is provided along with the computer; it is used for entering the text data with the help of the different types of keys present on it. When you press a key on your keyboard, a signal travels through the keyboard cable to your computer. When the data is being typed, the computer displays a character on the monitor or processes an instruction.

Keyboard

A computer keyboard is comprised of different types of keys like Numeric keys (0-9), Alphabetic keys (A-Z & a-z), Function keys (F1-F12), Symbolic keys (%, #, < >, @, ?, *) and Special keys (Enter key, Spacebar, Caps lock, Tab key, Shift key, etc.) There are different types of keyboards. The most popular type is the QWERTY design, which is based on typewriter keyboards.

Mouse

Mouse

A mouse is an input device that fits under the palm of your hand comfortably. It is used to draw and select the objects on the computer screen. It is also called a pointing device. A mouse consists of two buttons and a scroll wheel. The bottom of the mouse is flat and contains a mechanism that detects the movement of the mouse.

Mouse Pointer

Whenever you move the mouse in any direction, the pointer on display the screen moves in the same direction. This pointer is called mouse pointer. There are many different types of computer mouses. Both the wired and wireless mouse are popular and good for working with the computer.

Joystick

A joystick is also a pointing device which is mainly used to play and control the actions of video games on the computer. The device features a directional pad for moving characters or objects up, down or to the left or right, and several buttons that execute a variety of game-related tasks.

Joystick

Scanner

Scanner

A scanner is an input device that accepts paper document as an input. It is used to input data directly into the computer from the source document without copying and typing the data. The input data to be scanned can be a picture, a piece of text or a mark on paper.

A scanner is only able to send information to the computer and cannot receive information from the computer like a printer.

Light Pen

Light Pen

It looks like a pen, which works as a pointing device. It is used to select objects on the display screen. With the help of a light pen, we can also draw figures directly on the screen. The Computer Aided Design (CAD) applications commonly use light pens to draw directly on the screen.

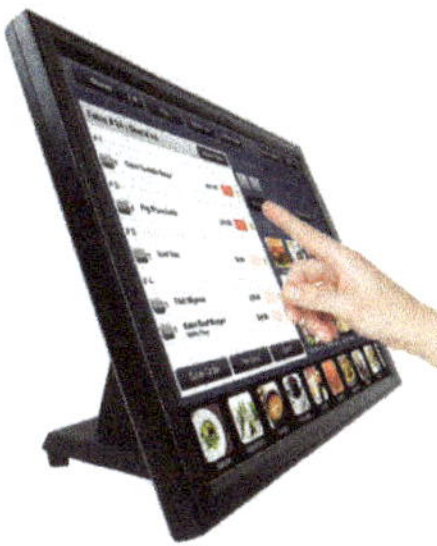

Touch Screen

It helps us to enter input by simply touching the screen. Here the input is recorded when a finger comes in contact with the screen. This finger acts as the pointing device. We use touch screens generally in the ATMs of banks.

Bar Code Reader

Bar Code Reader

A Bar Code Reader is a device used for reading bar coded data (data in the form of light and dark lines). Bar coded data is generally used in labelling goods, numbering books, etc. It may be a handheld scanner or may be embedded in a stationary scanner.

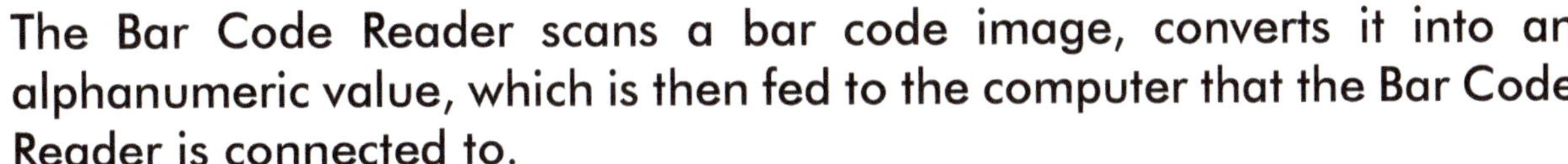

The Bar Code Reader scans a bar code image, converts it into an alphanumeric value, which is then fed to the computer that the Bar Code Reader is connected to.

Digital Camera

Digital Camera

A digital camera is an input device that allows users to take pictures and store photographed images digitally, instead of on traditional film. After taking the photograph, you can download a copy of the image from the digital camera to the hard disk of the computer. Many mobile devices such as smartphones, PDAs and portable media players often have built-in digital cameras.

Microphone

Microphone

A microphone is an input device to input sound that is stored in a digital form. It is used for various applications such as adding sound to a multimedia presentation or for mixing music.

MICR Reader

Magnetic Ink Character Recognition Reader (MICR Reader)

The MICR is a scanner that recognises numeric data printed with magnetically charged ink. The MICR reader detects characters and converts them into digital data. It is used on bank cheques and deposit slips.

The MICR serves as a deterrent to fraud, as a photocopied cheque will not be printed with magnetic ink.

Web Cam

Web Cam

A Web camera (or web cam) is a real-time camera that enables a user to capture videos and still images, make video telephone calls, etc. Web cameras usually come with software that helps you set up and use the Web camera.

PROCESSING

System Unit

Processing means an action taken by the computer on data to convert it into meaningful information. The main processing is done inside the system unit. The system unit is the box-like case that contains the electronic components of the computer that are used to process data.

Motherboard

Motherboard

The motherboard serves as a single platform to connect all the parts of a computer together. It connects the CPU, memory, hard drives, optical drives, video card, sound card, and other ports and expansion cards directly or via cables. It can be considered as the backbone of a computer.

Processor

Processor

The processor, also called a (Central Processing Unit), is the electronic component that interprets and carries out the basic instructions that operate the computer. Like your brain, the CPU is the brain of the computer which manages all the operations of the computer.

All types of processing is done by the CPU which receives the input from input devices and processes it before providing the processed result (information) to the output devices.

Components of Processor

Processors contain a Control Unit (CU) and an Arithmetic Logic Unit (ALU). These two components work together to perform processing operations.

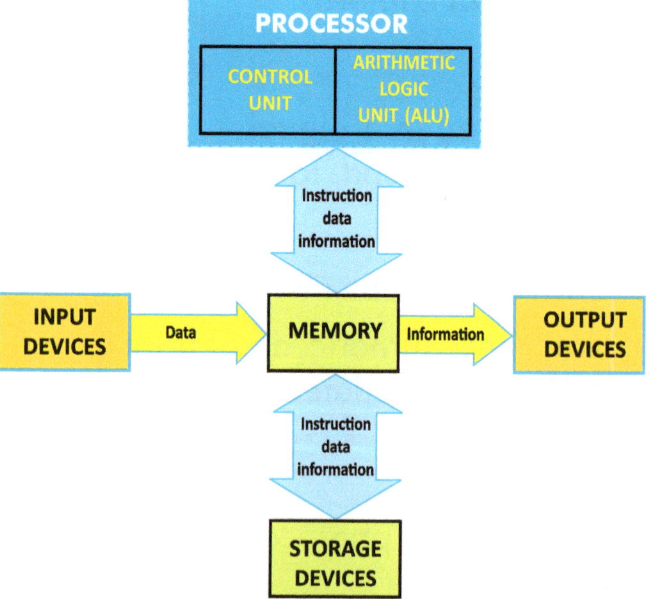

Most devices connected to the computer communicate with the processor to carry out a task. When a user starts a program, its instructions transfer from a storage device to memory. Data needed by programs enters memory from either an input device or from a storage device. The control unit interprets and executes instructions in memory, and the ALU performs calculations on the data in memory. Resulting information is stored in memory, from which it can be sent to an output device or a storage device for future access, as needed.

ALU : This unit consists of two subsections namely Arithmetic Section and Logic Section.

Arithmetic Section

The function of arithmetic section is to perform arithmetic operations like addition, subtraction, multiplication, and division. All complex operations are done by making repetitive use of the above operations.

Logic Section

The function of logic section is to perform logic operations such as comparing, selecting, matching, and merging of data.

Control Unit : This unit controls the operations of all parts of the computer but does not carry out any actual data processing operations.

Functions of this unit are –

It is responsible for controlling the transfer of data and instructions among the other units of a computer. It manages and coordinates all the units of the computer.

It obtains the instructions from the memory, interprets them, and directs the operation of the computer. It communicates with Input/Output devices for the transfer of data or results from storage. It does not process or store data.

Memory

A memory is just like a human brain. It is used to store data and instructions. Computer memory is the storage space in the computer, where data is to be processed and instructions required for processing are stored.

Memory is primarily of three types –

Cache Memory

Cache memory is a very high-speed semiconductor memory which can speed up the CPU. It acts as a buffer between the CPU and the main memory. It is used to hold those parts of data and program which are most frequently used by the CPU. The parts of data and programs are transferred from the disk to cache memory by the operating system, from where the CPU can access them.

Primary Memory (Main Memory)

Primary memory holds only those data and instructions on which the computer is currently working. It has a limited capacity and data is lost when power is switched off. It is generally made up of a semiconductor device. These memories are not so fast as registers. The data and instruction required to be processed resides in the main memory. It is divided into two subcategories, namely RAM and ROM.

Secondary Memory

This type of memory is also known as external memory or non-volatile namely it is slower than the main memory. It is used for storing data/information permanently. CPU directly does not access this memory, instead it is accessed via input-output routines. The contents of secondary memory are first transferred to the main memory, and then the CPU can access it. For example, disk, CD-ROM, DVD, etc.

Ports

Ports are slots on the motherboard into which a cable of external device is plugged in.

Examples of external devices attached via ports are the mouse, keyboard, monitor, microphone, speakers, etc.

A port is also a programmatic docking point through which information flows from a program to the computer or over the Internet.

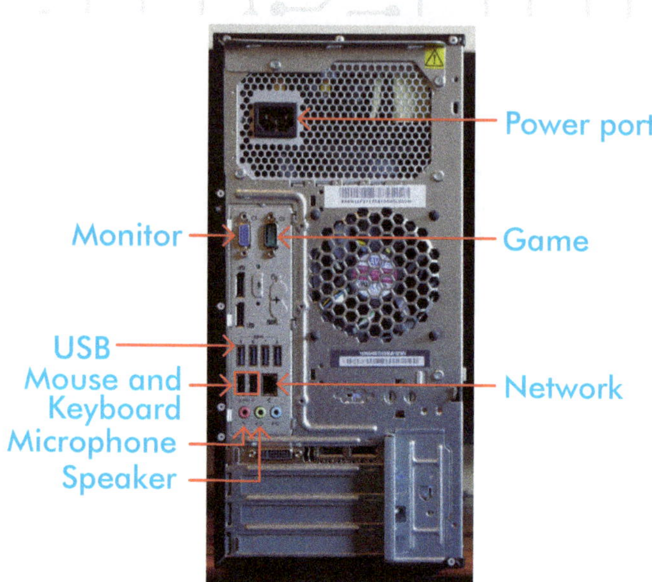

Ports on the back of System Unit

OUTPUT DEVICES

The result you get after processing the data is known as output. The output is provided by the different output devices either in the form of hard copy or soft copy. Output devices are mainly used to display information on a screen, create printed copies or generate sounds.

Monitor

A monitor is the most commonly used output device that displays you the output on the screen. A monitor looks like a television-screen, which displays both text and graphics. The text or graphics you see on the monitor exists electronically and is displayed for a temporary period of time. For this reason information displayed on the monitor is also referred to as soft copy.

Monitor

There are various sizes of a monitor such as 14″, 15″, 17″, 22″, 26″, etc. Whatever you type on the keyboard, it appears on the monitor. A monitor is also known as screen, display, video screen, Video Display Unit (VDU), etc.

Monitors come in two major types: CRT (Cathode Ray Tube) and LCD (Liquid Crystal Display). A CRT monitor is a desktop monitor that contains a cathode-ray tube. A cathode-ray tube (CRT) is a large, sealed glass tube. CRT monitors take up more desk space than LCD monitors. An LCD monitor is a desktop monitor that uses a liquid crystal display to produce images. These monitors produce sharp, flicker-free images. LCD monitors have lightweight, compact screens that consume less than one-third of the power unlike a CRT monitor.

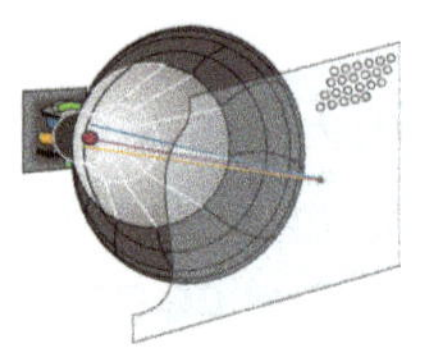

CRT Monitor

LCD Monitor

Printer

Printer

A printer is an output device, which takes processed data (information) from the computer to generate a printable copy of it. A printer provides the information in a permanent and readable form. Printed information, which exists physically, is called hard copy. After the monitor, the printer is the most used output device on the computer; it is commonly used to print text data, images, etc.

There are three main types of computer printers, namely dot matrix, inkjet and laser printers. Each of these printer types uses a different technology to print the data.

A dot-matrix uses hammers and a ribbon to form images out of dots. The more dot hammers use, the higher the resolution of the printed image.

An inkjet forms characters and graphics by spraying tiny drops of liquid ink onto a piece of paper.

A laser is a high-speed printer that works like a photocopier to produce high-quality images on a page.

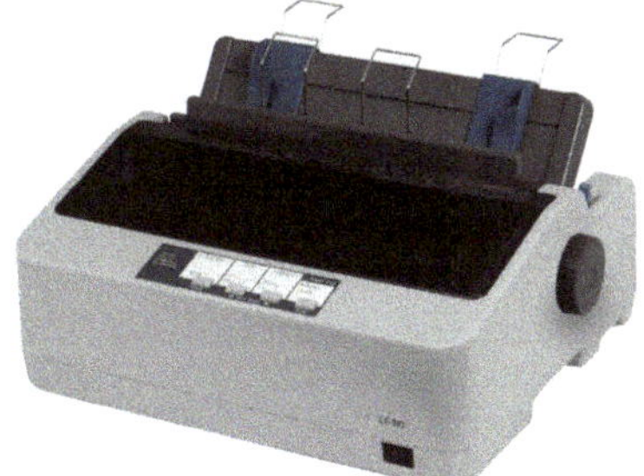
Dot Matrix Printer

Inkjet Printer

Laser Printer

Plotter

A plotter is an output device that produces hard copy output like a printer but in a different way. It produces high-quality graphics on paper using the variety of colours. It has one or more pens that draw onto the paper. Plotters are usually used for producing very accurate plans and drawings that have been created using Computer-Aided Design (CAD). Plotters are generally used by architects and engineers.

Plotter

Speakers

Speakers

Speakers are output device basically used to produce music, speech or other sounds, such as beeps. A speaker is connected to the sound card, fitted inside the computer, which outputs sound generated by the card. Audio data generated by the computer is first sent to the sound card, which is located on the motherboard. The card translates the data into audio signals, which are then sent to speakers.

STORAGE DEVICES

Storage, also called secondary memory, auxiliary storage or mass storage, holds items such as data, instructions and information for future use. Any hardware component used to store data, instructions and information is called a Storage device. The computer has many types of data storage devices. Some of them are classified as the removable data Storage Devices and the others as the non-removable data Storage Devices.

Floppy disk

A floppy disk or diskette is a portable, inexpensive storage medium that consists of a thin, circular, flexible plastic disk with a magnetic coating enclosed in a square-shaped plastic shell. While discussing a storage medium, the term portable means you can remove the medium from one computer and carry it to another computer.

Floppy Disks

Hard disk

Hard disk

The Hard disk, also called Hard disk drive, is the most important storage device used to store a large amount of digital information in the computer. It is a disk pack consisting of many inflexible, circular platters that use magnetic particles to store data, instructions and information. Most current hard drives have storage capacities from 500 GB (Gigabyte) to 6 TB (Terabyte) and more. The hard disk is fitted inside the System unit.

Re-writable CDs and DVDs

Rewritable CDs and DVDs look exactly like CDs and DVDs which you can buy in a store with music and movies on them. In case of rewritable CDs & DVDs, you can store information on them. They are often used to store music, text files, photos and other data. A re-writable CD can hold up to about 700 MB (Megabyte); A re-writable DVD can hold up to about 4.7 GB (Gigabyte) and Blu ray re-writable diskes, which are becoming popular nowadays, can hold about 25 GB (Gigabyte) of data.

CDs

USB Flash Drive

USB Flash Drives

A USB (Universal Serial Bus) flash drive is a small, portable device that plugs into the USB port of the computer. USB flash drives vary in sizes and shapes and can hold gigabytes of information. They are sometimes called thumb drives because they are about the size and shape of a person's thumb. They can be carried around easily, which makes them a good choice for transferring information from one computer to another. USB flash drives are also called pen drives, key drives or memory sticks.

LET'S HAVE A LOOK

- A computer is an electronic device that can store, transmit and manipulate data into information.
- Data is the input given to the computer.
- Processing means an action which is taken by the computer on data to convert it into meaningful information.
- Information is the processed data on which decisions and actions are based.
- The person who uses the computer and the information generated by it is called a user.
- Hardware is the term given to all the physical and mechanical equipments attached together to make a computer system.
- The computer accepts input (data) from the user via an input device like a keyboard.
- A keyboard is a common input device that is used for entering the text data with the help of the different types of keys present on it.
- A mouse is a pointing device that fits under the palm of your hand comfortably.
- A joystick is also a pointing device which is mainly used to play games on the computer.
- A digital camera is an input device that allows users to take pictures and store the photographed images digitally, instead of on traditional film.
- The MICR is a scanner that recognizes numeric data printed with magnetically charged ink.

BRAIN TEASER

1. Multiple Choice Questions

Tick (✓) the correct answer:

a. Raw information for data processing is:

i. Information ☐ ii. User ☐ iii. Data ☐

b. The person who uses a computer is known as:

i. Programmer ☐ ii. User ☐ iii. Operator ☐

c. A computer software is a set of:

i. Instructions ☐ ii. Hardware ☐ iii. Monitor ☐

d. An action which is taken by the computer on data is called:

i. RAM ☐ ii. Processing ☐ iii. Motherboard ☐

e. The devices which are used to input the data in the computer are known as:

i. Output devices ☐ ii. Input devices ☐ iii. Light pen ☐

f. A set of lines of different thicknesses that represent a number:
   i. Bar code ☐ ii. Microphone ☐ iii. Hard disk ☐

g. An input device is:
   i. CPU ☐ ii. Monitor ☐ iii. Scanner ☐

h. An output device is:
   i. Monitor ☐ ii. Hard disk ☐ iii. Keyboard ☐

2. Fill in the blanks:

a. A person who uses the computer and the information generated by it is called a ________________.

b. ________________ is the collection of facts which have no meaning to the user.

c. ________________ stands for 'Magnetic Ink Character Recognition Reader'.

d. CPU has two parts : ________________ and ________________.

e. At the back of the system unit, there are slots called ________________.

f. Printed information, which exists physically, is called ________________.

g. The USB flash drive is also called ________________.

3. Write '**T**' for True and '**F**' for False in the boxes:

a. A joystick is mainly used to play games on the computer. ☐

b. Input devices do all logical and mathematical work. ☐

c. CPU displays the processed information. ☐

d. A mouse is an input device. ☐

e. Rewritable CDs and DVDs look exactly like CDs and DVDs. ☐

f. A plotter is the output device used by architects and engineers. ☐

g. The hard disk is fitted inside the System unit. ☐

h. A rewritable CD drive is an input device used to enter data. ☐

i. The person who uses a computer is called a programmer. ☐

j. USB flash drives are also called pen drives. ☐

k. A keyboard has two buttons on the top of it. ☐

4. Answer the following questions

(i) Answer each in a few lines:

a. Name any two hardware components.

b. What are the four operations involved in the working of a computer?

c. Name the circuit board inside the system unit.

d. Which are the two components of processor?

e. Name the device used to play games on the computer.

f. Name the two types of computer memory.

g. What can you do with the help of a mouse?

h. Name two types of monitors.

i. Name different kinds of printers.

j. Name any two storage devices.

k. Name the output device used by architects and engineers.

(ii) Answer each comprehensively:

a. Differentiate between:

   i. Hardware and software   ii. Data and Information

b. Who are users?

c. Explain the steps involved in the working of a computer. Show it with the help of examples.

d. What is memory?

e. What is the role of the MICR in banks?

f. Draw and explain any two output devices.

g. What is a Processor? What are its different parts?

h. What is USB Flash Drive?

i. Define the following:

   i. Motherboard   ii. Touchscreen   iii. Printer   iv. Mouse

5. Write full forms for the following Acronyms.

a. CU ____________________

b. RAM ____________________

c. ALU ____________________

d. CPU ____________________

Operating System

In this chapter, we will learn:

⇒ Meaning of Operating System
⇒ Functions of Operating System
⇒ Types of Operating System
⇒ Categories of Operating System

INTRODUCTION

An operating system (OS) is the most important software that runs on the computer. It manages the memory of the computer, processes and controls all of its software and hardware. The operating system recognises input from an input device; coordinates the display of output and manages data and instructions in memory and information stored on the disk. The operating system works as a platform between you and your computer. It allows you to communicate with the computer without knowing how to speak the language of the computer.

In other words, we can say that an operating system is the first step to make the computer in working condition. It monitors different programs and users, making sure everything runs smoothly, without any interference.

Applications

Printer

Monitor

Operating System

Mouse

Keyboard

Disk Drive

MAIN FEATURES OF OPERATING SYSTEM

The main features of Operating System are shown below:

⇒ Managing the sharing of Internal memory among multiple applications.

⇒ It handles and monitors input, output and storage to and from the attached hardware devices, such as hard disks, printers, etc.

⇒ Scheduling the activities of the CPU and resources to achieve efficiency and prevention.

⇒ It sends messages to each application about the status of operations.

⇒ In a multiple operating system where multiple programs can be run at the same time, the operating system determines which applications should run in what order and how much time should be allowed for each application before giving another application a turn.

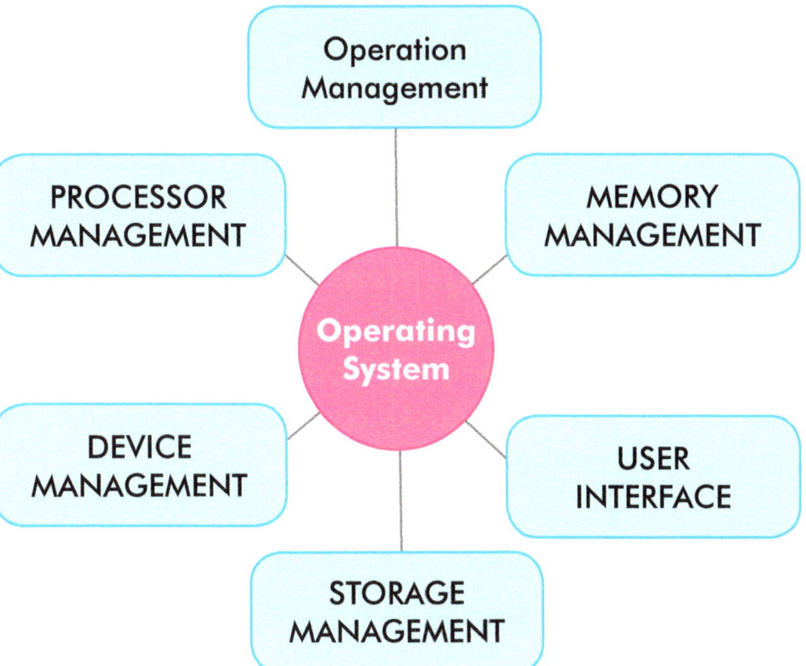

FUNCTIONS OF OPERATING SYSTEM

Many different operating systems exist, designed for all types of computers. Regardless of the size of the computer, most operating systems provide similar functions. The following sections discuss functions common to most operating systems. The operating system handles many of these functions automatically, without requiring any instructions from a user.

Booting the Computer

The process of starting or restarting the computer is known as booting. A cold boot is when you turn on a computer that has been turned off completely. A warm boot is the process of using the operating system to restart (turn off and then turn on automatically) the computer.

Performs Basic Computer Tasks

The operating system performs basic computer tasks, such as managing the various peripheral devices, for example, mouse, keyboard and printer. Most operating systems now are plug and play, *i.e.* a device such as a printer will automatically be detected and configured without any user's intervention.

Provides a User Interface

A user interacts with software through the interface. The two main types of user interfaces are: command line and a graphical user interface (GUI). With a command line interface, the user interacts with the operating system by typing commands to perform specific tasks. An example of a command line interface is DOS (Disk Operating System). With a graphical user interface, the user interacts with the operating system by using a mouse to access windows, icons and menus. An example of a graphical user interface is Windows 10.

Handles System Resources

The operating system also handles system resources, such as the memory of the computer and sharing of the central processing unit (CPU) time by various applications or peripheral devices.

Provides File Management

The operating system also handles the organization and tracking of files and directories (folders) saved or retrieved from a computer disk. The file management system allows the user to perform such tasks as creating files and directories, renaming files, copying and moving files and deleting files.

TYPES OF OPERATING SYSTEM

Within the broad family of operating systems, there are many types, based on the types of computers they control and the sort of applications they support.

Real-time Operating System (RTOS)

It is a multitasking operating system that aims at executing real-time applications. A real-time operating system (RTOS) is an operating system that guarantees a certain capability within a specified time constraint. A very important part of an RTOS is managing the resources of the computer so that a particular operation may be executed in precisely the same amount of time, every time it occurs. A real-time operating system offers programmers more control over process priorities.

Single-user, Single task

As the name implies, this operating system is designed to manage the computer so that one user may effectively do one thing at a time.

The Palm OS for the palm handheld computer is a good example of a modern single-user, single-task operating system.

Single-user, Multi-tasking

This is the type of operating system most people use on their desktop and laptop computers today. Both Microsoft Windows and Apple's Mac OS platforms are the examples of operating systems that will let a single user have several programs in operation at the same time. For example, it's entirely possible for a Windows user to write a note in a word processor while downloading a file from the Internet or while printing the text of an e-mail message.

Multi-user

A multi-user operating system allows many different users to take advantage of the resources of the computer simultaneously. The operating system must make sure that the requirements of the various users are balanced and that each of the programs they are using has sufficient and separate resources so that a problem with one user may not affect the entire community of users. Unix, VMS and mainframe operating systems, such as MVS, are the examples of multi-user operating systems.

Batch Processing Operating System

In a batch processing operating system interaction between the user and the processor is limited or there is no interaction at all during the execution of work. Data and programs that need to be processed are bundled and collected as a 'batch' and executed together.

Distributed Operating System

In a distributed system, software and data may be distributed around the system; programs and files may be stored on different storage devices which are located in different geographical locations and may be accessed from different computer terminals.

CATEGORIES OF OPERATING SYSTEM

Operating systems come in a variety of forms and can be upgraded and changed in the computer, whenever required. Basically, an operating system comes in three basic categories, *i.e.* stand-alone, server and embedded.

Stand-alone Operating System

A stand-alone operating system is a complete operating system that works on a desktop or notebook computer. A stand-alone OS or application is the one that actually executes locally on a "client computer" (a common desktop PC), not on a "server computer".

Microsoft Windows : It is a series of software operating systems and graphical user interfaces produced by Microsoft. Windows 3.1, Windows 95, Windows 98, Windows 2000, Windows NT, Windows Vista, Windows XP, Windows 7, Windows 8 and Windows 10 are some of the different versions available for Microsoft Windows.

Windows 7 is a series of operating systems produced by Microsoft for use on personal computers, including home and business desktops, laptops, netbooks, tablet PCs and media centre PCs. Windows 10 is intended to be a more focused, incremental upgrade to the Windows line, with the goal of being compatible with applications and hardware.

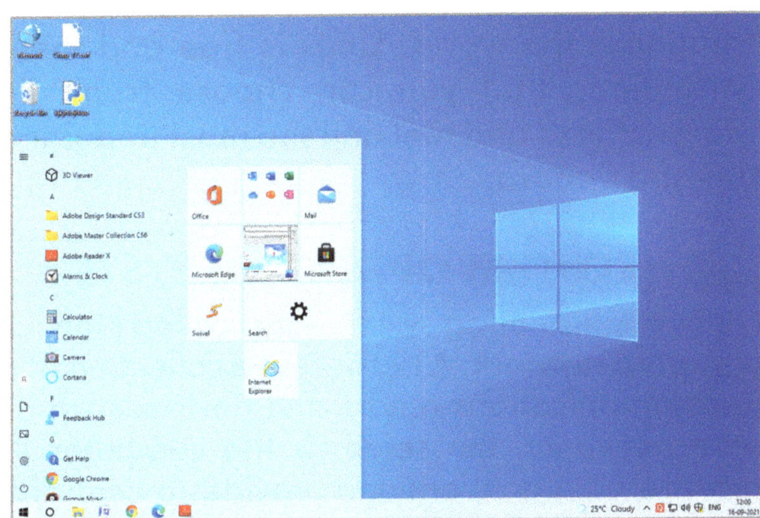

Windows 10

Windows 8 and Windows 10 are the next versions of Microsoft Windows, a family of operating systems produced by Microsoft. It is a successor of Windows 7. Windows 11 is also launched after Windows 10 that includes a slew of new features, such as the ability to download and run Android apps on your Windows PC and updates to Microsoft Teams, the Start menu and the overall look of the software, which is more clean and Mac-like in design.

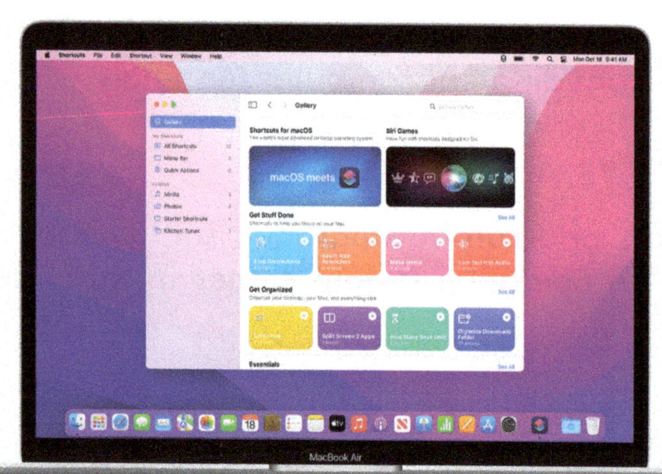

Mac OS : It is the trademark-protected name for a series of graphical user interface-based operating systems developed by Apple Inc. It comes pre-loaded on all new Macintosh computers or Macs. The latest version, Mac OS X, is a multitasking operating system available only for computers manufactured by Apple. It is also designed to be run on the server. The specific version names of Mac OS X are Lion, Snow Leopard and Leopard.

Linux : It is a free open-source operating system based on Unix. Linux was originally created by Linus Torvalds with the assistance of developers from around the globe. Linux is free to download, edit and distribute. Linux is a very powerful operating system throughout the world. Linux is free and there are many different distributions that you can choose from. Each distribution has different looks and feel and the most popular ones include Ubuntu, Mint and Fedora.

NETWORK OPERATING SYSTEM

A network operating system (also called Network OS or NOS) is an operating system that supports a network. A network is a collection of computers and devices connected together via communications media and devices such as cables, telephone lines and modems. In some networks, the server is the computer that controls access to the hardware and software on a network and provides a centralised storage area. The other computers on the network, called clients, rely on the server(s) for resources.

A server operating system is software that was specially developed to serve as a platform for running multi-user computer programs. Windows Server 2019, Unix, Netware and Solaris are the different types of Server Operating System.

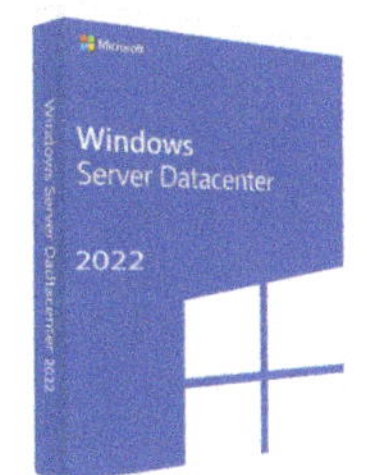

Windows Server 2022

Unix

Solaris

Netware

EMBEDDED OPERATING SYSTEM

Embedded operating systems are not anything new to the world of electronics. They have been installed on a wide variety of consumer electronics to allow them to function in a variety of different tasks. Embedded operating systems aren't even new to the world of computers. Handheld computers such as the Palm and Windows Mobile, all use the versions of embedded operating systems that are stored on an internal memory chip rather than booted from a disk.

Windows Embedded CE, Windows Mobile, Palm OS, iphone OS, Blackberry, Google Android, Symbian OS are the different examples of Embedded Operating System.

Windows CE

Windows Mobile

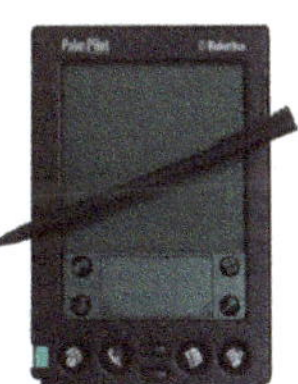
Palm OS

iPhone OS

Blackberry OS

Google Android

Symbian OS

LET'S HAVE A LOOK

- An operating system manages the memory of the computer, processes and controls all of its software and hardware.
- An operating system works as a platform between you and your computer.
- The process of starting and restarting the computer is known as booting.
- The Real time OS, Single User-Single task, Single User, Multitasking and Multiuser–are the four main types of OS.
- The three basic categories of OS all stand-alone, server and embedded OS.
- Window 11 is the latest generation operating system most commonly used in the computer.
- A network operating system is a software that supports network.
- Hand-held computers such as Palm OS and Windows Mobile, use the version of Embedded OS.

BRAIN TEASER

1. Multiple Choice Questions:

Tick (✓) the correct answer:

a. The software that allows you to communicate with the computer:

i. LOGO ☐ ii. Games ☐ iii. Operating System ☐

b. The process of starting or restarting a computer is called:

i. Running ☐ ii. Booting ☐ iii. Start UP ☐

c. The latest version of Windows OS is:

i. Window XP ☐ ii. Windows 10 ☐ iii. Windows 11 ☐

d. A user interacts with the operating system by using a mouse is:

i. RTOS ☐ ii. DOS ☐ iii. GUI ☐

e. A multitasking operating system:

i. RTOS ☐ ii. Multiuser ☐ iii. Single User ☐

f. An OS that works on a desktop or notebook computer:

i. Network OS ☐ ii. Embedded OS ☐ iii. Stand-alone OS ☐

g. An OS used in Windows Mobile is:

i. MAC OS ☐ ii. Network OS ☐ iii. Embedded OS ☐

2. Fill in the blanks:

a. ______________ is the first step to make the computer in working condition.

b. A ______________ is the process of using the OS to restart the computer.

c. A user interacts with the computer through the ______________.

d. An example of GUI interface is ______________ or ______________.

e. The OS handles the organization and tracking of ______________ and ______________.

f. In ______________, interaction between the user and the processor is limited during the execution of work.

g. Microsoft Windows and Macintosh are the ______________ types of an OS.

h. ______________ is an operating system designed by Google.

i. ______________ is the current release of Microsoft Windows.

3. Write 'T' for True and 'F' for False in the boxes:

a. An OS is the most important software that runs on the computer. ☐

b. The process of starting or restarting the computer is known as booting. ☐

c. Window 10 OS is a good example of single-user, single-task operating system. ☐

d. The OS also keeps the track of all files and folders. ☐

e. The latest version, Mac OS X, is a multitasking operating system. ☐

f. Linux was originally created by Microsoft Corp. ☐

g. Symbian OS is an example of Embedded Operating System. ☐

4. Match Column A with Column B:

	Column A		Column B
a.	Command Line User Interface	(i)	Open Source OS
b.	Cold Boot	(ii)	Multi User
c.	Single User, Multitasking	(iii)	Embedded OS
d.	UNIX	(iv)	Turn ON computer that has turned OFF
e.	Linux	(v)	Window and Mac OS
f.	Google Android	(vi)	DOS

5. Answer the following questions.

(i) Answer each in a few lines:

a. Name the software that manages the memory of the computer and controls its hardware and software.

b. Define booting.

c. Name the two types of User Interface.

d. Name the different types of OS.

e. What are the three categories of OS?

f. Name the categories of OS used in handheld computers and mobiles.

(ii) Answer each comprehensively:

a. What is an operating system? Explain.

b. Explain the different functions of an operating system.

c. Explain the different categories of an operating system.

d. Discuss the different types of an operating system.

Formative Assessment-1
(Chapters 1-2)

1. Tick (✓) the correct answer:

a. The person who works on the computer:
   i. programmer ☐ ii. user ☐ iii. operator ☐

b. The part that controls the working of all the hardware devices:
   i. RAM ☐ ii. Hard disk ☐ iii. Processor ☐

c. A Volatile memory:
   i. RAM ☐ ii. Keyboard ☐ iii. Hard disk ☐

d. An input device used to scan the images into the computer is:
   i. Keyboard ☐ ii. Mouse ☐ iii. Scanner ☐

e. A user interacts with the operating system by using a mouse:
   i. RTOS ☐ ii. DOS ☐ iii. GUI ☐

f. The process to start or restart the computer is:
   i. Turn ON ☐ ii. Booting ☐ iii. Processing ☐

g. An OS used in Windows Mobile is:
   i. MAC OS ☐ ii. Network OS ☐ iii. Embedded OS ☐

h. An Operating System allows us with the computer to:
   i. Play ☐ ii. Communicate ☐ iii. Process ☐

2. Complete the following chart:

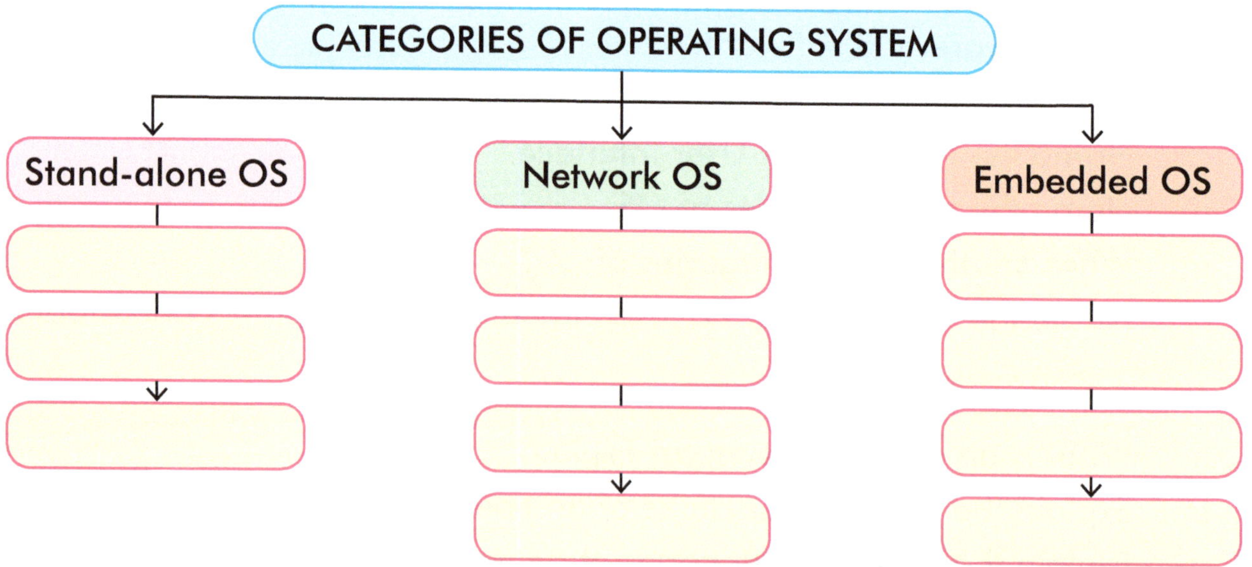

3 Taking Care of Your Computer

In this chapter, we will learn:

⇒ Maintaining hardware
⇒ Keep your computer physically clean
⇒ Maintenance inside the computer
⇒ Cleaning files
⇒ Defragment disk
⇒ Scan Disk
⇒ Scan for viruses
⇒ System Restore

MAINTAINING HARDWARE

Computer Maintenance of the computer is very important for keeping it running smoothly. A computer which is left untreated, can accumulate dust and debris, which may result in slow performance.

It is not difficult to keep our computer healthy and in good working order. Some of the tips and preventive measures can keep our computer faster, long-lasting and give peak performance.

Maintaining your computer involves three things:

⇒ Keeping your computer physically clean
⇒ Protecting it from Malware (Virus)
⇒ Keeping it internally clean

KEEPING YOUR COMPUTER PHYSICALLY CLEAN

While dealing with the computer, dust can potentially destroy the parts of your computer. By cleaning your computer regularly, you can help to keep it working and avoid expensive repairs.

Cleaning the Keyboard

A dirty keyboard can hamper your work. Dust, food and other particles can get stuck underneath the keys, which can cause trouble. The following steps are the basic cleaning tips that will help you to keep your keyboard clean:

⇒ Unplug the keyboard from the USB or PS/2 port.

⇒ Turn the keyboard upside down and gently shake it to remove the dirt and dust between the keys.

⇒ Use a can of compressed air to clean between the keys.

⇒ Moisten the cotton cloth or paper towel with rubbing liquid and use it to clean the top of the keys.

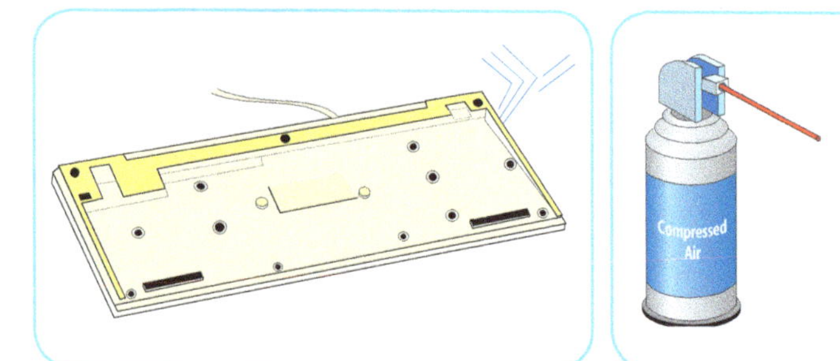

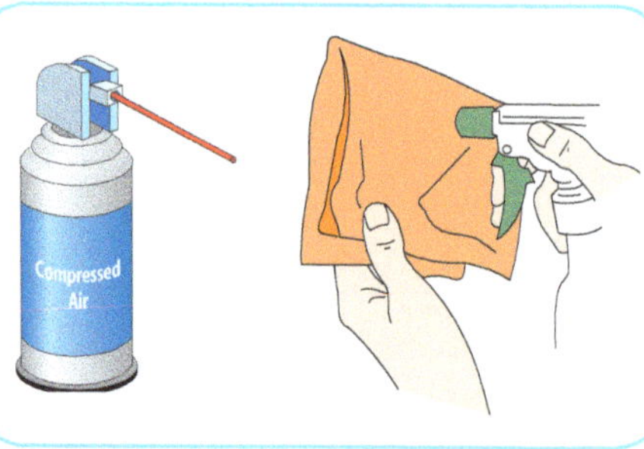

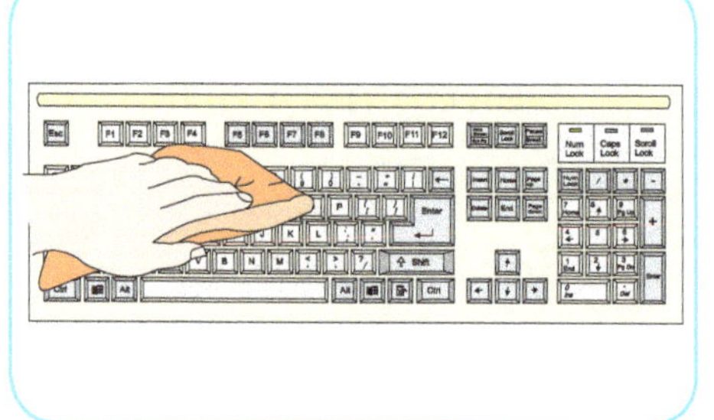

If you spill liquid on the keyboard, quickly shut down the computer and unplug the keyboard from the port. Then turn the keyboard upside down to allow the liquid to drain.

***Compressed air**: You can use a can of compressed air to blow dirt, debris and dust from inside a computer. Cans of compressed air are inexpensive and are available at most computer stores.*

Cleaning the Mouse

The mouse can get sticky over time as dust collects near the light emitter. This can cause an erratic cursor movement or prevent the mouse from working. To clean the mouse, follow these cleaning tips:

⇒ Unplug the mouse from the USB or PS/2 port.

⇒ Moisten the cotton cloth or paper towel with rubbing liquid and use it to clean the top and bottom of the mouse.

⇒ Take the cotton bud and gently wipe lens and the LED on the back side of the mouse.

⇒ If you want to give the mouse a quick cleaning, place it on a clean white sheet of paper and move the mouse back and forth. Some of the dust particles should rub off onto the paper.

Cleaning the Monitor

Dirt, fingerprints and dust can make your computer screen difficult to read. However it is easy to clean your screen whenever needed. The safest method to clean your monitor is simply to use a piece of soft, clean cloth moistened with water.

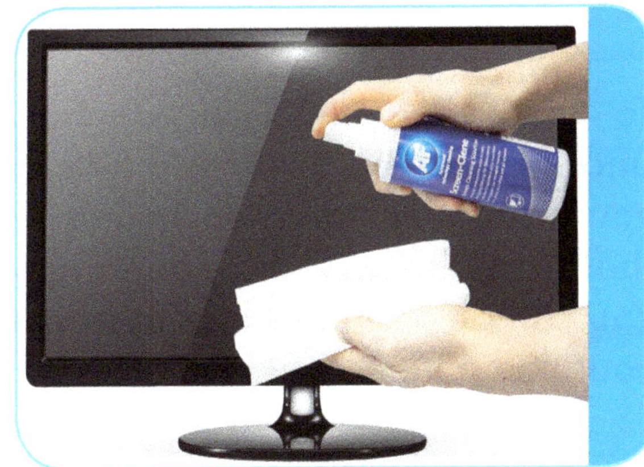

⇒ Do not use a glass cleaner to clean a monitor screen. Many screens have anti-glare coating that can be damaged by a glass cleaner. Use a piece of soft clean cloth moistened with water to wipe the screen clean.

⇒ Do not spray liquid directly onto the screen. The liquid could leak into the monitor and can damage the internal components.

Cleaning the Computer Case

Overheating, dust and dirt are the three mortal enemies of the computer. Dust can slow down air flow inside your computer casing by building up on your cooling fan, which can raise the temperature of the computer to dangerous levels. This can cause your computer to fail prematurely, and you can lose data. Here are a few tips you can use while cleaning your computer case:

⇒ Dust is the main enemy of your computer. Use an anti-static wipe to gently clean the area in order to remove the dust.

⇒ Use a can of compressed air with a narrow nozzle to blow out debris from the air intake slots.

⇒ Keep your computer cool. Don't restrict the airflow around your computer.

⇒ A computer can generate a lot of heat, so the case has a cooling fan that does not let it overheat. Avoid stocking papers, books or other items around your computers.

SAFEGUARDING AGAINST MALWARE

Malware is any type of software that is designed to damage your computer or gain unauthorised access to your personal information. It includes viruses, worms, Trojan horses, spyware and other types. Most malware is distributed over the Internet, often bundled with other software.

The best way to guard against malware is to install an anti-virus software such as Norton or Kasperky. An anti-virus software helps to prevent malware from being installed and it can also remove malware from your computer. New malware is being created all the time, so it is important to update your anti-virus software frequently.

INTERNAL MAINTENANCE TECHNIQUES

To keep the computer system running smooth and fast you need to perform routine internal maintenance to enhance performance and reduce the risk of computer failure.

Disk Clean-Up

To keep your computer running smoothly, it is important to keep files and folders uncluttered. The unwanted files can eventually fill up your hard drive, which will make your computer slower down and harder to use. Windows provides a Disk cleanup program that scans the hard drive for temporary files and other unwanted files that can be deleted. You can delete these files to free up space on your hard drive and improve the speed of your computer.

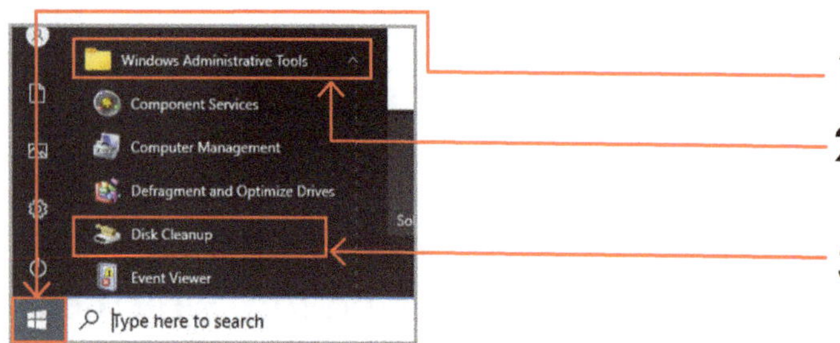

1. Click on Start button.
2. Scroll down the menu and click on Windows Administrative Tools.
3. Click on Disk Cleanup. The Disk Cleanup Options dialog box will appear.

The Drive Selection dialog box appears if your computer has more than one drive.

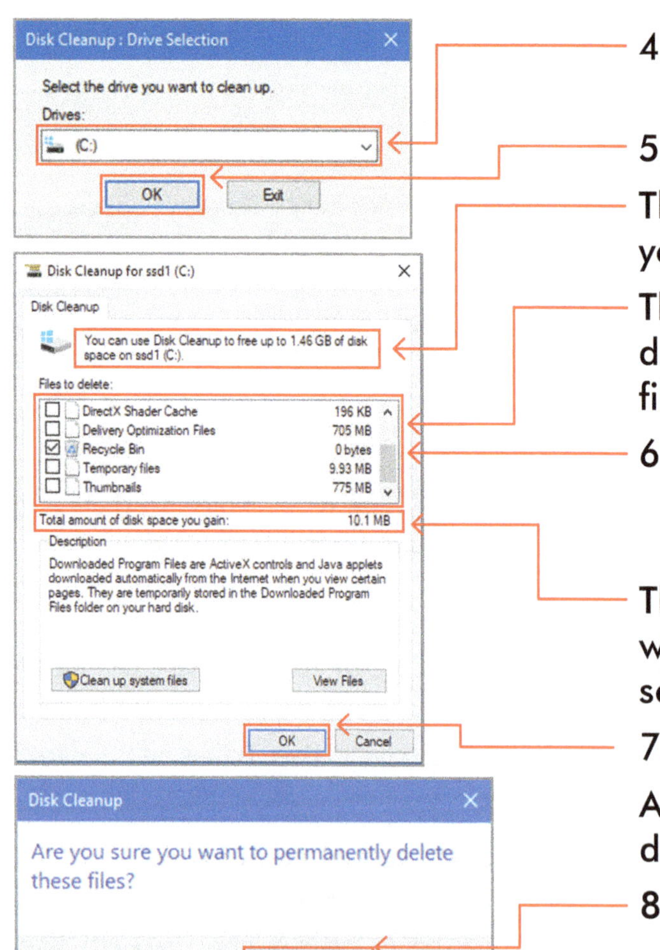

4. Click on the down arrow of Drives and then click on the hard drive you want to clean up.
5. Click on OK.

This area displays the total amount of disk space you can free up.

This area displays the type of files Windows can delete and the amount of disk space each type of files uses.

6. Windows will delete each of files that displays a check mark. You can click the box beside a type of file to add or remove a check mark.

This area displays the total disk space Windows will free up by deleting the types of files you have selected.

7. Click on OK to delete the files.

A dialog box appears, confirming that you want to delete the files.

8. Click on Delete Files to delete the files permanently.

Disk Defragmenter

Disk Defragmenter is a program which is used to increase the speed of the computer speed by rearranging files stored on a hard disk.

If your computer is running slowly, running Disk Defragmenter can help to speed it up.

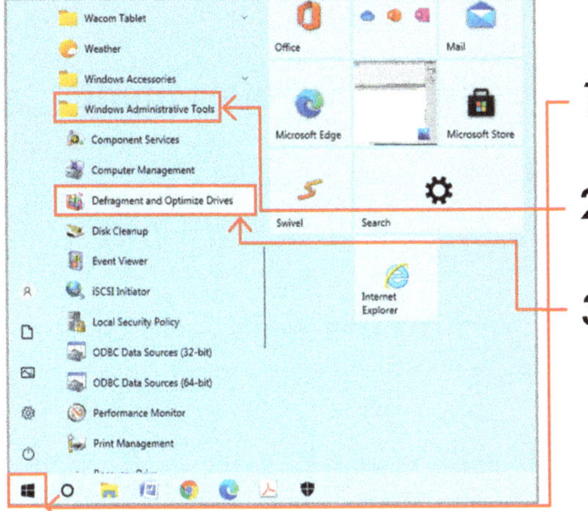

1. Click on Start button.
2. Click on Windows Administrative Tools.
3. Click on Defragment and Optimize Drives. The Defragment and Optimize Drives window will appear.

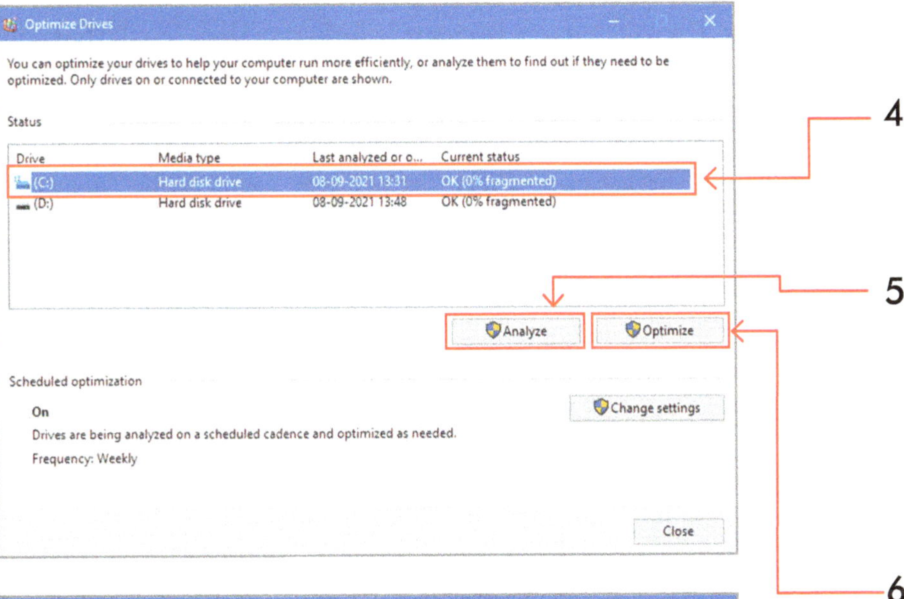

4. Select the disk drive you want to defrag.
5. Click the "Analyze" button on the Optimize Drives window.
6. Click the "Optimize" button to start defragmenting your drive.
7. Click on Close when you have finished.

Disk Scanner

A disk scanner is a program that detects and corrects problems on a hard disk or floppy disk. A disk scanner searches for and removes unnecessary files from your computer. Windows includes two disk scanner utilities. One detects problems and the other searches for and removes unnecessary files such as temporary files.

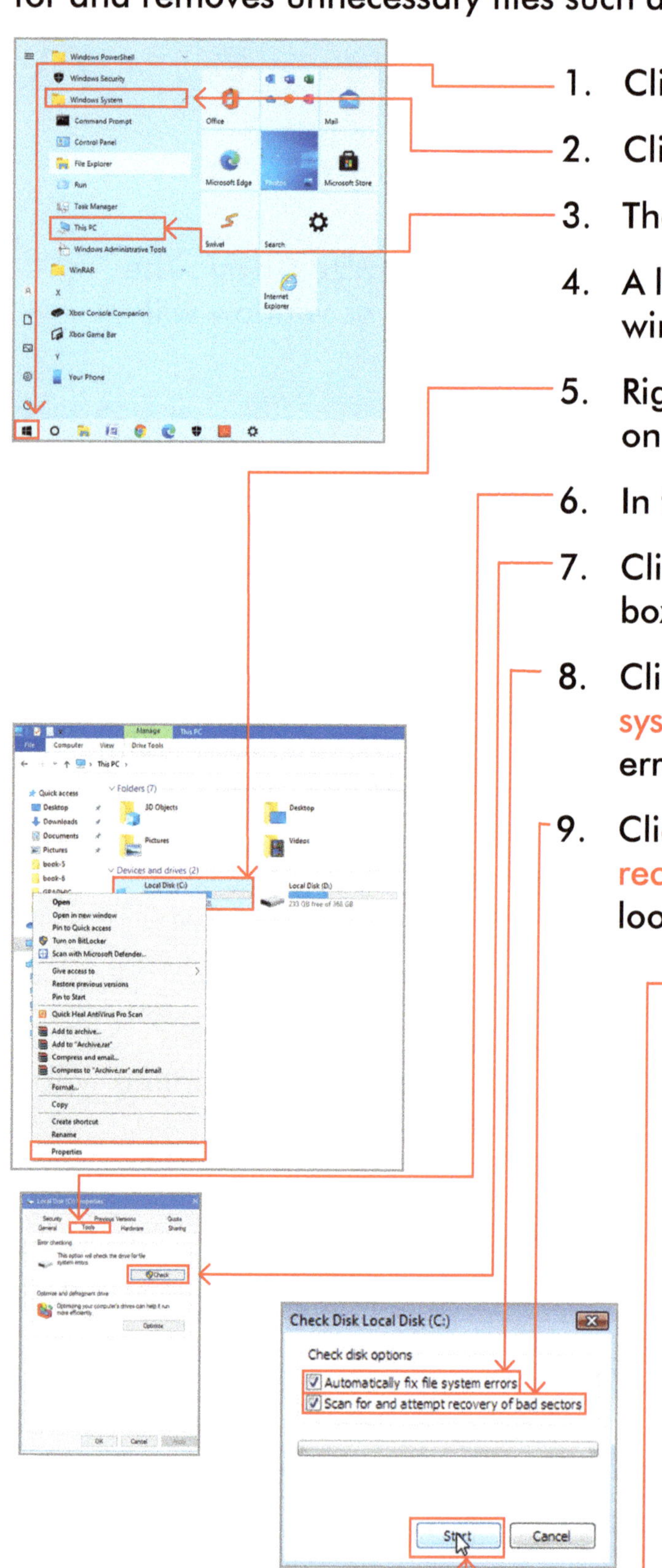

1. Click on Start button to display the Start menu.
2. Click on Windows System.
3. Then click on This PC option.
4. A list of drives is displayed on the right side of the window.
5. Right-click on the drive you want to run Scan disk on and select Properties.
6. In the Properties window, click on the Tools tab.
7. Click the Check button. The Check Disk dialog box appears.
8. Click on the check box of Automatically fix file system errors if you want Check Disk to fix any errors it finds.
9. Click on the check box of Scan for and attempt recovery of bad sectors if you want Check Disk to look for bad sectors.
10. Click on Start.

    The hard drive check begins.

    A dialog box appears when the drive check is over.

11. Click on Close to return to the Properties dialog box of the hard drive.
12. Click on OK in the Properties dialog box of the hard drive.

System Restore

If your computer faces any problem, you can use System Restore. System Restore helps you to restore your system files to an earlier point in time when the computer was problem - free. It is a way to Undo system changes to your computer without affecting your personal files such as e-mail, documents or photos.

System Restore uses a feature called system protection to create and save restore point regularly on your computer. These restore points contain information that Windows uses.

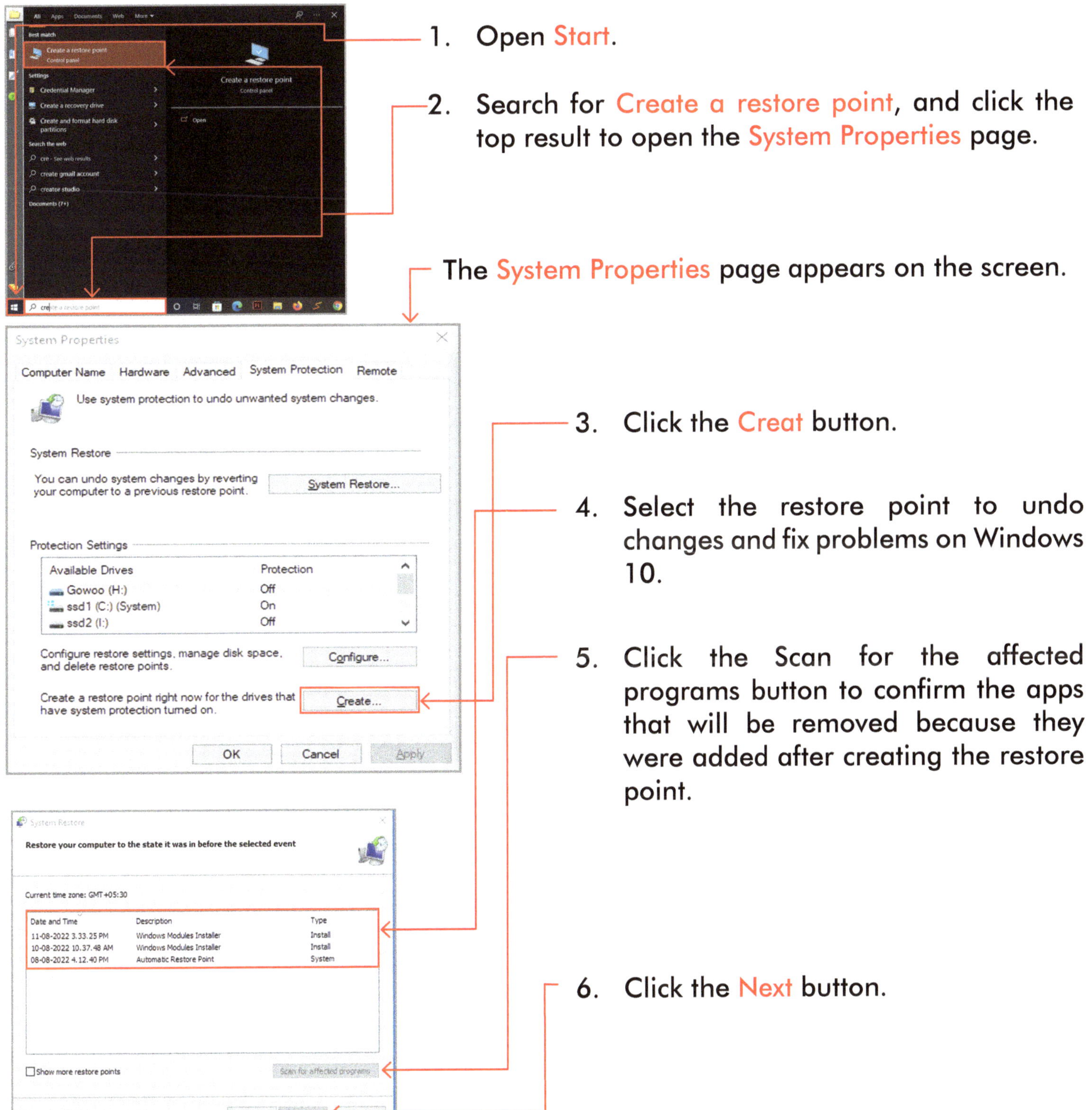

1. Open Start.
2. Search for Create a restore point, and click the top result to open the System Properties page.

The System Properties page appears on the screen.

3. Click the Creat button.
4. Select the restore point to undo changes and fix problems on Windows 10.
5. Click the Scan for the affected programs button to confirm the apps that will be removed because they were added after creating the restore point.
6. Click the Next button.

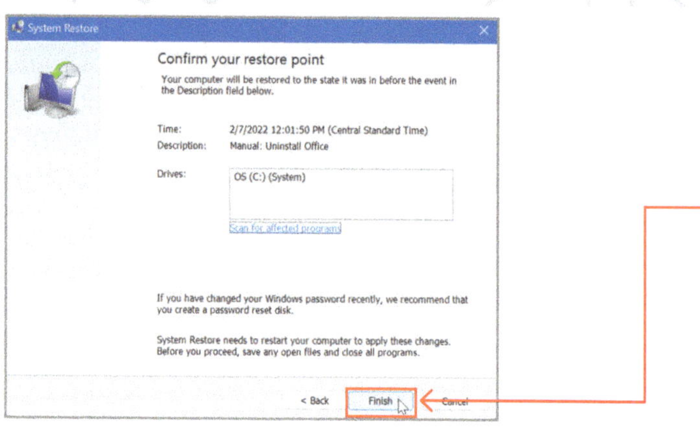

7. Click the Finish button.

LET'S HAVE A LOOK

- Taking care of the computer can make your computer faster, long-lasting and give the peak performance.
- Maintaining a computer involves three steps: keeping it physically clean, protecting it from Malware and keeping it internally clean.
- Always unplug the parts of the computer before cleaning them.
- Do not spray liquids directly onto the parts of the computer.
- Always use a piece of soft moistened cloth to clean the parts of the computer.
- Use an updated anti-virus software to protect your computer from Malware.
- Use Internal maintaining techniques regularly to keep the computer working properly.
- System Restore helps you to restore your system files to an earlier point in time.

BRAIN TEASER

1. Multiple Choice Questions

Tick (✓) the correct answer:

a. A can used to clean between the keys of the keyboard:

i. coke can ☐ ii. can of compressed air ☐

iii. cleaner Can ☐

b. What should we not spray directly onto the screen?

i. Powder ☐ ii. Ink ☐ iii. Liquid ☐

c. The main enemy of the computer:

i. Dust ☐ ii. Finger prints ☐ iii. Games ☐

d. Which helps you to restore your system files to an earlier point in time?

i. Disk cleanup ☐ ii. Scan Disk ☐ iii. System Restore ☐

2. Fill in the blanks:

a. A computer system requires both the __________ and __________ maintenance.

b. Always __________ the parts of the computer before __________ them.

c. The most common causes of the overheating of the computer are __________ and __________ .

d. Do not spray __________ directly on the parts of computer.

e. Clean the screen of the monitor with a piece of __________ cloth.

f. To clean the unnecessary files, you are required to run a __________ program.

g. Use can of __________ compressed air with a narrow nozzle to blow out debris from the air intake slots.

h. Always use an updated __________ software to protect your computer from Malware.

3. Write 'T' for True and 'F' for False in the boxes:

a. The cleaning of the computer does not affect the life of the computer. ☐

b. Only physical cleaning is sufficient for the computer. ☐

c. Always unplug the parts before cleaning them. ☐

d. Do not spray the liquid on the parts directly. ☐

e. The defragmentation of hard disk increases the speed of the computer. ☐

f. Malware does not affect the working of the computer. ☐

g. Internal cleaning affects the speed of the computer. ☐

h. A disk scanner detect and resolves problems on hard disk. ☐

i. The unwanted files benefits the computer. ☐

4. Answer the following questions

(i) Answer each in a few lines:

a. What can destroy the parts of your computer?

b. What can you use to clean the keyboard and its keys?

c. What can happen if the dust collects near the light emitter of a mouse?

d. What is the safest method to clean the monitor?

e. Name the software used to protect your computer against Malware.

f. Which technique can you use to delete the unwanted files from the hard disk?

g. What is disk defragmenter?

h. How we can keep our computer running smoothly?

i. How to clean a keyboard without any damage?

(ii) Answer each comprehensively:

a. Why is the cleaning of the computer needed?

b. What are the three steps involved in the cleaning of the computer?

c. What are the tips that will help you to keep your keyboard clean?

d. What will happen if dust collects near the light emitter of a mouse? How can we prevent it?

e. 'Do not spray liquid directly to the part of the computer.' Why?

f. How can malware affect your computer?

g. How does a disk defragmenter help the computer?

h. What is the use of a disk cleanup program?

i. How we can safeguard against malwares?

j. What are anti virus programs? Name some of popular anti-virus softwares.

5. Complete the following:

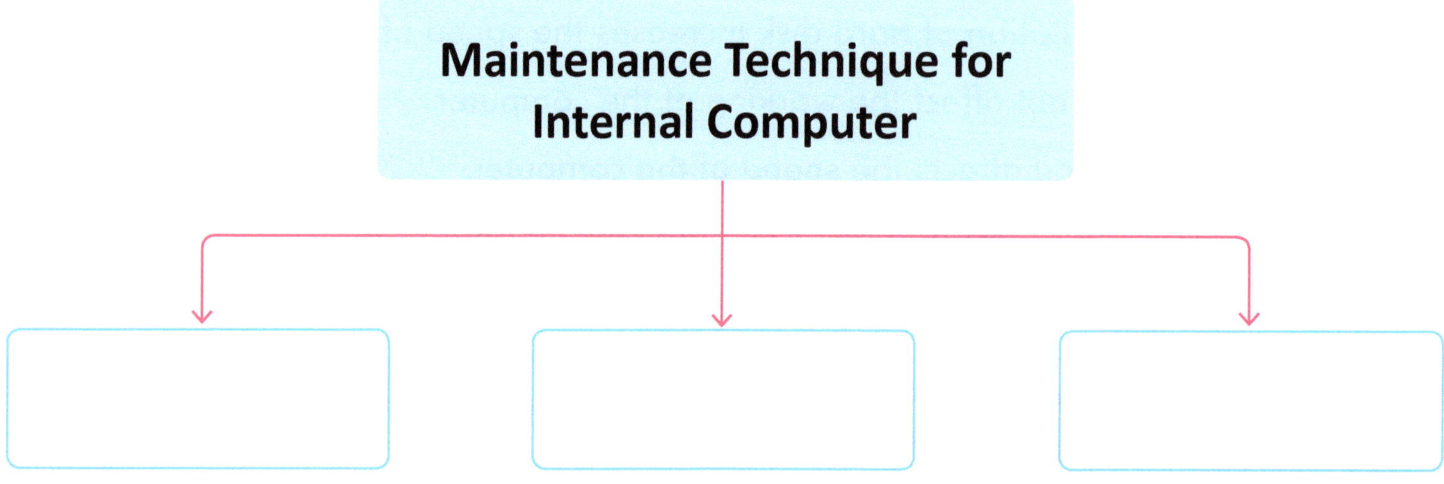

4 Formatting and Creating Tables in MS-Word 2016

In this chapter, we will learn:

⇒ Introduction to MS-WORD
⇒ Formatting in a document
⇒ Adding a picture in a document
⇒ Adding clipart
⇒ Adding word art
⇒ Creating a table

MS-WORD 2016

All of you studied in a previous class that MS-Word 2016 is a word processing software and is a part of Microsoft Office package. It is used to create a text based document like typing letters, making reports, etc. It provides you with so many good-features that can be used to create an attractive and efficient document. In this chapter, you will learn about some of its features.

FORMATTING THE TEXT

Formatting refers to the appearance or presentation of your document in an attractive manner by making the required changes to the text through different formatting options provided in MS-Word. Some of the formatting options are font, font size, alignment, numbering and bulleting, etc.

You can format a text by using Font and Paragraph Group in Home tab.

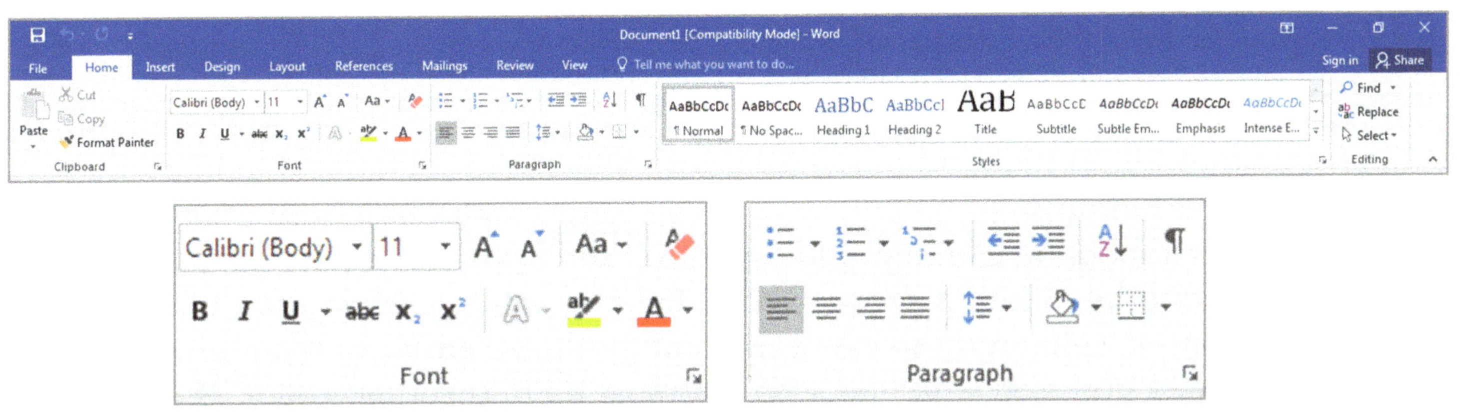

Font and Paragraph Group in Home tab

OPTIONS PRESENT IN THE HOME TAB

There are many options present in Home tab that are used for formatting the text.

Font

A font is a design and style of a character. Word 2016 lets you change the text in different fonts and gives your text an attractive look.

Font Size

You can increase and decrease the size of the text as per your need. The text size in a document is measured by the point, where one point is equal to 1/72 inch.

Font | Font size

Bold, Italic and Underline

You can make the text Bold, Italic and Underline to give a special attraction towards the particular text by using **B** *I* U buttons present in the Font group in Home tab.

Heaven	**Heaven**	*Heaven*	Heaven
Normal	Bold	Italic	Underline

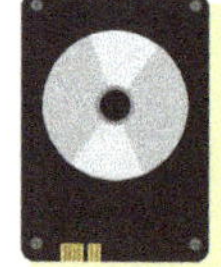

Remember

You can also use a keyboard shortcut to make the text bold, italic and underline. Press Ctrl+B to apply bold formatting, press Ctrl+I to apply italics and press Ctrl+U to apply underlining.

Alignment and Justification

Alignment refers to the appearance and orientation of the edges of the document. There are four different types of alignments (left, centre, right and justify) available in Microsoft Word. Here is an example that will show you the different alignments.

Align Left	Centre	Align Right	Justify
The Microsoft Office 2016 is the most recent version of Microsoft's productivity suite. It is the successor of Microsoft Office 2013.	The Microsoft Office 2016 is the most recent version of Microsoft's productivity suite. It is the successor of Microsoft Office 2013.	The Microsoft Office 2016 is the most recent version of Microsoft's productivity suite. It is the successor of Microsoft Office 2013.	The Microsoft Office 2016 is the most recent version of Microsoft's productivity suite. It is the successor of Microsoft Office 2013.

Bullets and Numbering

The Bullets and Numbering allows you to organize text in lists. Bullets are used to list items that do not have to be in any particular order. Bullet points are often used in documents and presentations to help organize information and make it easier to read or understand. Numbers or letters are used when information must be in a certain order. Numbering is useful in describing a procedure containing steps that must be followed consecutively.

INSERTING PICTURES AND CLIPART

You can insert pictures and clipart into the document along with the text wherever needed. Inserting pictures and clipart makes the document more attractive and presentable.

Inserting Pictures

To illustrate the concept of document, you can insert a picture in your document.

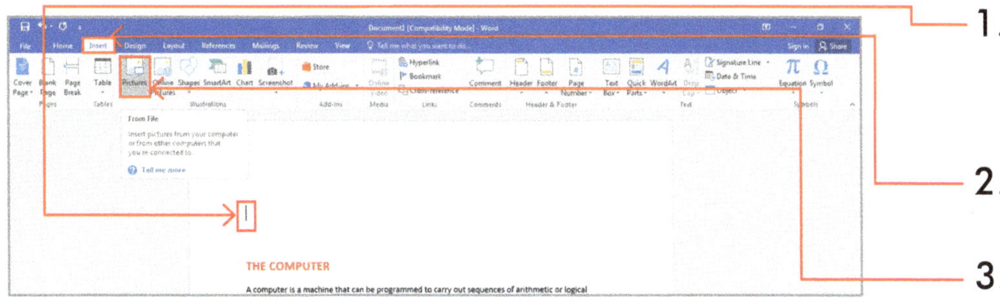

1. Click on the location in your document where you want to add a picture.
2. Click on Insert tab.
3. Click on Pictures.

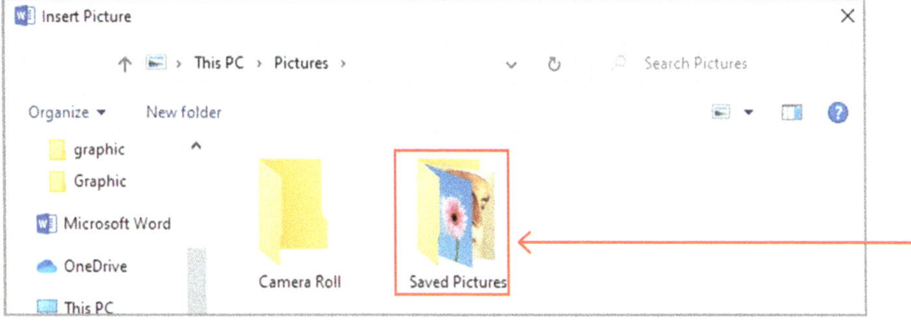

4. Navigate to the folder where your image is located.

The Insert Picture dialog box appears.

5. Select the image you want to add to your document.
6. Click on Insert to add the picture to your document.

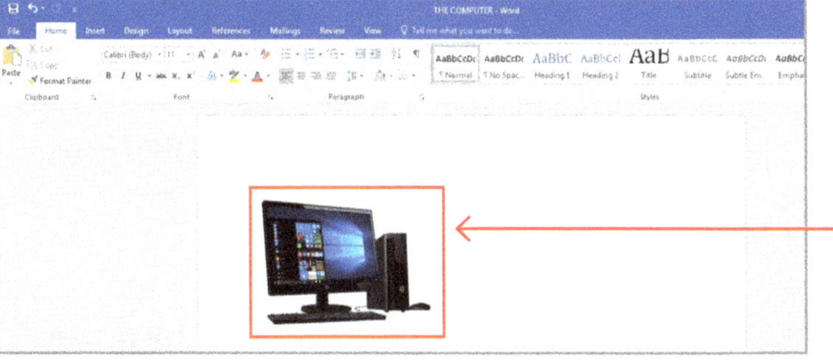

The picture appears in your document.

To delete the picture, just click on the picture you want to delete. Handles (●) appear around the picture. Then, press Delete key to delete the picture.

Wrapping Text Around a Graphic

Text wrap is a feature that enables you to surround a picture or diagram with the text. The text wraps around the graphics. To wrap the text, follow the given steps:

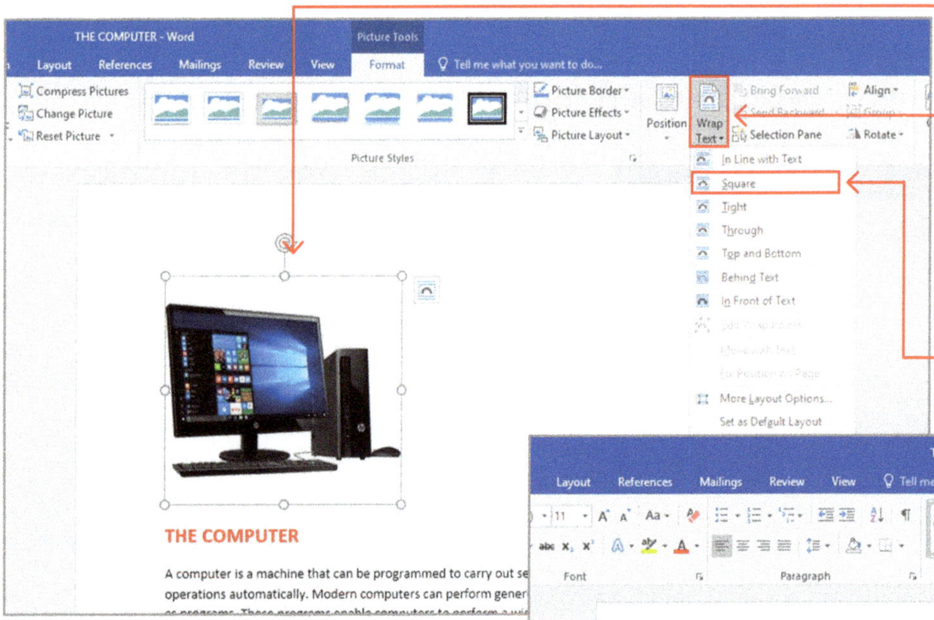

1. Click on the object or picture that you want to wrap.
2. Click on Wrap Text button on the Format tab.
3. Click on Square.

The Square wrap style is applied.

This example wraps the text squarely around the object.

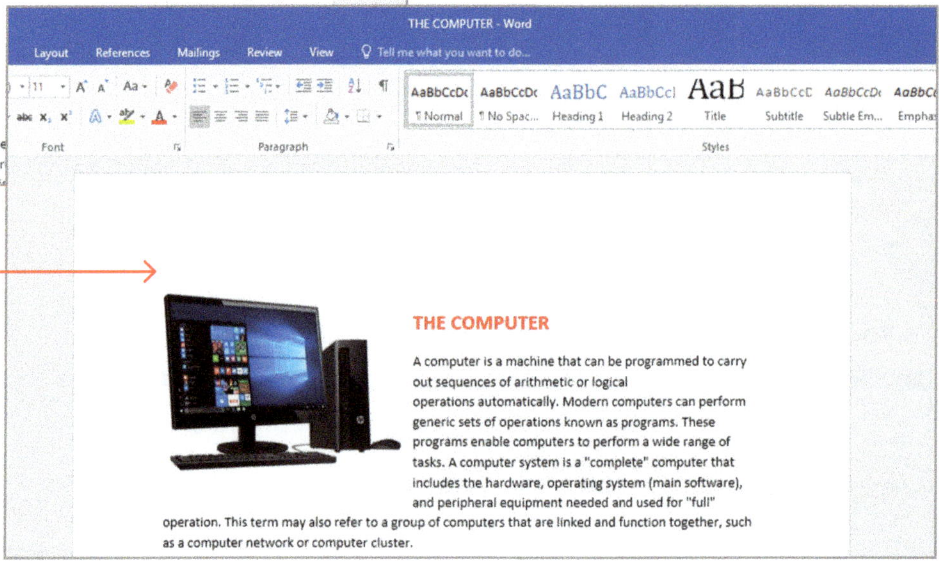

Moving and Resizing an Object

The picture you inserted in the document can be moved anywhere and can be resized (small and large) according to the requirement. To resize and move the picture, the steps are:

MOVE AN OBJECT

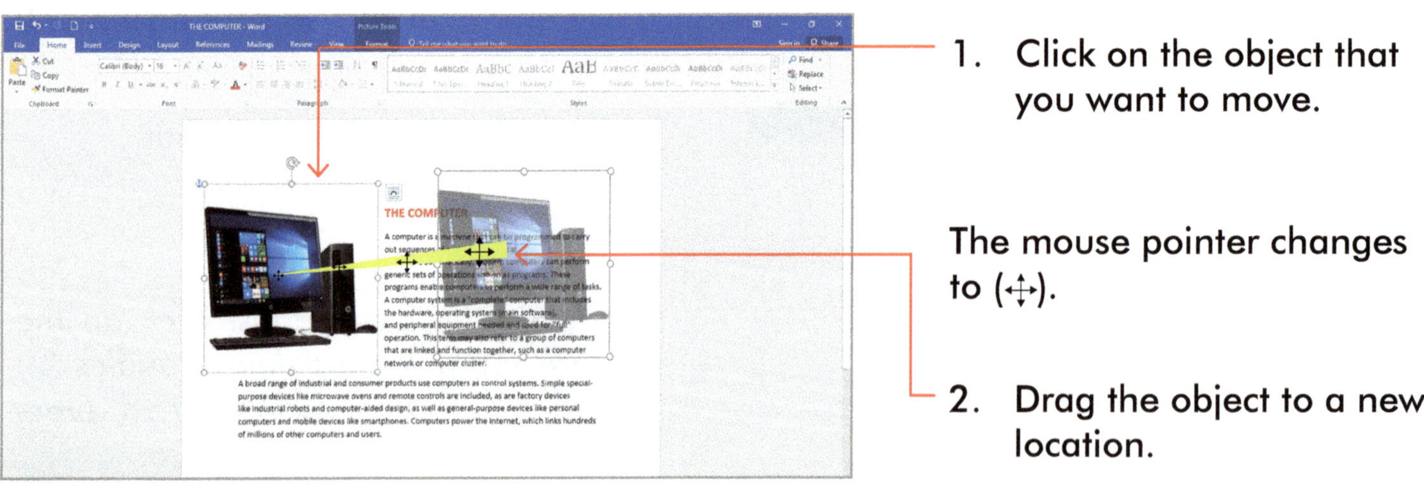

1. Click on the object that you want to move.

The mouse pointer changes to (✣).

2. Drag the object to a new location.

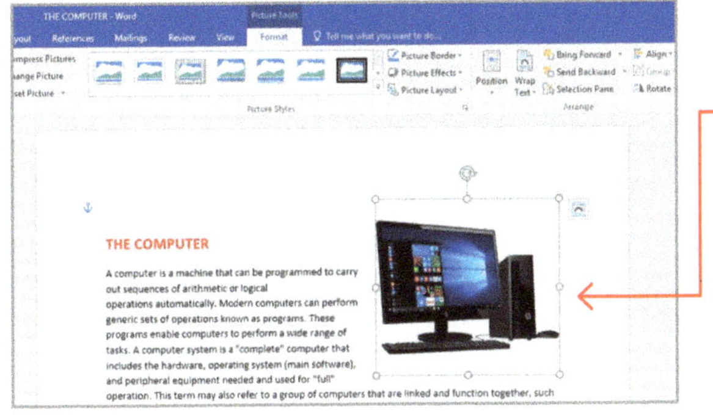

The object moves to the new location, as soon as you release the mouse.

Note

If you are not able to drag the object from its place--

Right-click the picture, click Wrap Text , and choose another option, such as "Square," and you'll be able to drag and drop the picture.

RESIZE AN OBJECT

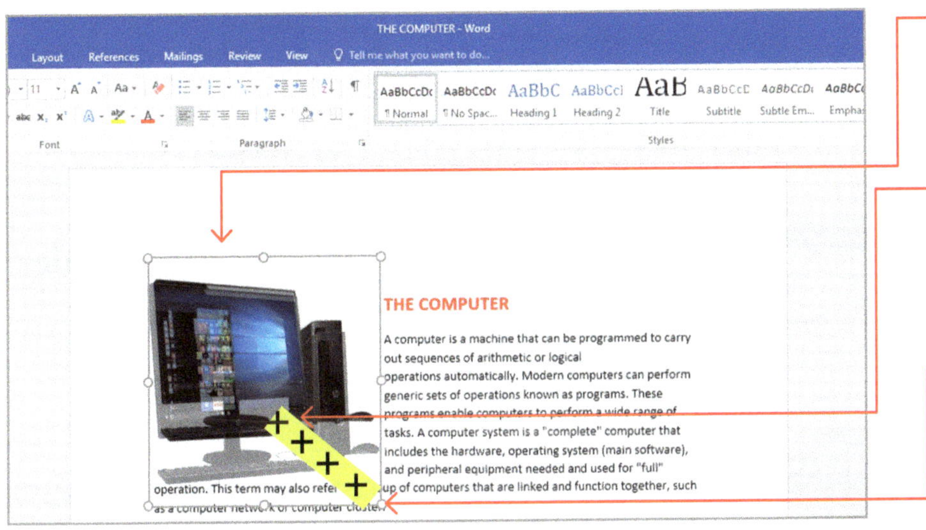

1. Click on the object that you want to resize.
2. Place your mouse on the selection handle.

The mouse pointer changes into (+).

3. Drag a selection handle to resize the object.

As soon as you release the mouse, the object is resized.

Adding Picture Effects

You can add special visual effects to the picture or clipart inserted in the document by using the new Picture Effect tool.

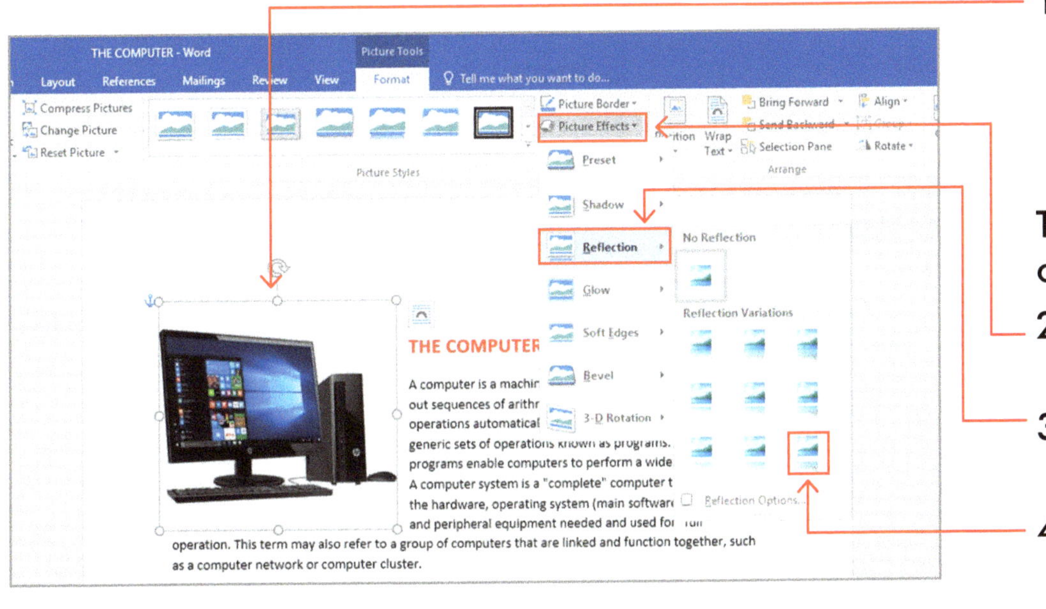

1. Double-click the picture you want to edit.

The Format tab appears on the Ribbon.

2. Click on Picture Effects button.
3. Click on Reflection category.
4. Click on Full Reflection 4 pt offset style.

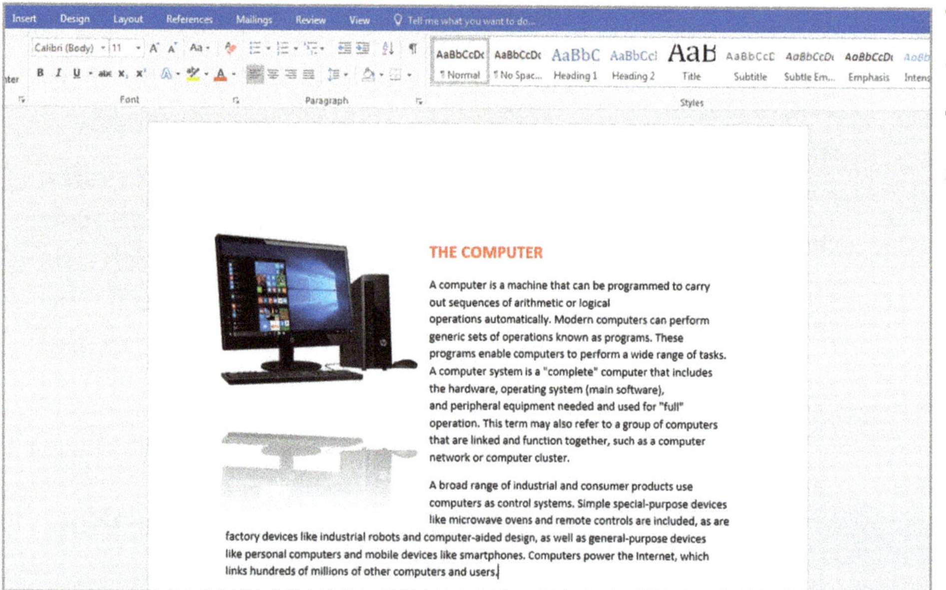

The new effects are assigned to the picture.

To remove the effect, repeat steps 1 to 3; then click on No Reflection.

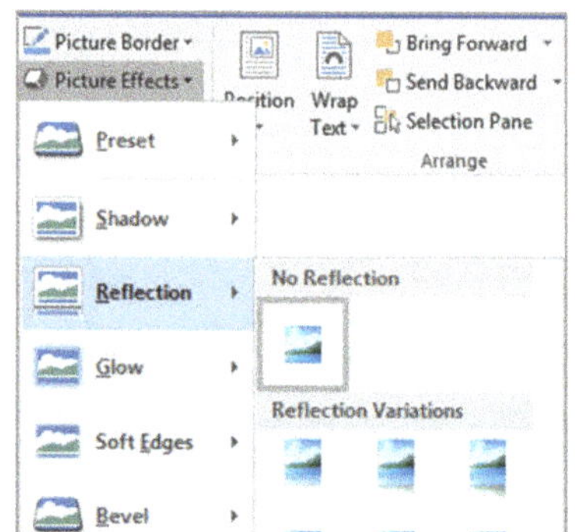

We can also find a picture from OneDrive option which is powered by Bing.

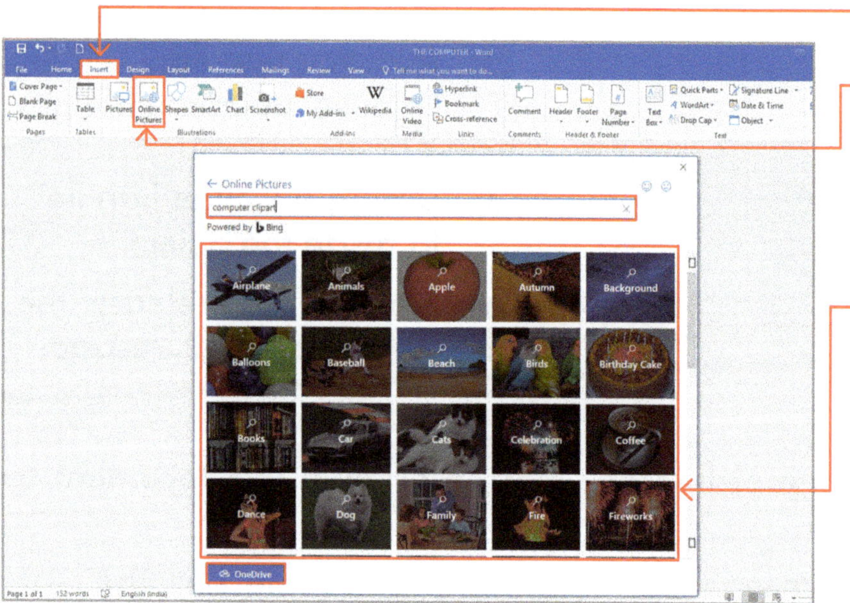

1. Click on Insert Tab
2. Click on Online Pictures under Illustrations group.
3. Click on Browse (in One Drive - Personal box).

Online pictures box shows images with different categories.

Click on the category you want the image from.

Select the image. Click on Insert.

The image appears in the desired location.

Inserting Clipart

You can add clipart images to your document to help get your message across and add graphic interest to your document.

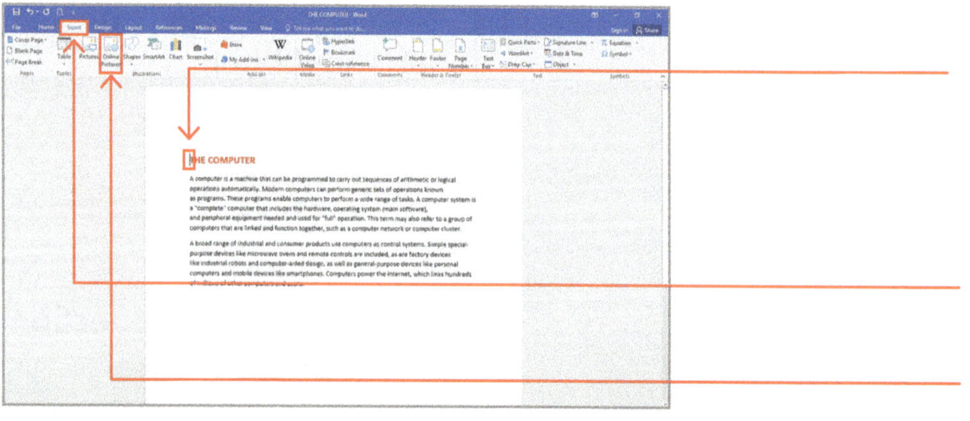

1. Click on the location where you want to add clipart.
2. Click on Insert tab.
3. Select Online Pictures.

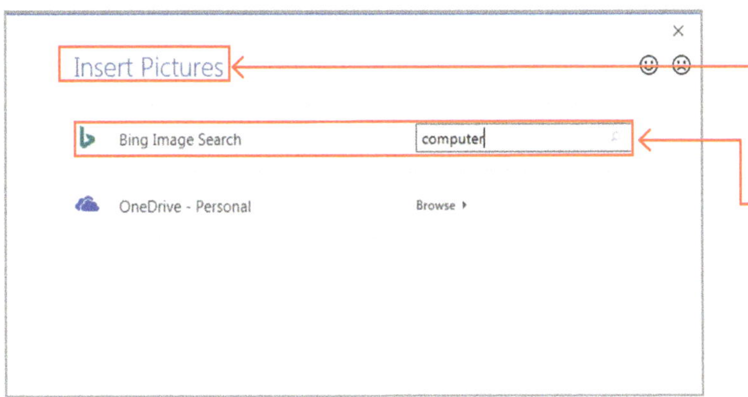

Insert Pictures dialog box appears.

Choose Bing Image Search or your OneDrive. In our example, we'll use Bing Image Search. Type the name of the picture in Bing Image Search box. Press the Enter key.

Your search results will appear in Online Pictures dialog box

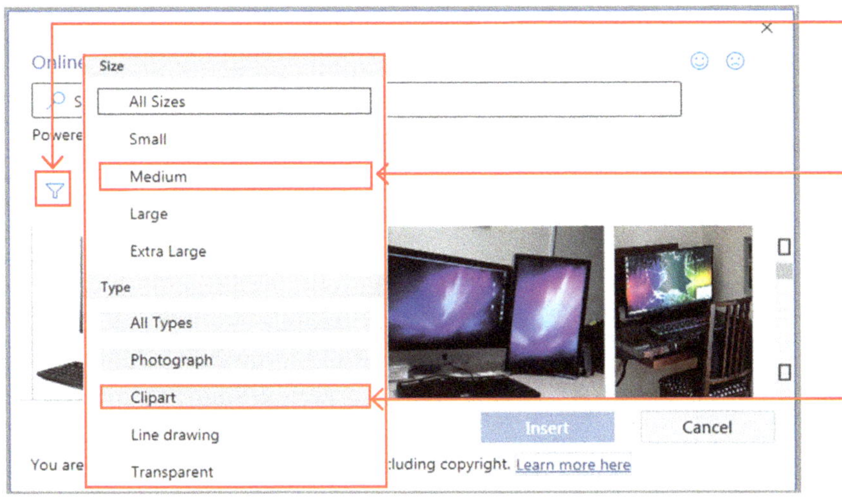

Click on the Filter icon.

A menu list appears.

Click on the size you want for your picture.

Click on the Type(clipart) you want for your picture.

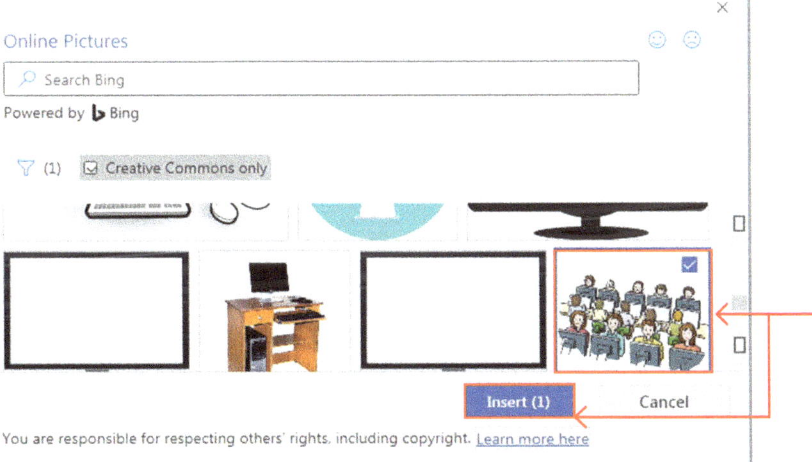

Search results will appear in the box.

Select the desired image and then click Insert.

The image will appear in the document.

Inserting WordArt

WordArt is decorative text that you can add to a document as an eye-catching visual effect. You can create WordArt text or you can apply a WordArt style to the existing text. It is mainly used to give the title an impressive look. To insert a WordArd text, follow these steps:

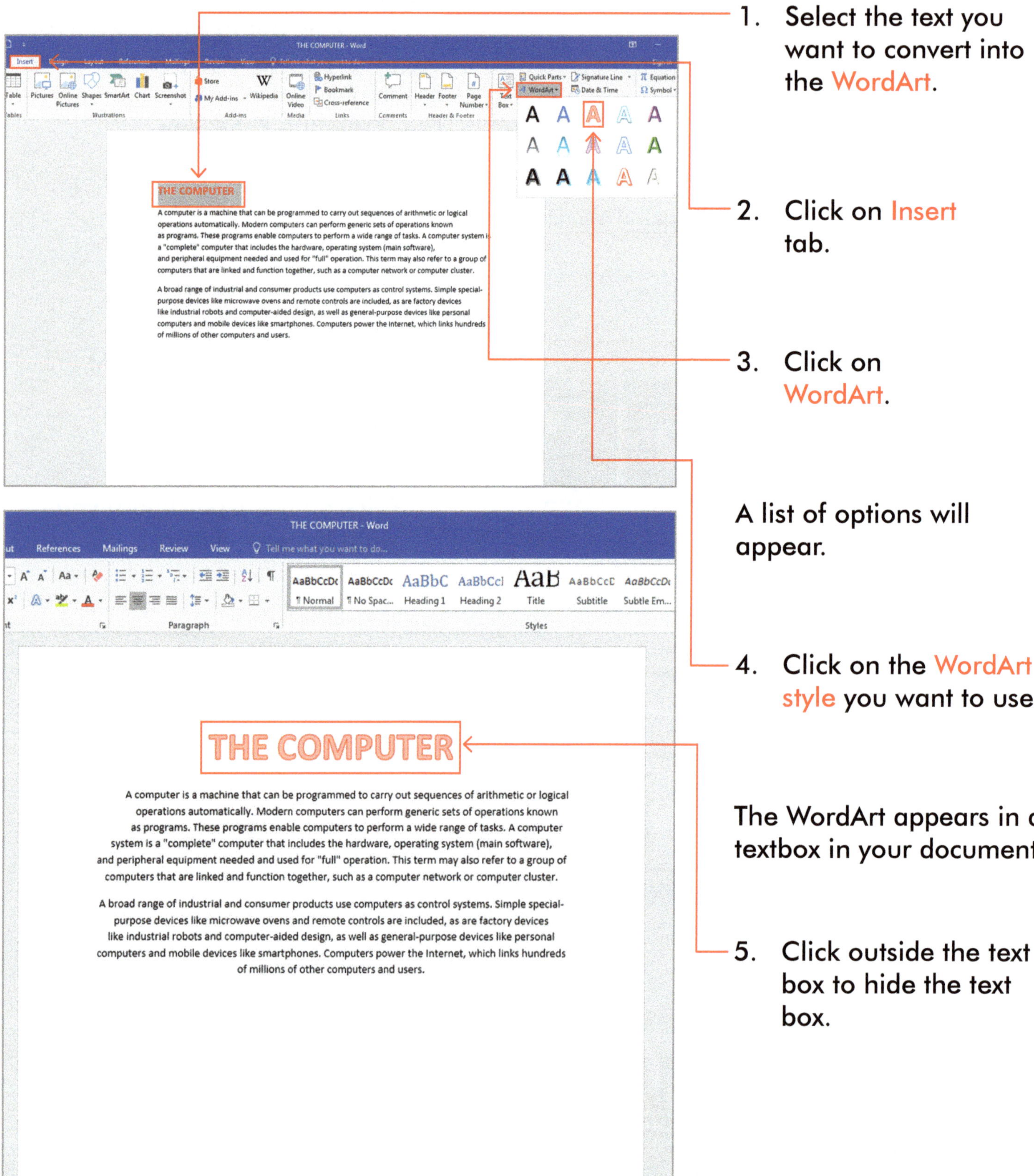

1. Select the text you want to convert into the WordArt.
2. Click on Insert tab.
3. Click on WordArt.

   A list of options will appear.
4. Click on the WordArt style you want to use.

   The WordArt appears in a textbox in your document.
5. Click outside the text box to hide the text box.

TABLES

When you want your text in the form of rows and columns, you can insert the ready-made rows and columns in a tabular form provided in Table feature. The table in Word consists of a grid of boxes arranged in rows and columns, somewhat like a spreadsheet. Tables are well suited to organize and display a large amount of data.

Inserting Table

To insert table in a document, follow the steps.

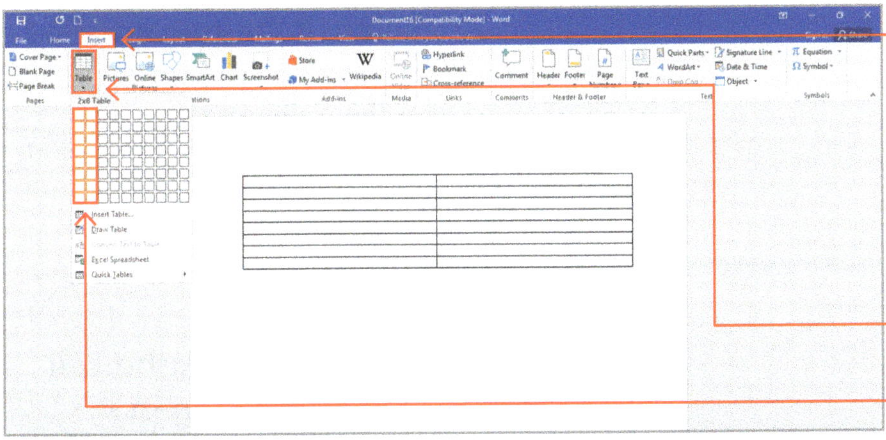

1. Click in the document where you want to insert a table.
2. Click on Insert tab on the Ribbon.
3. Click on Table button.
4. Drag the mouse pointer until you highlight the number of rows and columns, you want the table to contain.

Word previews the table as you drag over cells.

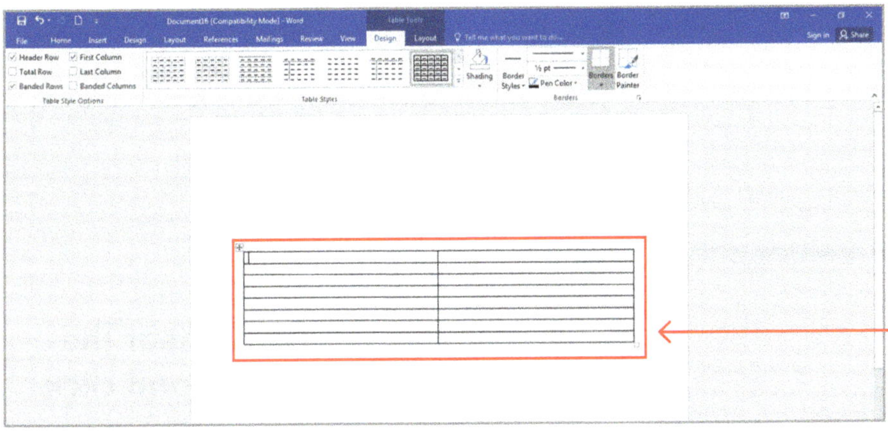

Word adds table to the document.

Entering Text in Table

The text can be entered in the boxes of a table with the help of the keyboard.

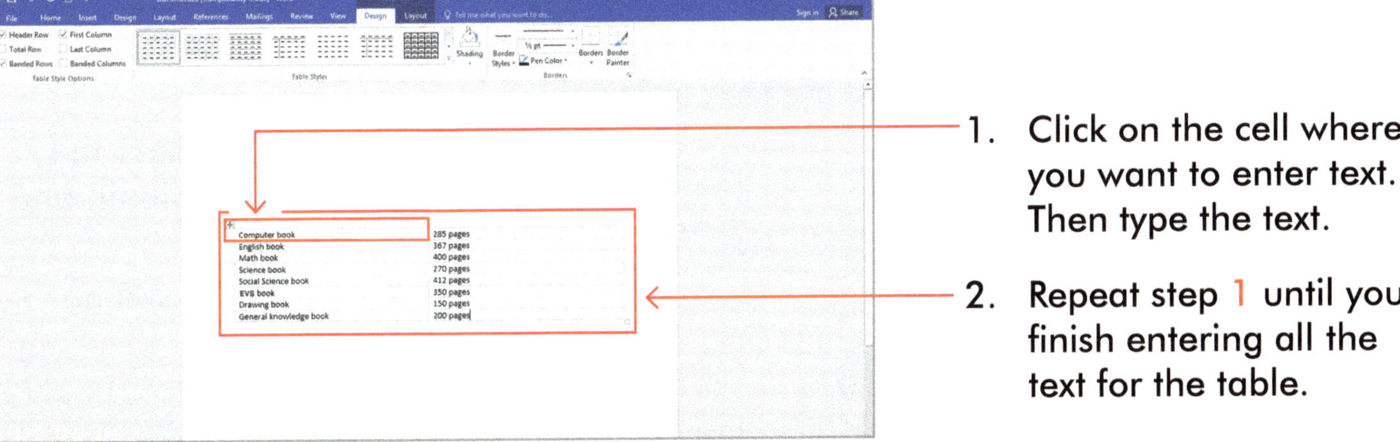

1. Click on the cell where you want to enter text. Then type the text.
2. Repeat step 1 until you finish entering all the text for the table.

Selecting Cells in Table

To work with or apply formatting in a table, first you have to select the particular cells, rows and columns. Selected cells, rows and columns appear highlighted.

TO SELECT A RANGE OF CELLS

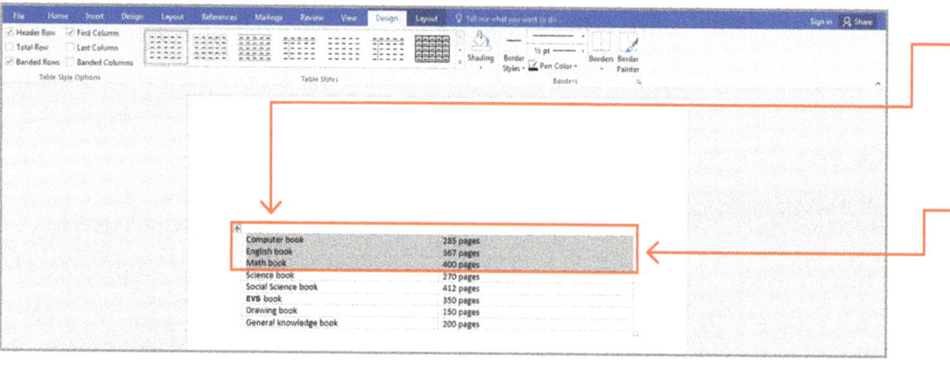

1. Click and drag the mouse over the cells that you want to select.
2. Release the mouse button to select the cells.

TO SELECT A SINGLE CELL

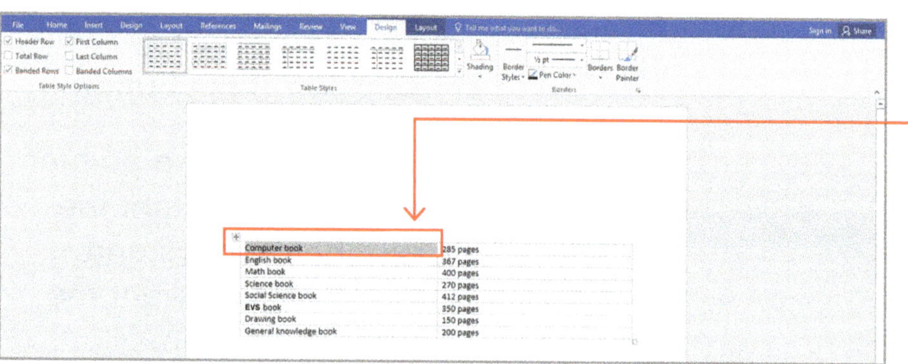

You can triple-click the cell to select everything in it.

TO SELECT AN ENTIRE ROW

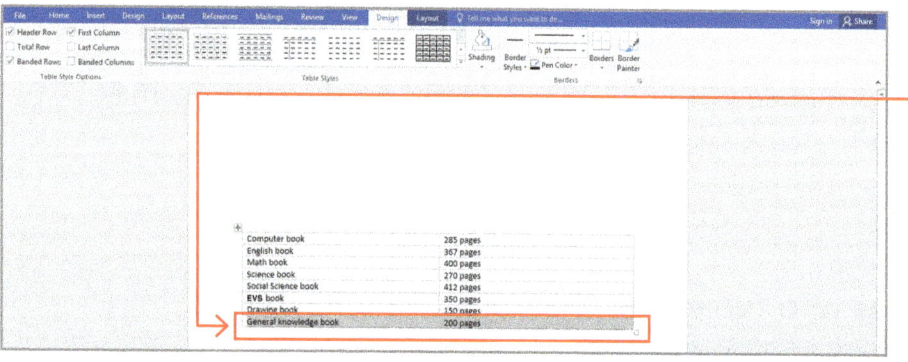

Take your mouse near the left border of row and click on it.

The entire row will be selected.

TO SELECT AN ENTIRE COLUMN

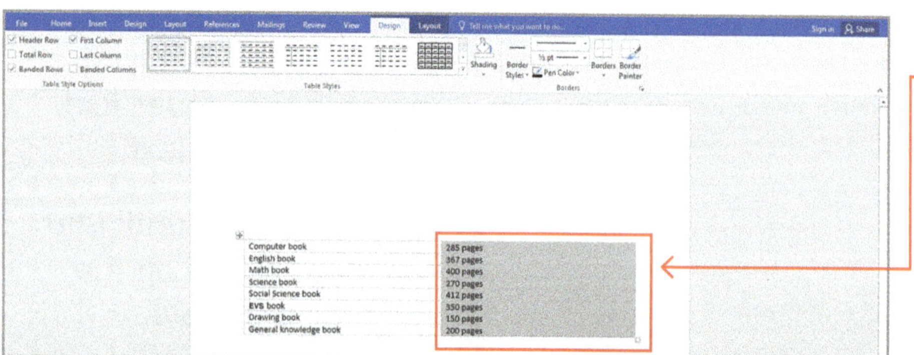

Take your mouse near the upper border of column and click on it.

The entire column will be selected.

Inserting Rows and Columns

You can also insert extra rows or columns, if required, in between the table.

Inserting Rows

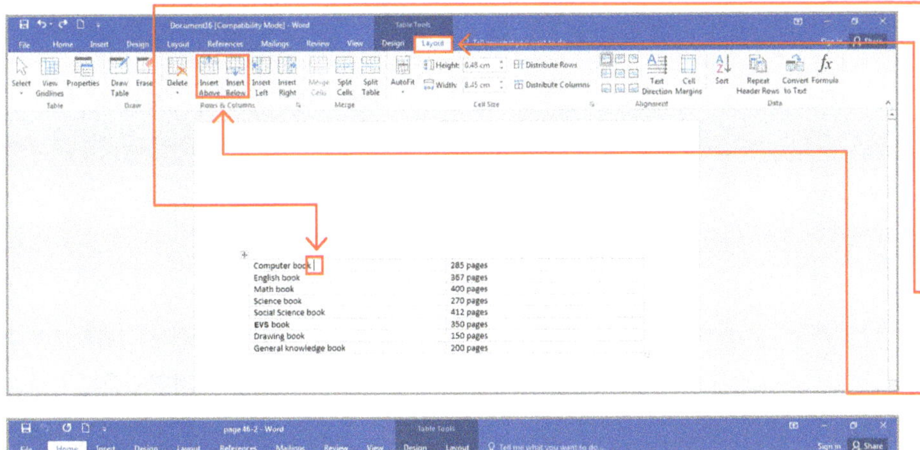

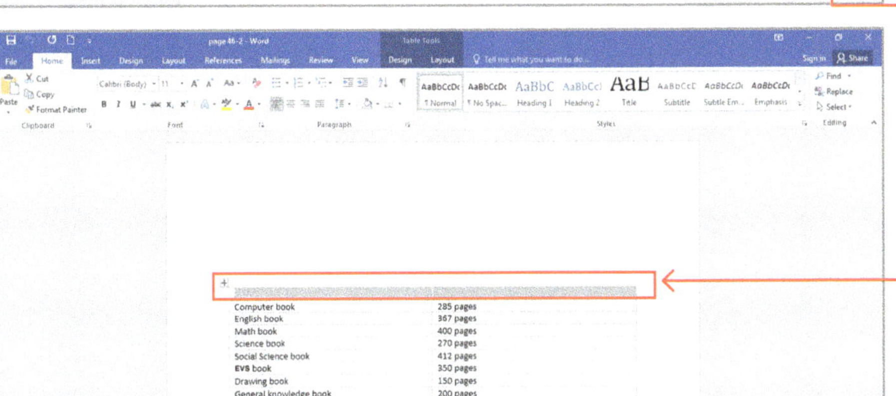

1. Click in the row where you want to add another row.

If you select more than one row, Word duplicates the number when you activate Insert command.

2. Click on Layout tab in Table Tools group.
3. You can click Insert Above or Insert Below to add new rows.

In this example, we click on Insert Above.

Word adds a row to the table.

Inserting Columns

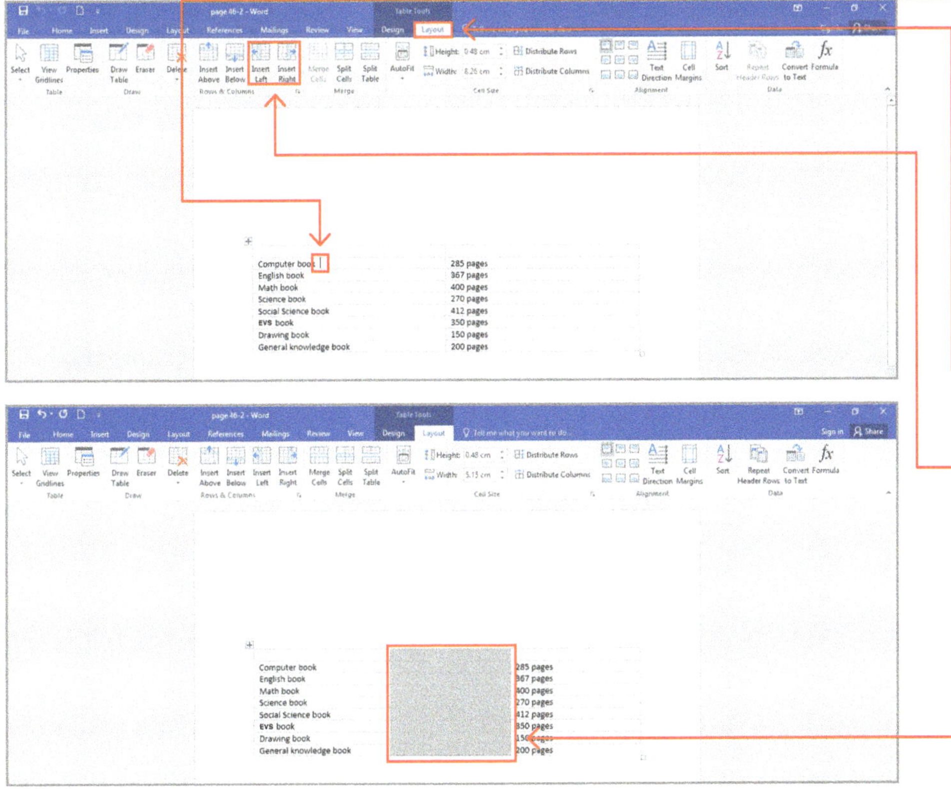

1. Click in the column where you want to add another column.

If you select more than one column. Word duplicates the number when you activate Insert command.

2. Click on Layout tab in Table Tools group.
3. You can click Insert left or Insert right to add new columns.

In this example, we click on Insert Right.

Word adds a column to the table.

Deleting Rows and Columns

You can also delete extra rows or columns, if not needed, from the table.

Deleting Row

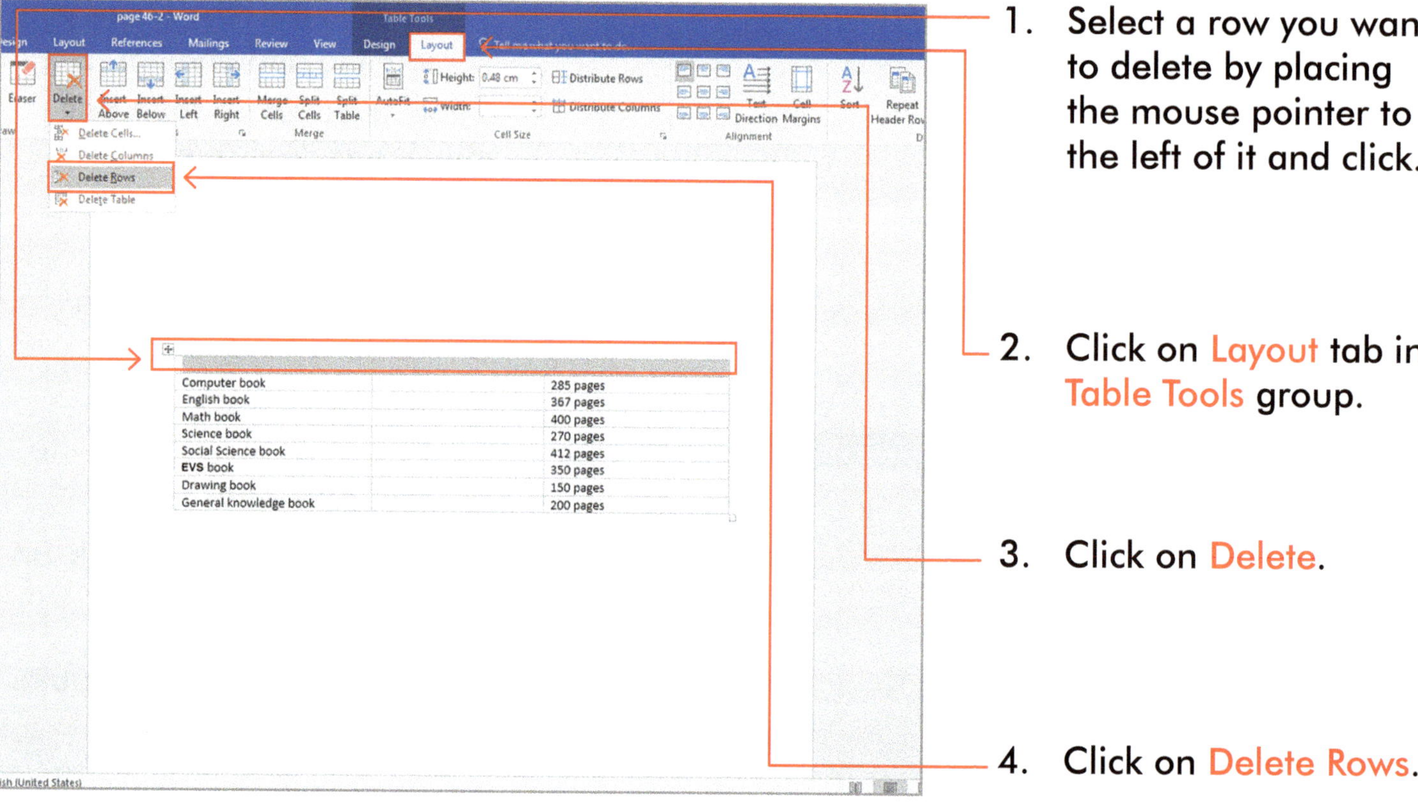

1. Select a row you want to delete by placing the mouse pointer to the left of it and click.
2. Click on Layout tab in Table Tools group.
3. Click on Delete.
4. Click on Delete Rows.

Deleting Column

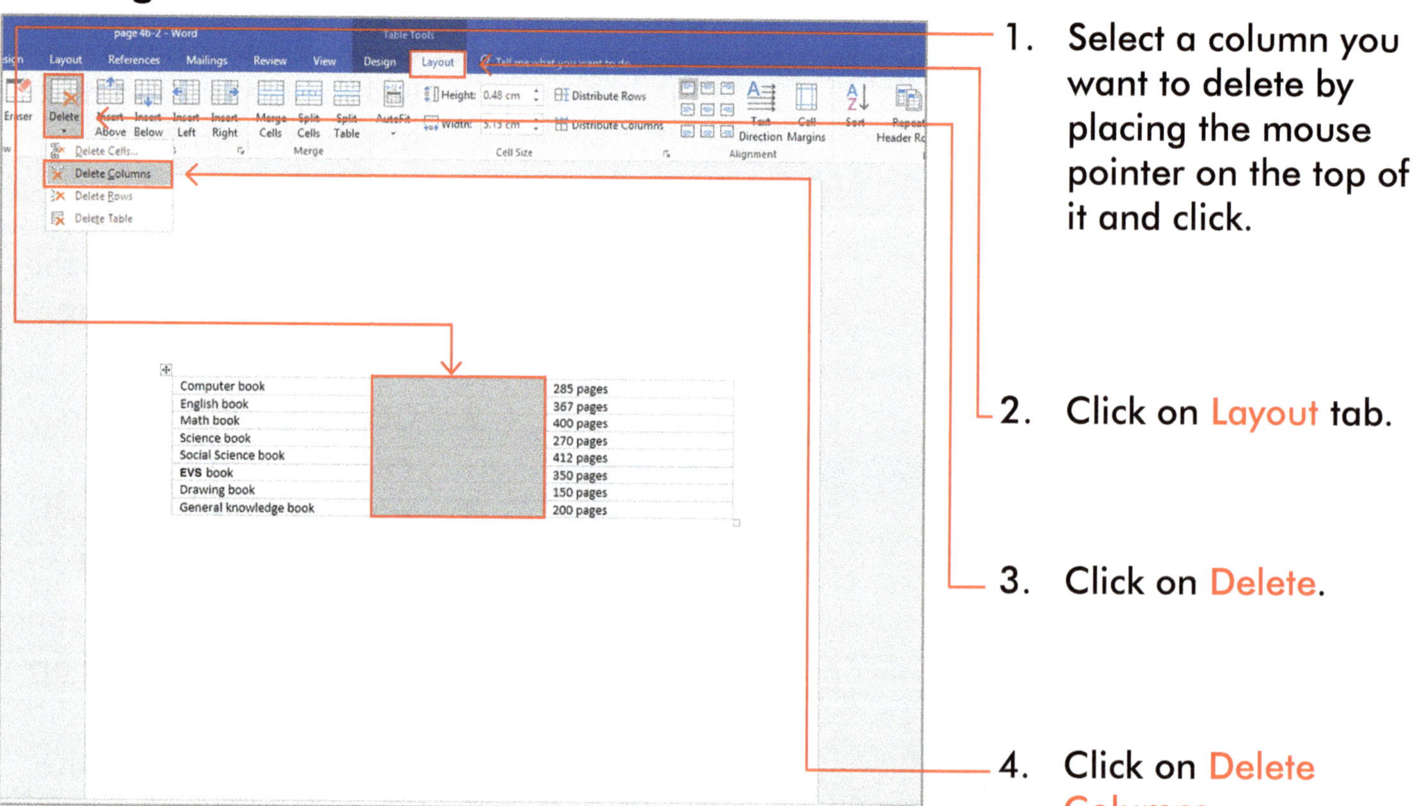

1. Select a column you want to delete by placing the mouse pointer on the top of it and click.
2. Click on Layout tab.
3. Click on Delete.
4. Click on Delete Columns.

Change the Row Height or Column Width

You can change the height of rows or the width of columns to accommodate your table information.

Changing Height of a Row

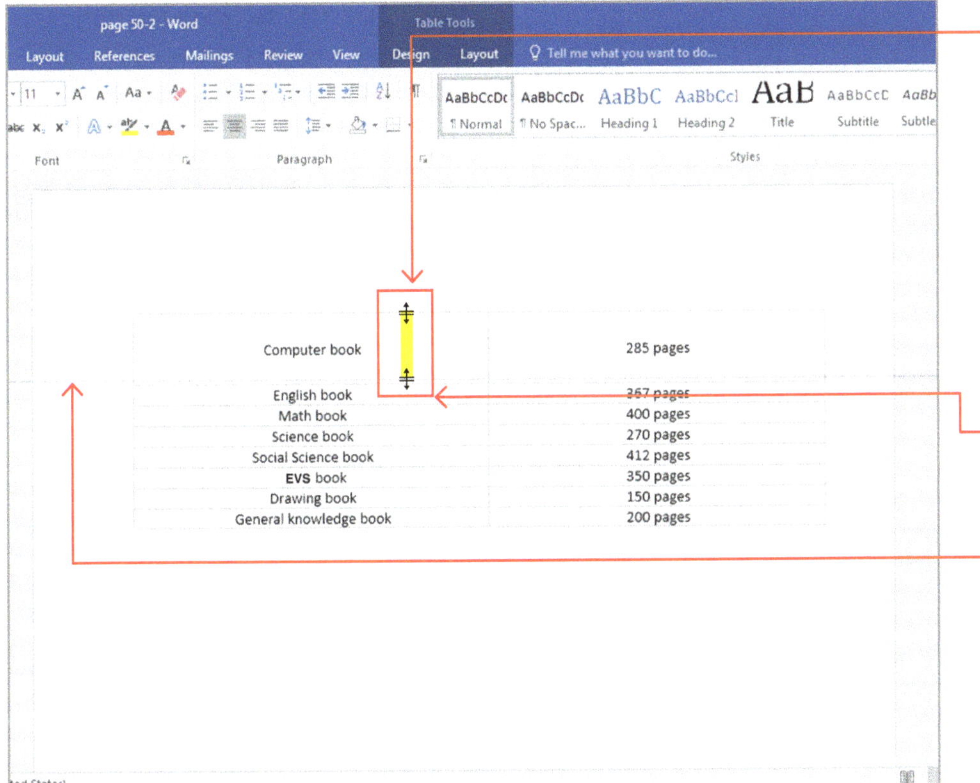

1. Place the mouse pointer over the bottom edge of the row you want to change into a new height.

The mouse pointer changes into (ǂ).

2. Drag the row edge to a new position.

A dotted line shows the new position.

Release the mouse pointer.

Word adjusts the row height.

Changing Width of a Column

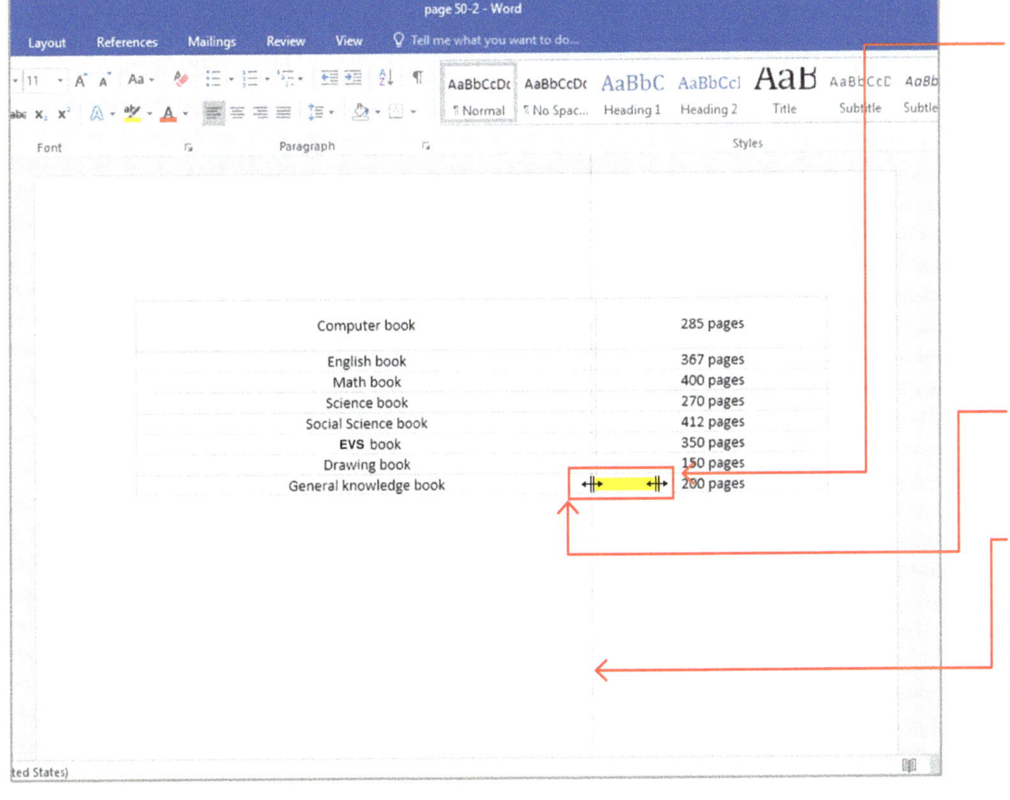

1. Place the mouse pointer over the edge of the column you want to change into a new width.

The mouse pointer changes into (⟛).

2. Drag the column edge to a new position.

A dotted line shows the new position.

Release the mouse pointer.

Word adjusts the column width.

Moving a Table

You can move a table to a different location in your document.

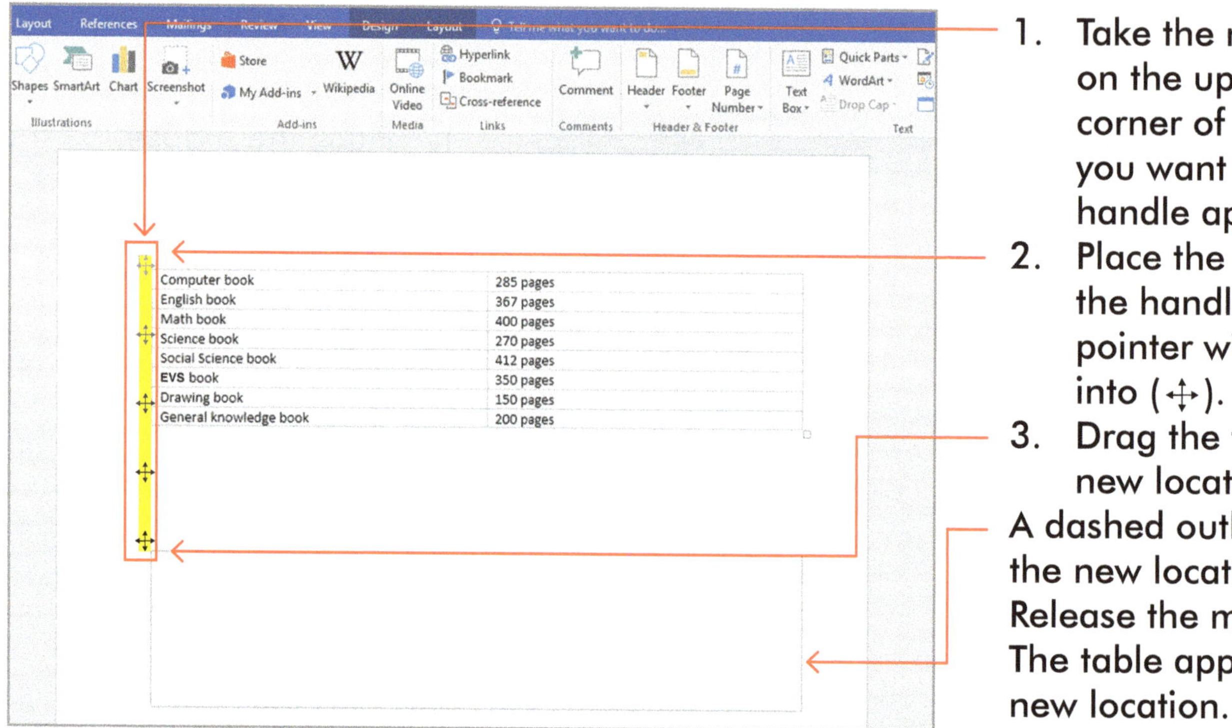

1. Take the mouse pointer on the upper-left corner of the table, you want to move. A handle appears.
2. Place the mouse over the handle. The mouse pointer will change into (✥).
3. Drag the table to a new location.

A dashed outline indicates the new location.

Release the mouse button. The table appears in the new location.

To copy a table, perform steps 1 to 3, except press and hold down the Ctrl key as you perform step 3.

Resizing a Table

You can change the size of a table if you find that your table dimensions do not suit your purpose.

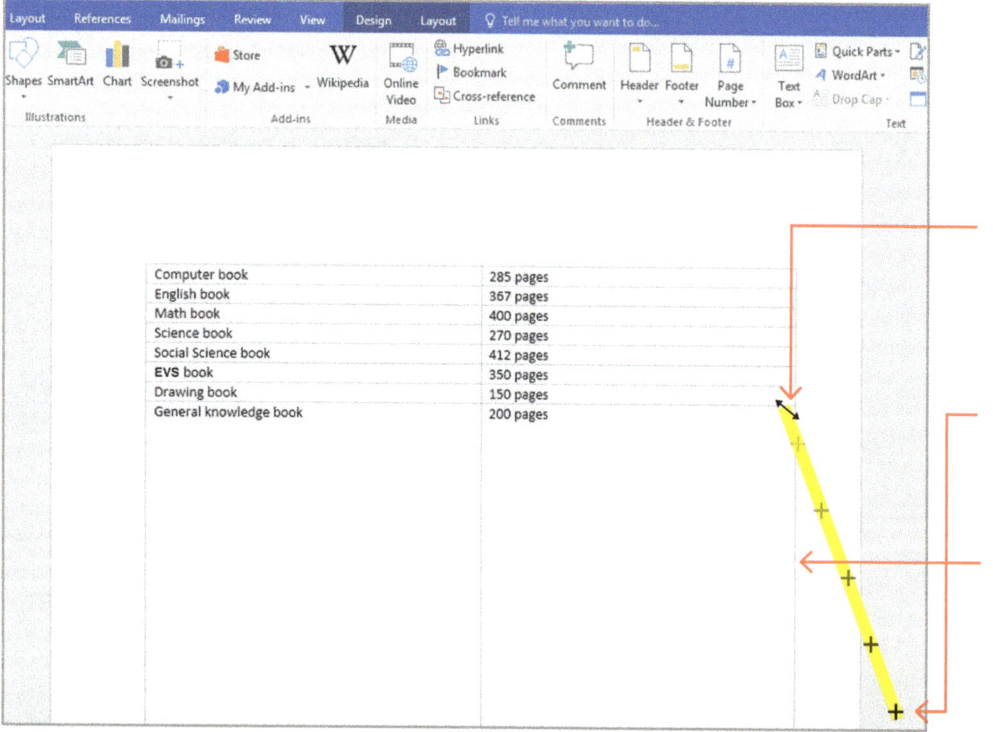

1. Point the mouse pointer over the table you want to resize.

A handle appears.

2. Place the mouse over the handle. The mouse pointer will change into (↘).
3. Drag the handle until the table is of the size you want.

A dashed outline indicates the new size of table.

Release the mouse button. Word resizes the table.

Aligning The Text In Cell

You can align text with the top, bottom, left, right or centre of cells to make your text look more uniform. By default, Word aligns your table text to the left, inside each cell.

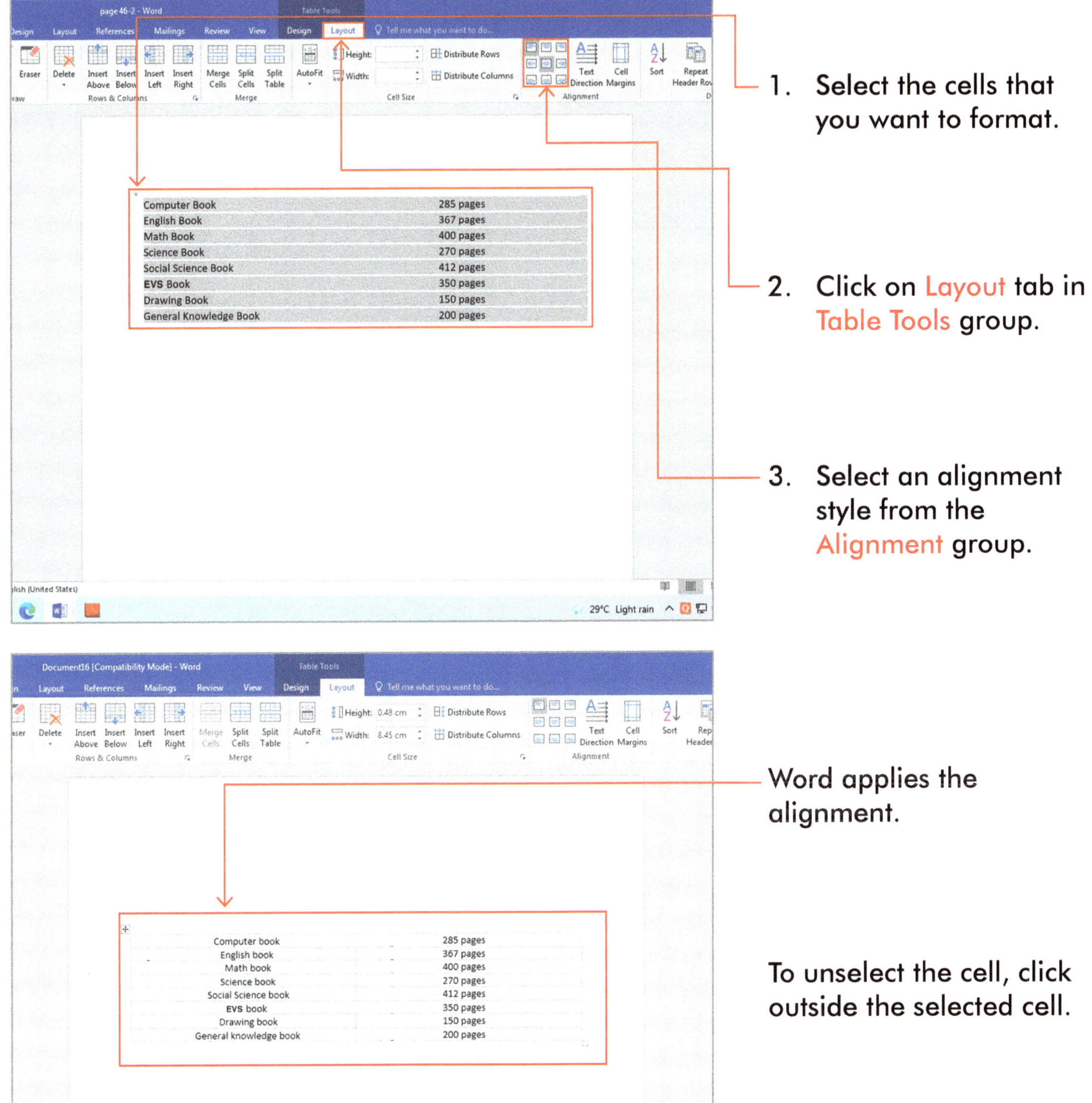

1. Select the cells that you want to format.
2. Click on Layout tab in Table Tools group.
3. Select an alignment style from the Alignment group.

Word applies the alignment.

To unselect the cell, click outside the selected cell.

This example centres the text in the cells.

Combining Cells In A Table

To create one large cell, you can combine two or more cells in your table. It is useful when you want to display a title across the top side of your table.

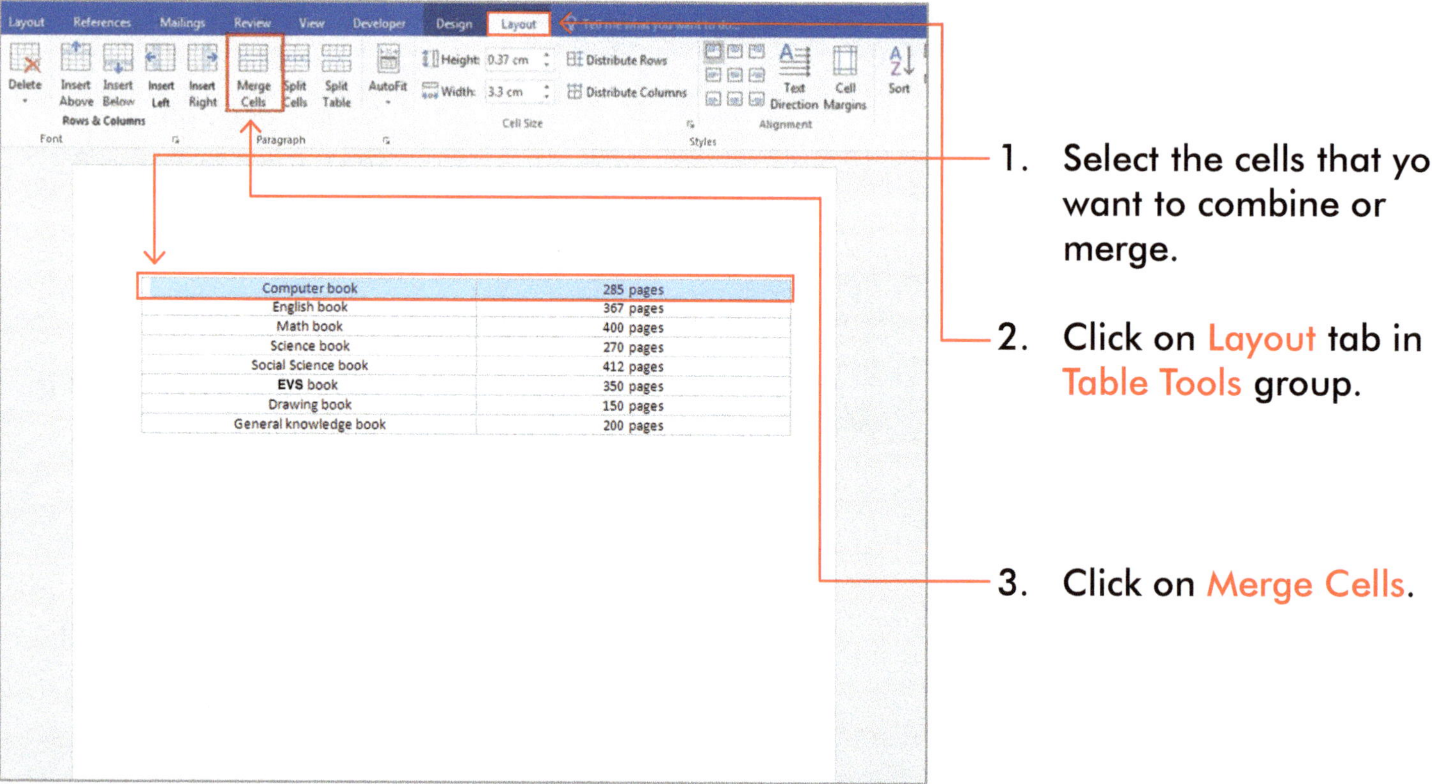

1. Select the cells that you want to combine or merge.
2. Click on Layout tab in Table Tools group.
3. Click on Merge Cells.

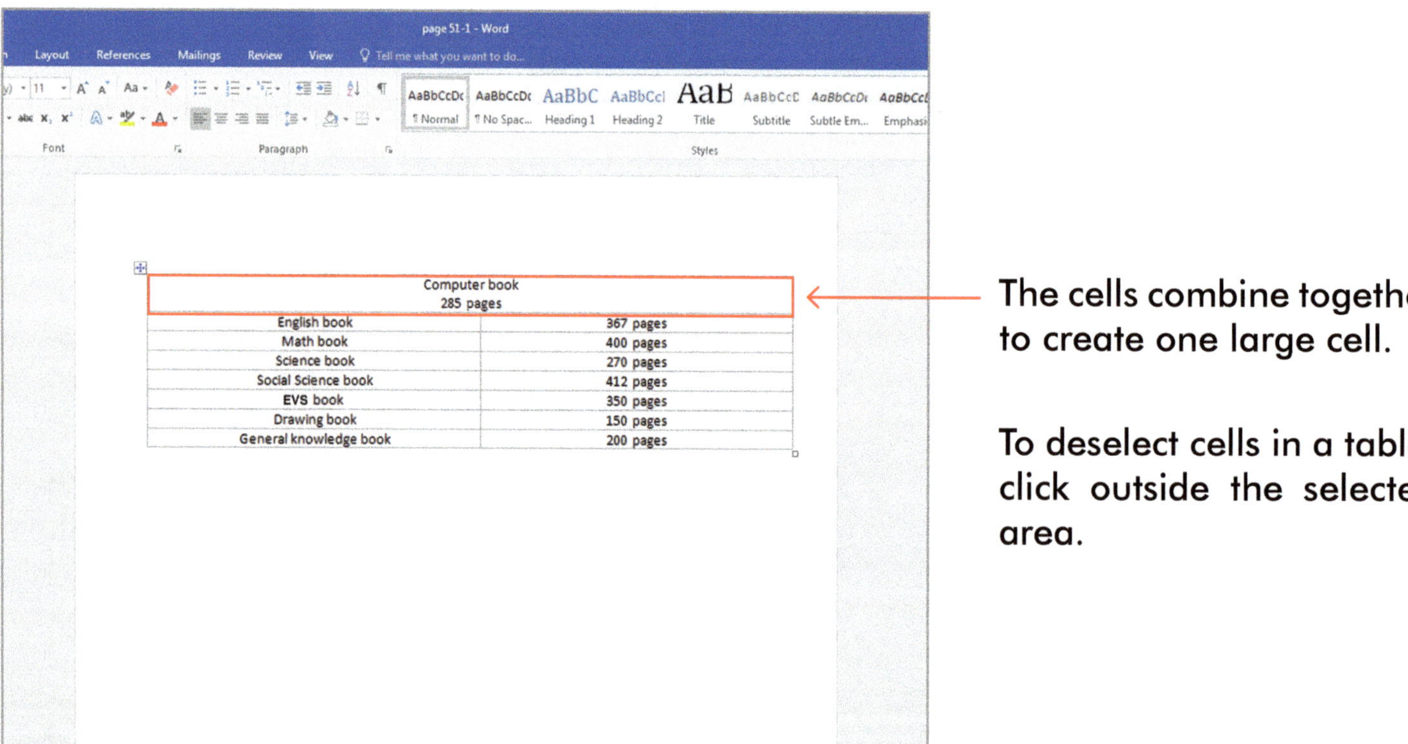

The cells combine together to create one large cell.

To deselect cells in a table, click outside the selected area.

Applying Table Styles

The ready-made table styles specifically designed can be applied to your table. Table styles provide you with a variety of ready-made designs that include shading, colour, borders and fonts of the table.

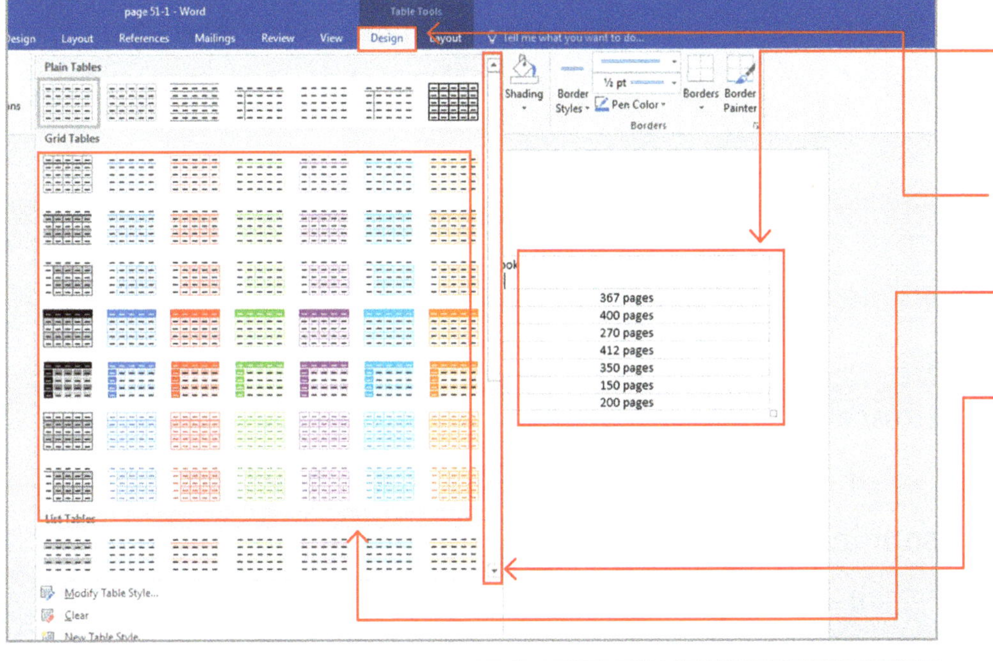

1. Click on anywhere in the table that you want to format.
2. Click on Design tab in Table Tools group.
3. Click on a styles from the Table Styles list.

You can click on the down arrow button of More to display the entire palette of available styles.

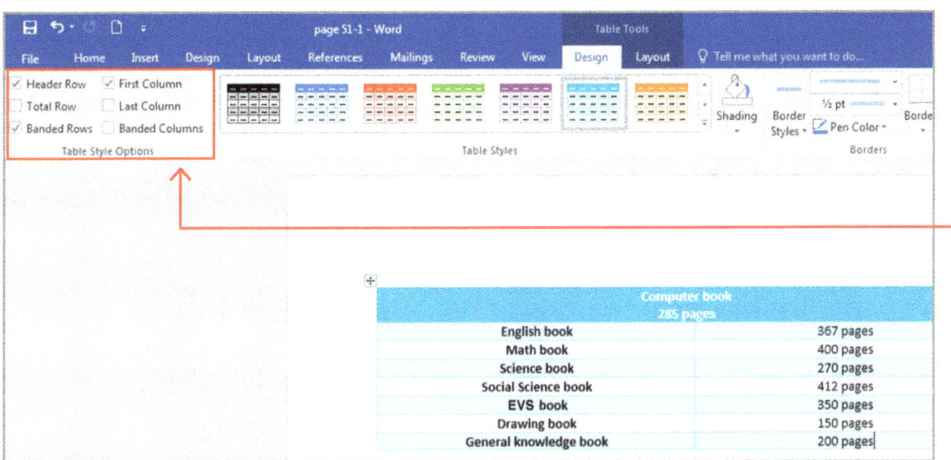

Computer book	285 pages
English book	367 pages
Math book	400 pages
Science book	270 pages
Social Science book	412 pages
EVS book	350 pages
Drawing book	150 pages
General knowledge book	200 pages

You can use the Table Style Options by clicking on check boxes.

Word applies the style.

LET'S HAVE A LOOK

- MS-Word is a word processing software used to create text-based documents.
- Formatting refers to the appearance or presentation of the document in attractive manner.
- Formatting can be done by using Font and Paragraph group in Home tab.
- A font in MS-Word is a design and style of a character.
- The text size in document is measured in points.
- Bold, italic and underline buttons are present in Font Group on Home tab.
- Text wrap is a feature that enables you to surround a picture or image with text.
- The WordArt feature provides you with ready-to-use text effects.
- Table is used to insert the text in tabular form.

SHORTCUT KEYS

Bold	:	Ctrl+B	Italic	:	Ctrl+I
Underline	:	Ctrl+U	Right Align	:	Ctrl+R
Left Align	:	Ctrl+L	Justification	:	Ctrl+J
Centre Align	:	Ctrl+E	Increase font size	:	Ctrl+]
Decrease font size	:	Ctrl+[			

BRAIN TEASER

1. Multiple Choice Questions

Tick (✓) the correct answer:

a. Changing the text appearance to make document attractive:
   i. Editing ☐ ii. Formatting ☐ iii. Entering ☐

b. The font options are present in:
   i. Insert tab ☐ ii. View Tab ☐ iii. Home tab ☐

c. The font size is measured in:
   i. Inch ☐ ii. CM ☐ iii. Points ☐

d. Shortcut key to make the text bold is:
   i. Ctrl+B ☐ ii. Ctrl+I ☐ iii. Ctrl+U ☐

e. Clipart feature is present in:
   i. Home tab ☐ ii. Insert tab ☐ iii. View tab ☐

f. Adjusting the text around the picture:
   i. ClipArt ☐ ii. WordArt ☐ iii. TextWrap ☐

2. Fill in the blanks:

a. MS-Word is a ______________ software.

b. Formatting can be done by using ______________ and ______________ group in Home tab.

c. You can ______________ and ______________ the size of the text as per your need.

d. ______________ and ______________ allow you to organise text in lists.

e. The ______________ feature provides you with the different text effects.

f. A table consists of a ______________ of boxes.

3. Answer the following questions

(i) Answer each in a few lines:

a. Where are formatting buttons present?

b. What feature is used to make changes in your document?

c. Name four types of alignments provided by MS-Word.

d. What are the different formatting buttons present in MS-Word?

e. Name the different types of tabs present in Word Window.

(ii) Answer each comprehensively:

a. What is MS-Word?

b. What is formatting. How is it useful?

c. Define font. Make a list of some common fonts available in MS-Word.

d. What is Alignment?

e. What are WordArt and Clipart feature used for?

f. What is the use of table feature?

g. Why do you use bullets and numbering in document?

4. Write the procedure for each of the following:

a. Inserting pictures

b. Inserting bullets and numbering

c. Inserting a table

d. Changing the column width

Create a calendar for the years 2022 and 2023 in Word by using Table.

5 Starting MS-Excel

In this chapter, we will learn:

⇒ About MS-Excel as a spreadsheet

⇒ Functions of Excel

⇒ Basic Features of Excel

⇒ Various Components of Excel

⇒ Spreadsheets and Workbooks

⇒ Entering data in MS-Excel

⇒ Arranging workbook in Excel

⇒ Closing a workbook

⇒ Exiting from MS-Excel

MS-EXCEL

MS-Excel is an electronic spreadsheet program that has many uses, for example, it can be used as a financial tool to perform calculations and other tasks automatically. Other uses include: creating contact lists, budgets, or just to track and analyze data for both business and personal use. Excel allows you to accomplish these tasks in a shorter period of time than writing or calculating by hand.

Functions of Excel

Various functions of the spreadsheet program are:

Organize data : Microsoft Excel is a great tool for organizing data in rows and columns. The row and column format of an Excel spreadsheet is perfect for entering many types of data you need to track. After entering the data, you can perform various sorting operations to control how the data is listed.

Store data in worksheet : Data you enter into Excel is stored in a file, called a workbook. Within each workbook, you can store many individual worksheets to hold your data. You can give your worksheets distinct names. You can even add and delete worksheets as needed.

Present your data : You can make your spreadsheet data easier to read with the help of the formatting tools in excel. You can add shading to cells, change the number, format or change the font and size of your data. You can also present your worksheet data to others using charts and graphs.

Used as an analytical tool : Besides the good use on managing data, Excel is a great analytical tool for business. With the Pivot table contained within Excel, you can easily analyze a large number of data, as the Pivot table can automatically sort, count and total the data stored in one table or spreadsheet and create a second table displaying the summarized data.

Create forms and consolidate result : You can use Excel to create not only a simple form that contains boxes, but also professional forms which include options buttons that allow you to select answers, drop down list to select a particular answer from the list of items.

Share data : You can share your data with other users. You can import data from other sources into your Excel worksheets or export your data into other file formats. You can also save your data as a PDF or HTML file to share with others or post on the Internet.

BASIC FEATURES OF EXCEL

There are a number of features that are available in Excel to make your task easier. Some of the main features are:

Edit and format data : You can enter, edit and format data in an Excel worksheet. You can quickly enter a series of numbers, find and replace data or check data for spelling errors. You can also make data stand out in a worksheet by adding borders or changing the font, colour, style or alignment of the data.

Autofill : This feature allows you to fill cells quickly with repetitive or sequential data, such as chronological dates or numbers, and repeated text. AutoFill can also be used to copy functions. You can also alter text and numbers with this feature.

Autoshapes toolbar : This toolbar will allows you to draw a number of geometrical shapes, arrows, flowchart elements, stars and more. With these shapes you can draw your own graphs.

Charts : This feature helps you present a graphical representation of your data in the form of Pie charts, Bar charts, Line charts and more.

Using formula and functions : Formulas and functions allow you to perform calculations and analyze data in a worksheet. Common calculations include : finding the sum, average or total number of values in a list.

Print worksheets : You can produce a hard copy of a worksheet you create. Before printing, you can see on your screen how the worksheet will look when printed.

Opening MS-Excel

Before you begin working with Excel, you must open the program window. The steps to open MS-Excel window are given below:

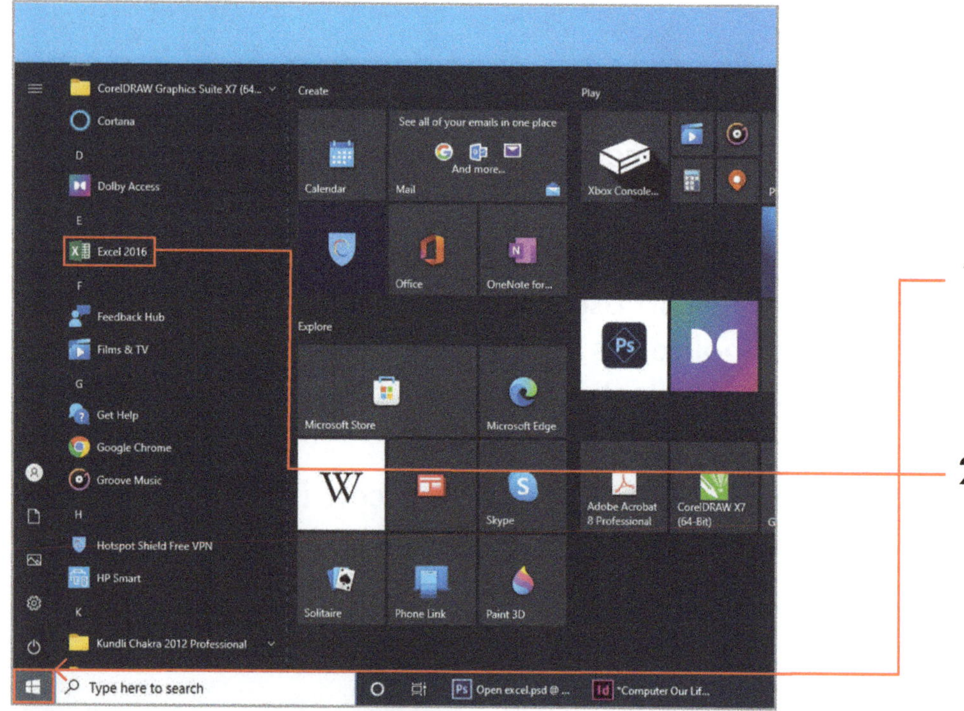

1. Click on Start button.

2. Scroll the menu and click Excel 2016.

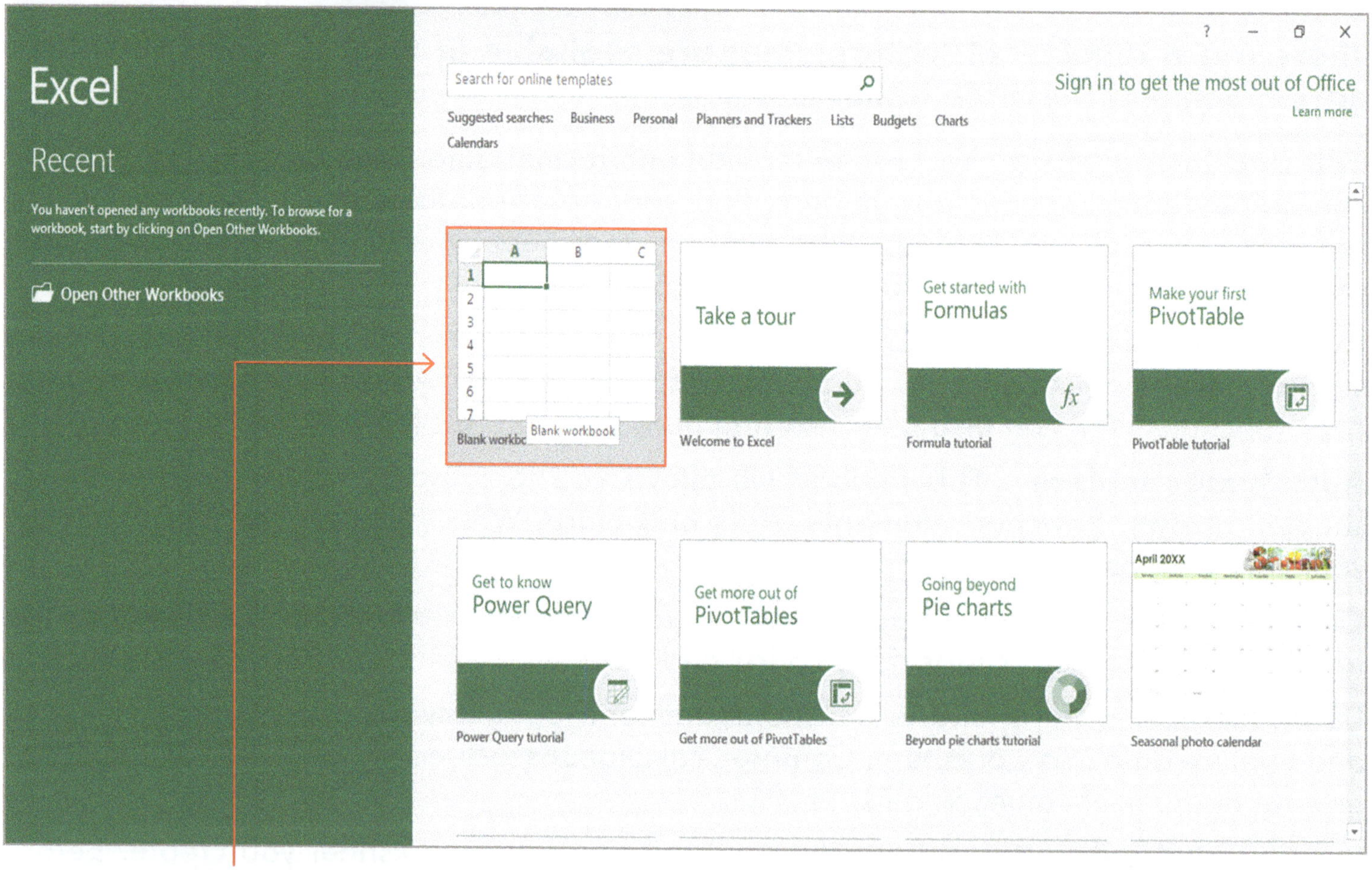

3. Click on the Blank workbook.

After following the above steps, a window will appear on the screen as shown below. The Excel 2016 program window displays several common elements found in MS-Word 2016 program, including a File tab, the Ribbon, the Quick Access toolbar and scroll bars. In addition, the Excel window features a Formula bar for entering mathematical formulas.

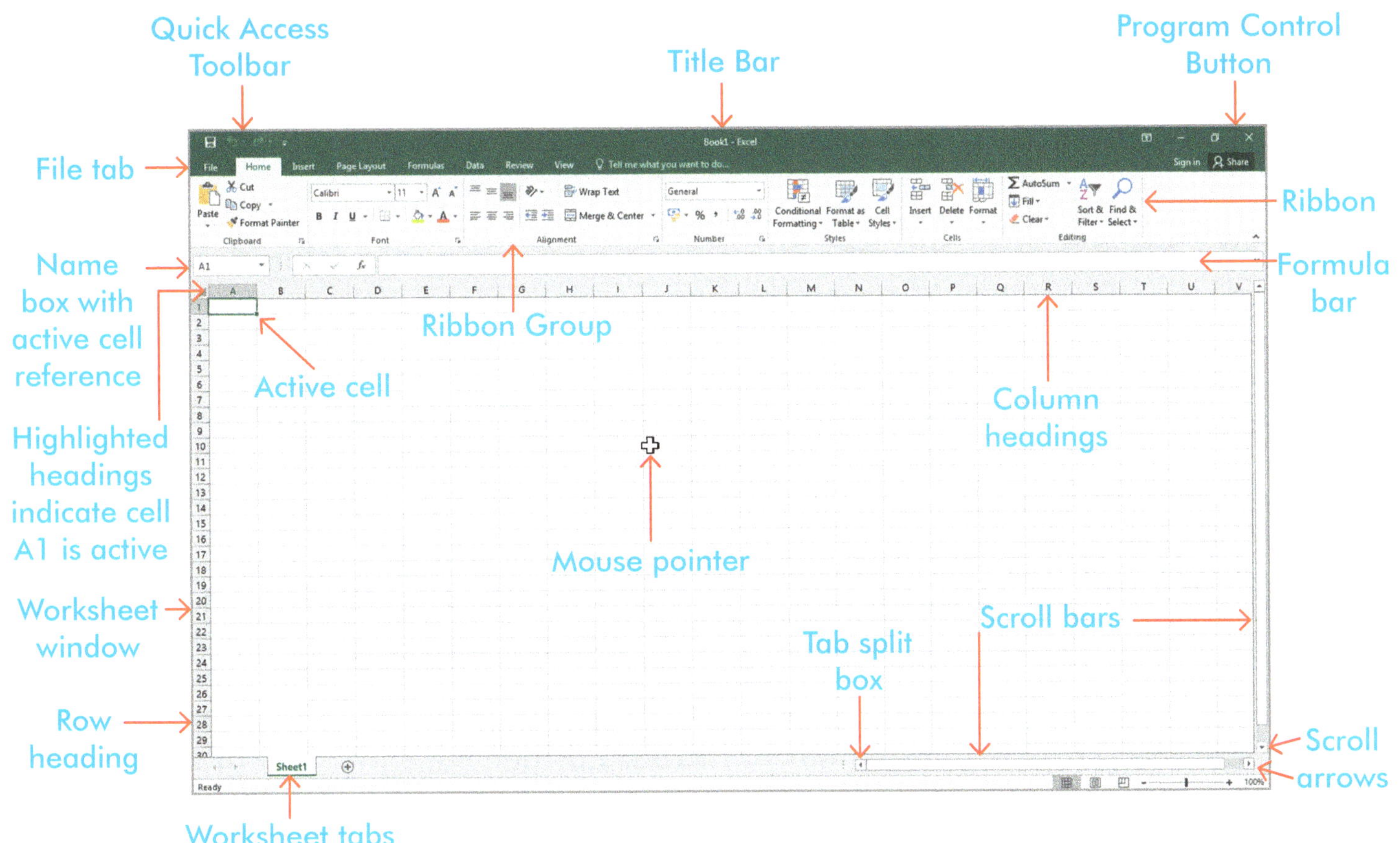

DIFFERENT COMPONENTS OF MS-EXCEL 2016 WINDOW

Title bar : It is located on the top of the window that shows the name of the current workbook.

File tab : A green button located at the left top corner that contains the file menu command, such as New, Open, Save, etc.

Quick Access Toolbar : It displays quick access buttons to the Save, Undo and Redo commands.

Ribbon : The menu tabs with the group of related command buttons are displayed on it.

Ribbon Group : Tools on the Ribbon are organized into groups by their respective functions.

Formula Bar : It is used to enter and edit formulas and perform calculations on your worksheet data.

Program Window Controls : On the right corner of the title bar, there are three buttons to minimize, maximize or close the worksheet window.

Name box : The address of the active cell is displayed in this box.

Worksheet Window : It is a single page in Excel, also called spreadsheet. By default, there are three worksheets present in an Excel workbook. Each worksheet of Excel 2016 typically has 16384 columns and 1048576 rows. The column letters begin with A and end with XFD; row numbers begin with 1 and end with 1048577. Only a small fraction of these columns and rows displays on the screen at one time.

Gridlines : The vertical and horizontal lines that divide the sheet into a row and a column are the Gridlines.

Active Cell : A cell is formed by the intersection of a row and a column. The currently selected cell that appears highlighted with dark black border is an active cell. The data is entered in the active cell.

Scroll bar : A worksheet window allows you to view the portion of the worksheet displayed on the screen. Below and to the right of the worksheet window are scroll bars, scroll arrows and scroll boxes, which you can use to move the window around in order to view the different parts of the active worksheet.

Worksheet Tab : There can be more than one worksheet in Excel and each has a specific name. Any worksheet can be activated by clicking on the worksheet tab.

Tab Split bar : To the right of the worksheet tabs at the bottom of the screen is the tab split box. You can drag the tab split box to increase or decrease the view of sheet tabs.

Mouse Pointer : The mouse pointer is displayed as a block plus sign [✚], whenever it is located in a cell on the worksheet. Another common shape of the mouse pointer is the block arrow.

Row and Column Heading Buttons : Work area is divided into rows and columns. Rows are meant for using numbers and columns for using letters.

Tab Scrolling button : It is arranged on the left side of the horizontal scroll bar. It is used to display the worksheet tabs which are invisible. To activate the worksheet, the tab is displayed and clicked.

SPREADSHEETS AND WORKBOOKS

The Excel file is often called a workbook and a workbook consists of different worksheets, also called spreadsheets.

The application software is known to be spreadsheet software generally when the work is done in tabular form with number and text including calculation and graphic operations.

Remember

Maximum 256 worksheets can be added in a workbook.

A spreadsheet is a grid of data divided into numbered rows and lettered columns. Each block in this grid is called a cell,and it can hold an individual piece of text or data. A cell has a lettered column and numbered row. In Excel, a file/document is considered a spreadsheet, although it is commonly referred to as a workbook.

A new MS-Excel workbook contains 3 worksheets by default - Sheet1, Sheet2 and Sheet3. You can add a worksheet to the workbook. The name of the worksheet that is currently in use is highlighted in bold letters. It is the active sheet.

Basic parts of a Spreadsheet

Workbook : A workbook is a collection of different worksheets. By default, a workbook contains three worksheets that can be increased or decreased as per the requirement.

Cell : The Intersection of rows and columns is called a cell. A cell in Excel worksheet looks like a rectangular box.

Cell Address : The cell address corresponds to the column name and the row name; each cell has a unique address.

Cell Range : It is a collection of two or more cells: A cell range is of two types: Contiguous Cell Range and Non-Contiguous Cell Range. Contiguous Cell Range is a collection of cells which are adjacent to one another. Colon (:) is used to specify this cell range, e.g. A1:A6. Non-Contiguous Cell Range is a collection of cells which are not adjacent to one another. Comma (,) is used to specify this cell range, e.g., (A1,B1,C3). A cell range can be referred to in a formula as well.

Block : A group of cells, when selected, forms a rectangle; it is called a block.

Data types : While working in Excel, the following types of data can be entered:

⇒ **Numbers** : Numbers include the digits (0-9) and their various combinations. All types of calculations can be done on numbers.

⇒ **Text** : Text includes the collection of alphabet, numbers and special characters. No mathematical calculation can be performed with text.

⇒ **Formula** : A formula includes digits and mathematical symbols. The formula should always start with an equal sign (=).

⇒ **Date and Time** : Date type is used to enter date in a different format but the default format is mm/dd/yy. Time data type is used to enter time in either hh:mm or hh:mm:ss format.

Creating a New Workbook

By default, every new workbook you open automatically contains three blank worksheets you can use to enter Excel data. But you can create a new workbook any time by following these steps:

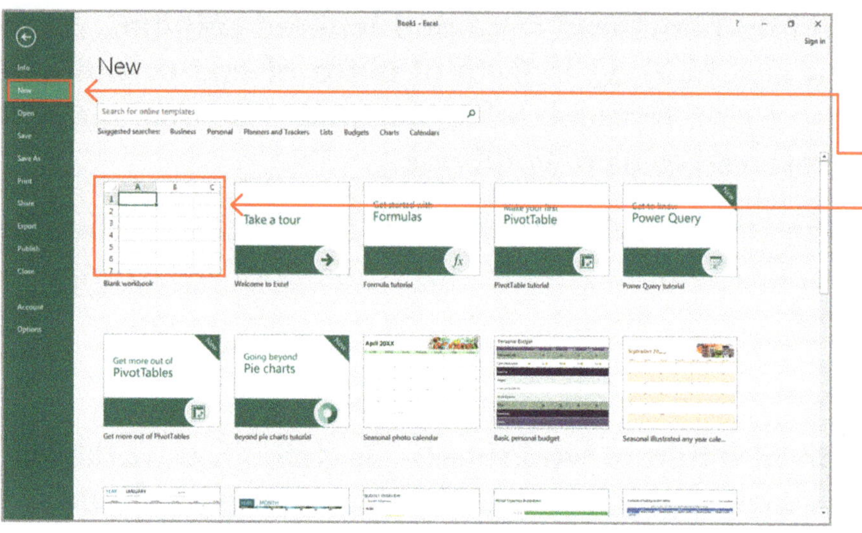

1. Click on File tab.

Backstage view will appear.

2. Click on the New button.
3. Click on Blank Workbook in the Templates list.

A sample View of your selected workbook appears in this area.

The new workbook file will open and you can start adding your own data.

Changing the Active Cell

The new worksheet displayed on screen shows the first cell as an active cell and the active cell can be changed as per requirement.

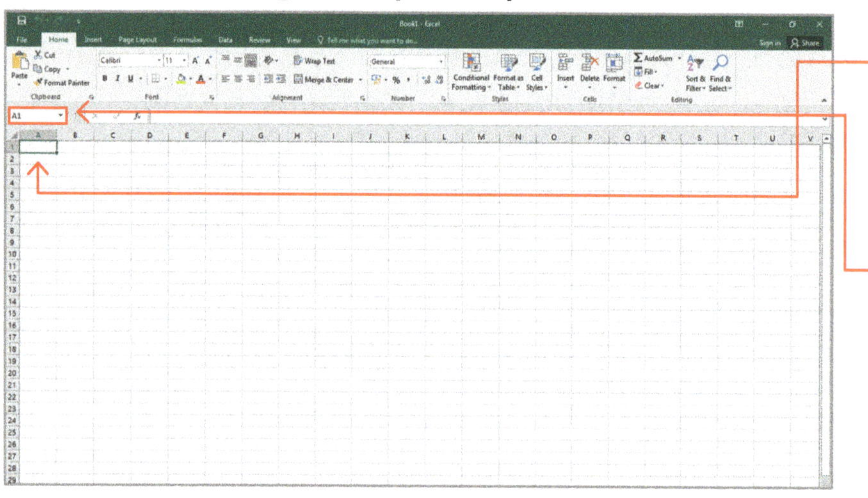

The active cell displays a thick dark border.

The Name box shows the cell reference for the active cell.

A cell reference identifies the location of each cell in a worksheet and consists of a column letter followed by a row number (example: A1).

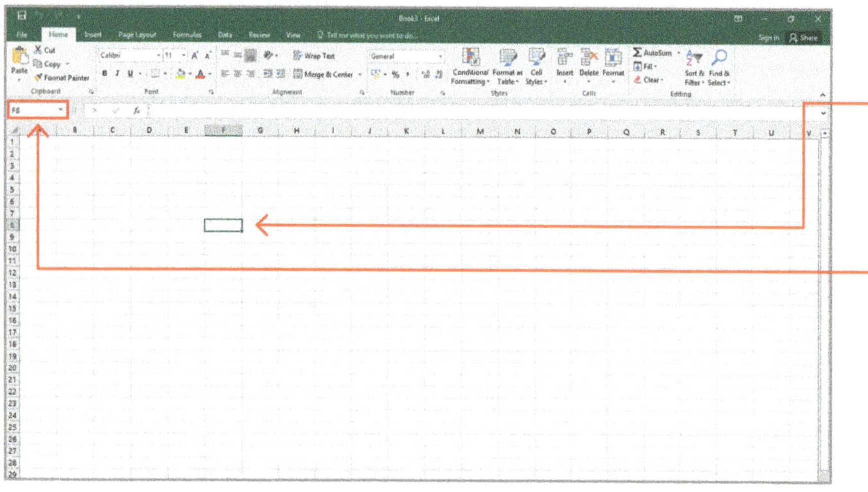

1. Click on the cell you want to make active cell.

The Name box again shows the cell reference for the new active cell (example: F8).

Entering Data in the Worksheet

The data in the form of numbers or text can be entered by just clicking on a cell and typing with the help of a keyboard. You can type data directly into the cell or you can enter data using the Formula bar.

Data can be mostly text or numbers in Excel. Excel automatically left-aligns text data in a cell and right-aligns numbers.

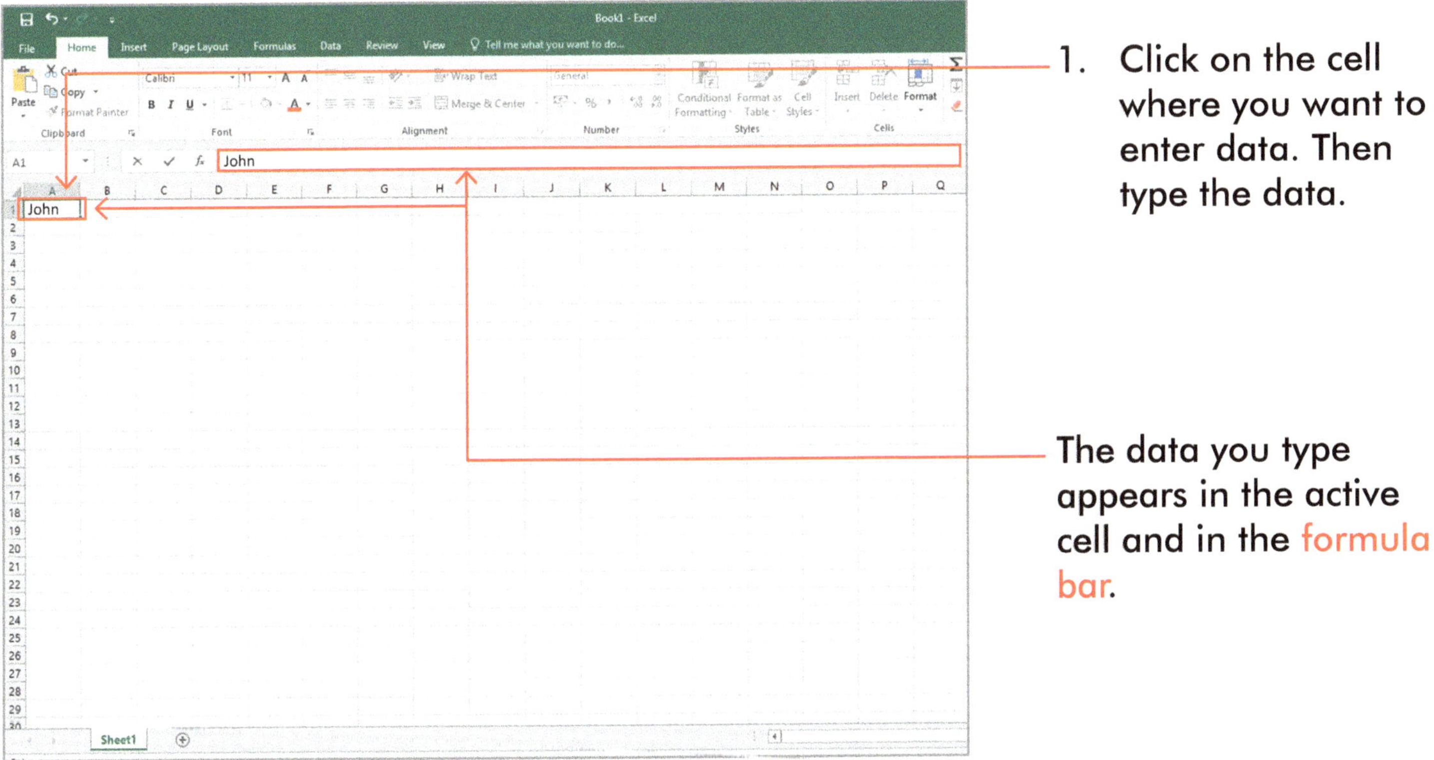

1. Click on the cell where you want to enter data. Then type the data.

The data you type appears in the active cell and in the formula bar.

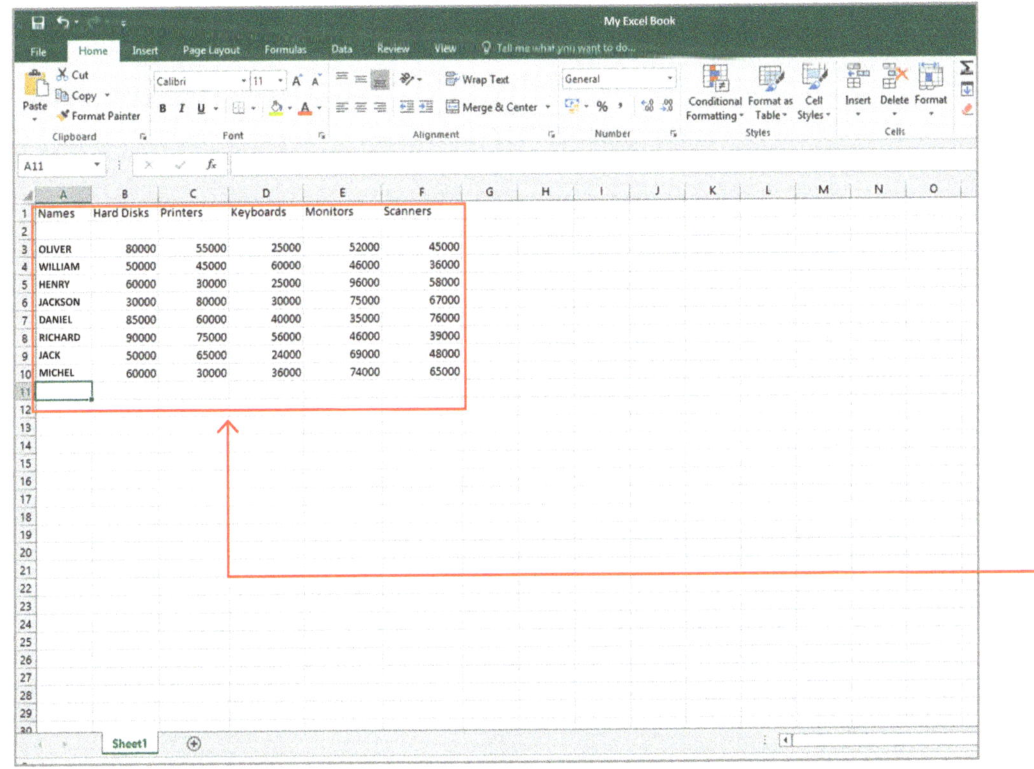

Names	Hard Disks	Printers	Keyboards	Monitors	Scanners
OLIVER	80000	55000	25000	52000	45000
WILLIAM	50000	45000	60000	46000	36000
HENRY	60000	30000	25000	96000	58000
JACKSON	30000	80000	30000	75000	67000
DANIEL	85000	60000	40000	35000	76000
RICHARD	90000	75000	56000	46000	39000
JACK	50000	65000	24000	69000	48000
MICHEL	60000	30000	36000	74000	65000

2. To enter the data and move down one cell, press Enter key from the keyboard.

You can also press arrow keys from the keyboard to enter the data and move one cell in any direction.

3. Repeat steps 1 and 2 until you finish entering all your data.

Saving a Workbook

You can save your data as a workbook file to reuse it or share it with others. To save the workbook in the memory of the computer, follows the steps as:

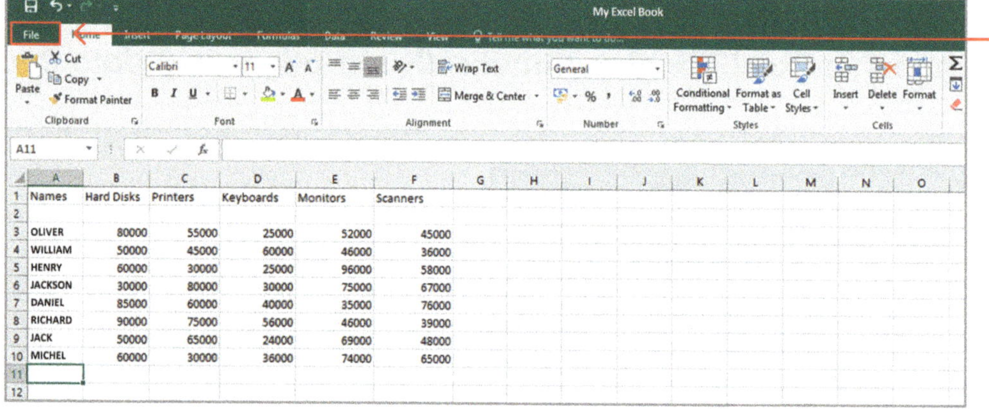

	A	B	C	D	E	F
1	Names	Hard Disks	Printers	Keyboards	Monitors	Scanners
2						
3	OLIVER	80000	55000	25000	52000	45000
4	WILLIAM	50000	45000	60000	46000	36000
5	HENRY	60000	30000	25000	96000	58000
6	JACKSON	30000	80000	30000	75000	67000
7	DANIEL	85000	60000	40000	35000	76000
8	RICHARD	90000	75000	56000	46000	39000
9	JACK	50000	65000	24000	69000	48000
10	MICHEL	60000	30000	36000	74000	65000

1. Click on File tab.

Backstage view will appear.

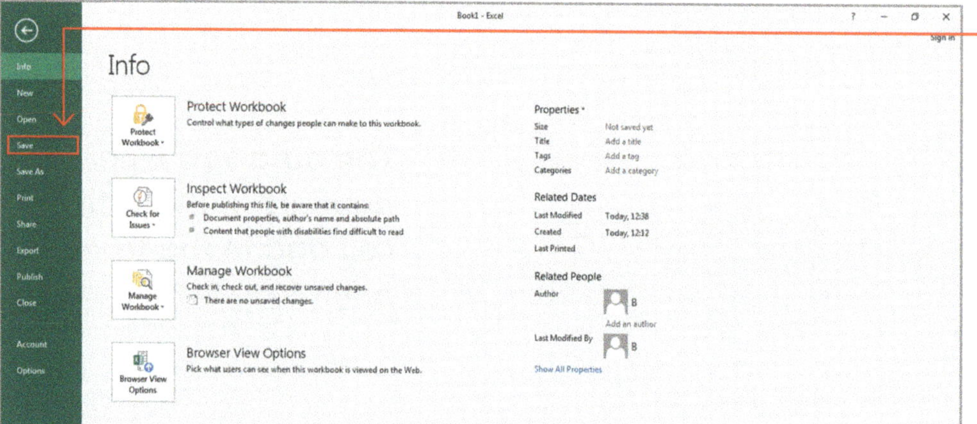

2. Click on the Save or Save As button.

You can also click the Save button ( ) on Quick Access toolbar to save the file.

The Save As dialog box appears.

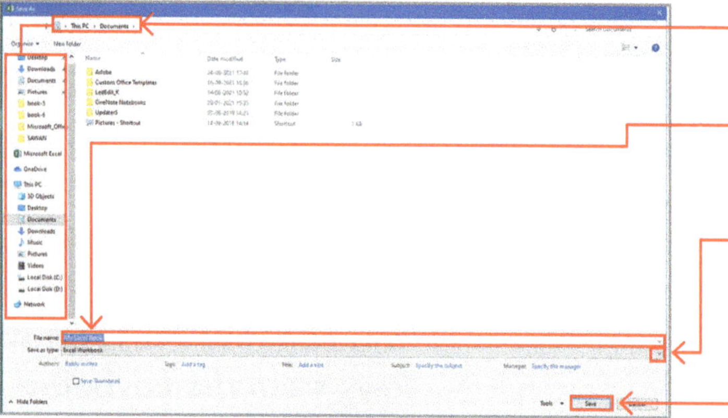

3. Click on these areas to navigate to the folder in which you want to save the file.
4. Click in the File name text box and type a name for the file.

You can click on the down arrow Save as type and choose a format to save the file in another format.

5. Click on Save.

Remember

The Excel file is saved with .xlsx file extension.

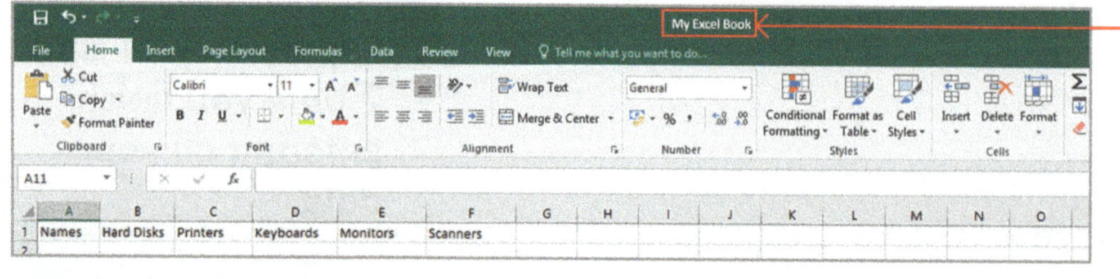

The Excel saves the workbook and the new filename appears on the title bar.

Opening An Already Existing File

You can open a workbook you have already saved. To open an already existing file, follow the given steps:

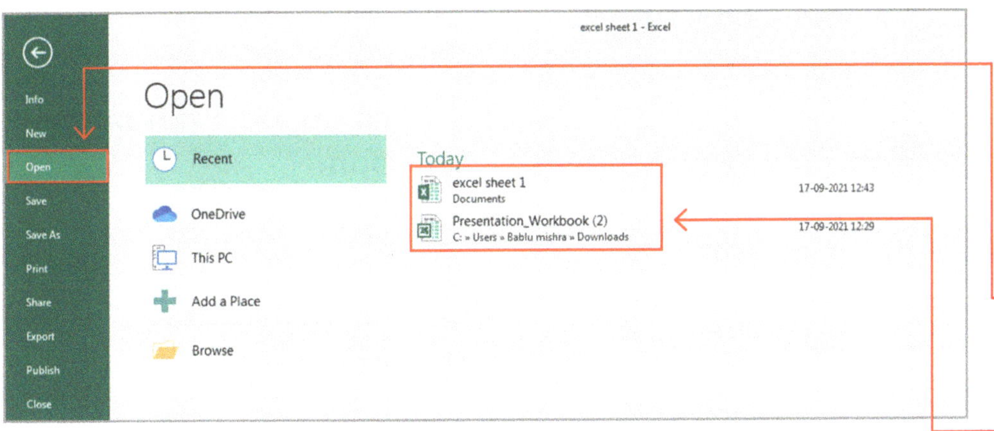

1. Click on File tab.

Backstage view will appear.

2. Click on the Open button.

The recently opened workbook appears on the File menu, and you can click any of these workbooks to open them.

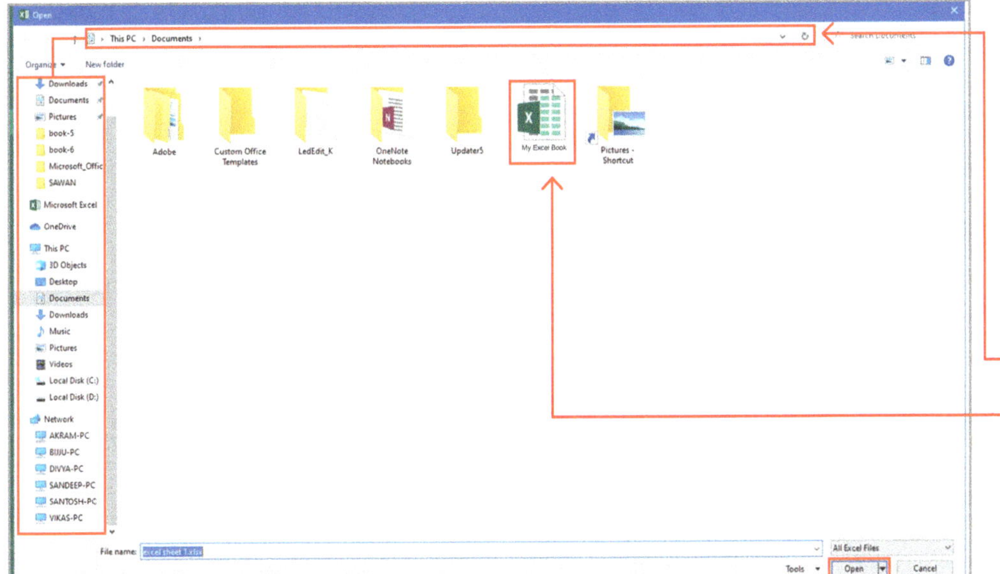

The Open dialog box appears.

3. Click on these areas to navigate to the folder or drive where you stored the file.

4. Click on the name of the file that you want to open.

5. Click on Open.

My Excel Book

Names	Hard Disks	Printers	Keyboards	Monitors	Scanners
OLIVER	80000	55000	25000	52000	45000
WILLIAM	50000	45000	60000	46000	36000
HENRY	60000	30000	25000	96000	58000
JACKSON	30000	80000	30000	75000	67000
DANIEL	85000	60000	40000	35000	76000
RICHARD	90000	75000	56000	46000	39000
JACK	50000	65000	24000	69000	48000
MICHEL	60000	30000	36000	74000	65000

The file opens in the program window.

The name of the opened file appears on the Title bar.

Viewing More Than One Workbook Simultaneously

To view and work in two or more worksheets simultaneously on the screen, Excel provides four display modes, namely tiled, horizontal, vertical or cascade.

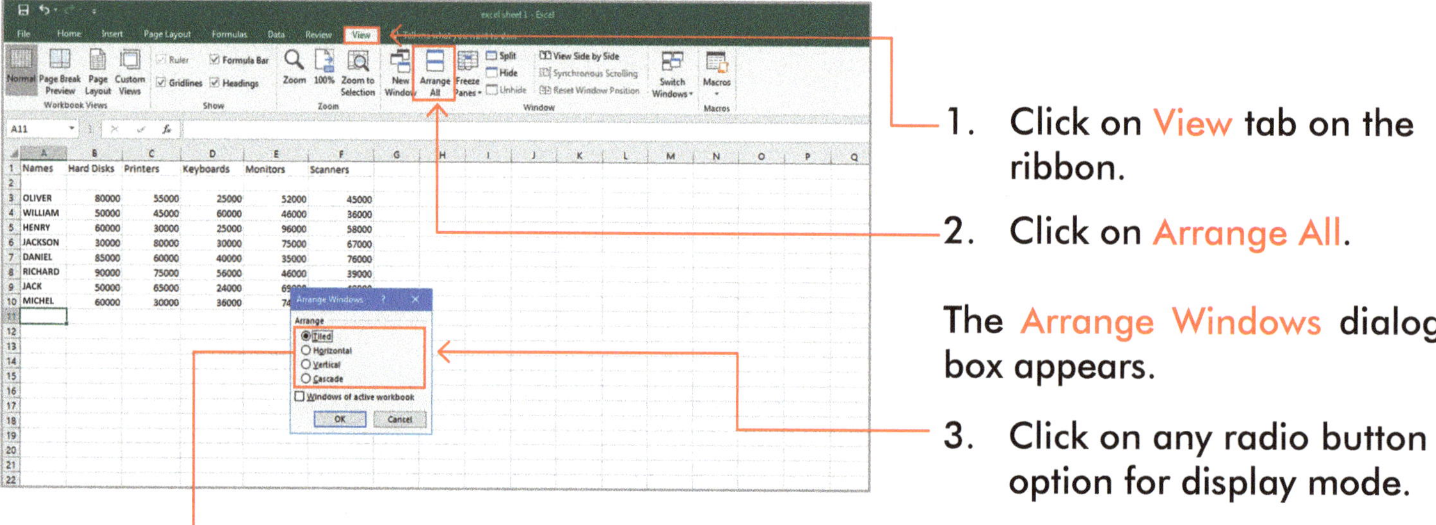

1. Click on View tab on the ribbon.
2. Click on Arrange All.

The Arrange Windows dialog box appears.

3. Click on any radio button option for display mode.

Tiled	:	It arranges the workbooks like mosaic tiles across the screen.
Horizontal	:	It arranges the workbooks stacked horizontally.
Vertical	:	It arranges the workbooks vertically.
Cascade	:	It arranges the workbooks stacked on top of one another in a cascading display.

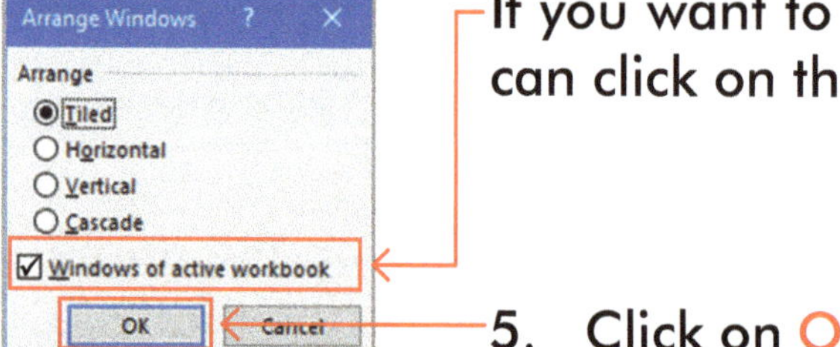

If you want to display only the sheets in the active workbook, you can click on the check box of Windows of active workbook.

5. Click on OK.

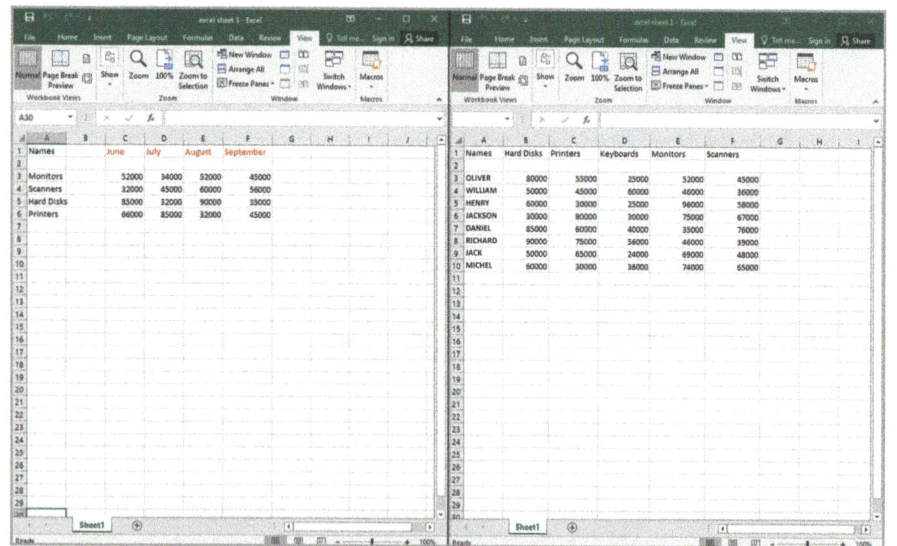

This example shows two workbooks arranged vertically.

The active workbook's title bar is highlighted.

Closing A Workbook

You can close your worksheet after finishing your work without closing the entire Excel program. Follow the steps to close the workbook.

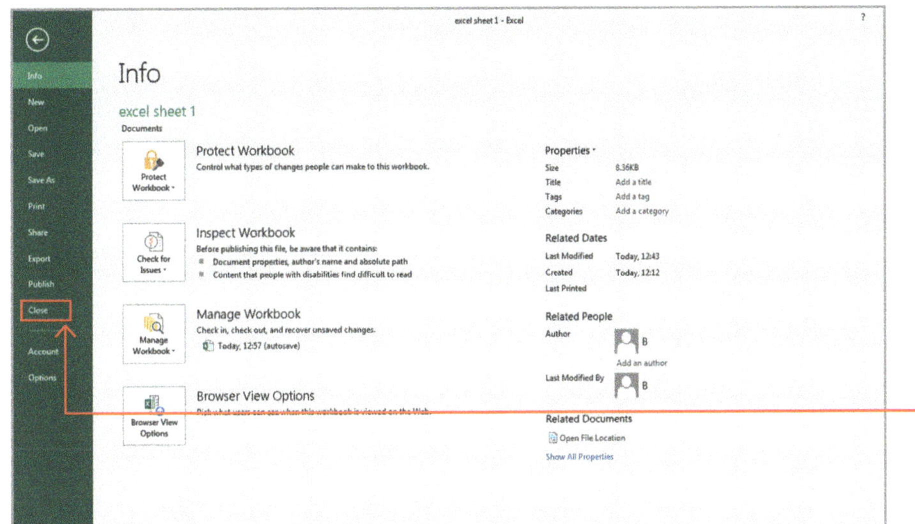

1. Click on File tab.

Backstage view will appear.

2. Click on the Close button.

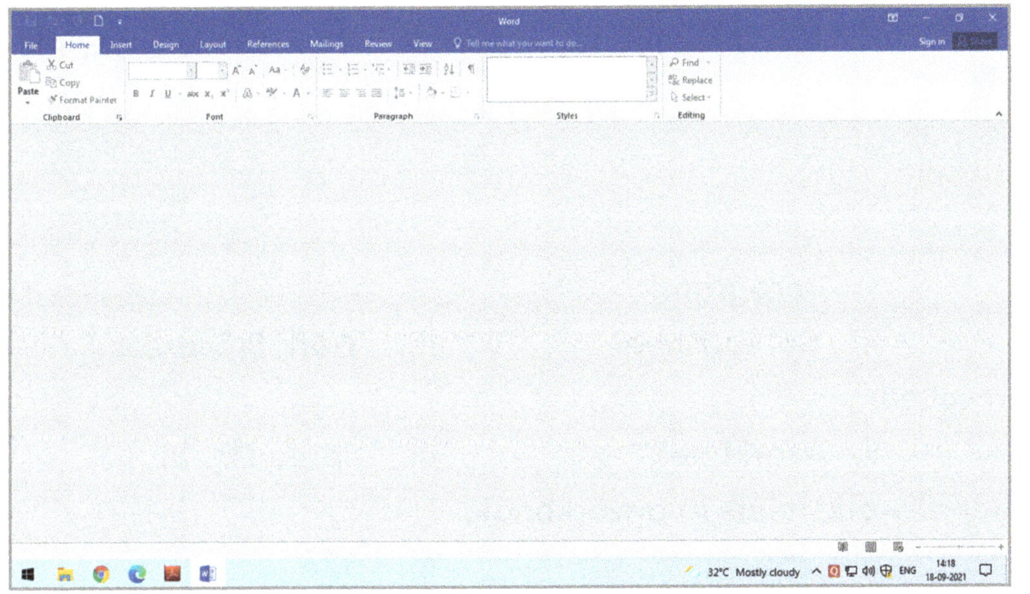

The File closes.

Exiting from Excel

When you finish your work, you can exit from Excel. If you want to save your work, do so before exiting from Excel completely.

1. Click on the File tab, Backstage view will appear.
2. Click Exit Excel.

   If you have not yet saved your work, Excel prompts you to do so before exiting.
3. Click on Yes to save.

   The Excel program window closes. (You can exit Excel by simply clicking Close button(X) in the upper-right corner of the Excel window.

LET'S HAVE A LOOK

- MS-Excel is an electronic worksheet, also called a spreadsheet.
- Excel file is often called a workbook.
- A workbook is divided into different worksheets.
- In Excel, the work is done in tabular form.
- A worksheet in an Excel is divided into rows and columns.
- A row and a column intersect and form a cell.
- An active cell appears highlighted with a dark black border.
- The data is entered either in the active cell or in the Formula bar.
- By default, an Excel workbook contains 3 worksheets.

SHORTCUT KEYS

Creating a new worksheet	: Ctrl+N		Opening a worksheet	: Ctrl+O
Exiting from Excel	: Alt+F4		Saving a workbook	: Ctrl+S

BRAIN TEASER

1. Multiple Choice Questions

Tick (✓) the correct answer:

a. MS-Excel is a ____________ program:
   i. Presentation ☐ ii. Spreadsheet ☐ iii. Work Processor ☐

b. The Excel file is often called:
   i. Worksheet ☐ ii. Workbook ☐ iii. Spreadsheet ☐

c. The maximum number of worksheets in a workbook:
   i. 258 ☐ ii. 256 ☐ iii. 526 ☐

d. The file extension of an Excel file:
   i. .xlsx ☐ ii. .exl ☐ iii. .excel ☐

e. By default, there are ____________ worksheets in an excel workbook.
   i. 5 ☐ ii. 3 ☐ iii. 2 ☐

f. The number of rows in a worksheet:
   i. 1048444 ☐ ii. 1048576 ☐ iii. 1048345 ☐

g. The horizontal and vertical lines in a worksheet:
   i. Ruler ☐ ii. Gridlines ☐ iii. Inserting lines ☐

h. The keyboard shortcut for saving an Excel file:
   i. Alt+O ☐ ii. Ctrl+S ☐ iii. Ctrl+O ☐

2. Fill in the blanks:

a. MS-Excel is an ______________ worksheet.

b. A collection of worksheets is called a ______________.

c. A worksheet contains ______________ rows and ______________ columns.

d. ______________ displays the address of an active cell.

e. The shortcut of opening a worksheet is ______________.

f. ______________ toolbar contains the buttons, such as save, Undo, Redo, etc.

g. The data is entered in the ______________ cell.

h. The intersection of rows and columns is called a ______________.

i. The mouse pointer is displayed as a ______________ sign whenever it is located in a cell on the worksheet.

j. The default format of date in excel is ______________ .

3. Write '**T**' for True and '**F**' for False in the boxes:

a. MS-Excel is Windows-based word processor software. ☐

b. Status bar is located at the top of the Excel window. ☐

c. New worksheets can be inserted in MS-Excel. ☐

d. The intersection of rows and columns is called a cell. ☐

e. A file in MS-Excel is known as a workbook. ☐

f. By default, there are 5 worksheets in a worksheet. ☐

4. Answer the following questions

(i) Answer in a few lines:

a. Name the spreadsheet program used to enter data in tabular form.

b. What is an Excel file known as?

c. What is Quick Access Toolbar?

d. How many numbers of rows and columns are there in a worksheet?

e. Differentiate between a workbook and a worksheet.

f. List the different components of an Excel window.

g. Name some commands displayed in File Tab.

h. What is the active cell?

i. Name the types of data entered in MS-Excel.

j. Write a keyboard shortcut to save a workbook.

k. What is the use of Formula bar?

(ii) Answer comprehensively:

a. Explain MS-Excel.

b. Write the different uses of MS-Excel.

c. What is a spreadsheet?

d. What are the different parts of a worksheet?

e. What are the features of MS-Excel?

f. Define the following:

i. Worksheet ii. Mouse Pointer iii. Cell iv. Worksheet Tab v. File tab

5. Label the following:

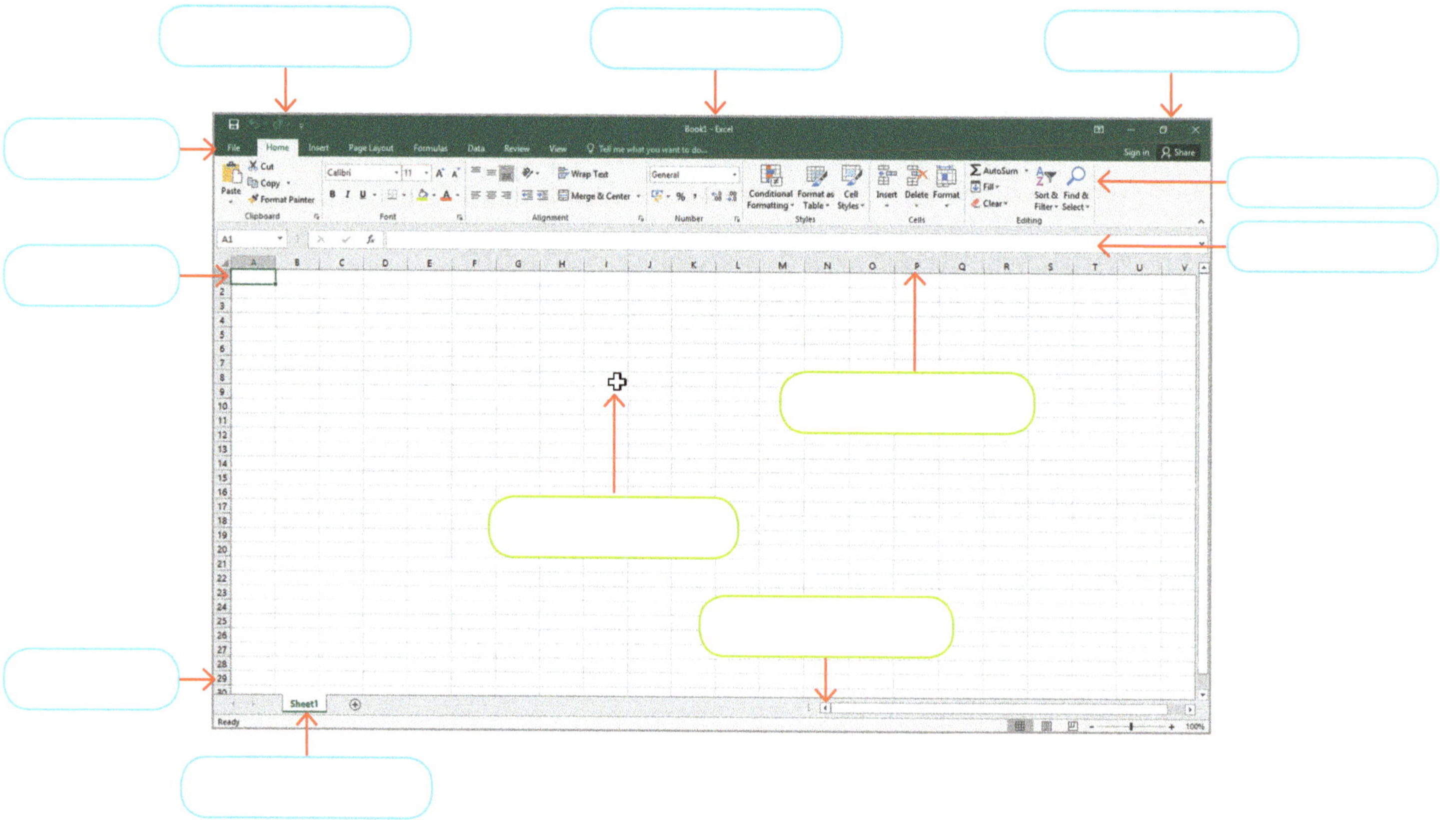

LAB ACTIVITY

Visit your computer room and switch on the computer. Start MS-Excel and watch carefully all the components of MS-Excel spreadsheet. Ask your computer teacher about the uses of different components of MS-Excel worksheet. Finally, close the MS Excel program.

- Try to create a new Workbook in MS-Excel.

Formative Assessment-2
(Chapters 3-5)

1. **In MS-Word, type about 80-100 words, on 'Keeping Your Computer Healthy' and save the file as Healthy Computer.**

2. **Look at the following figure and answer the questions given below:**

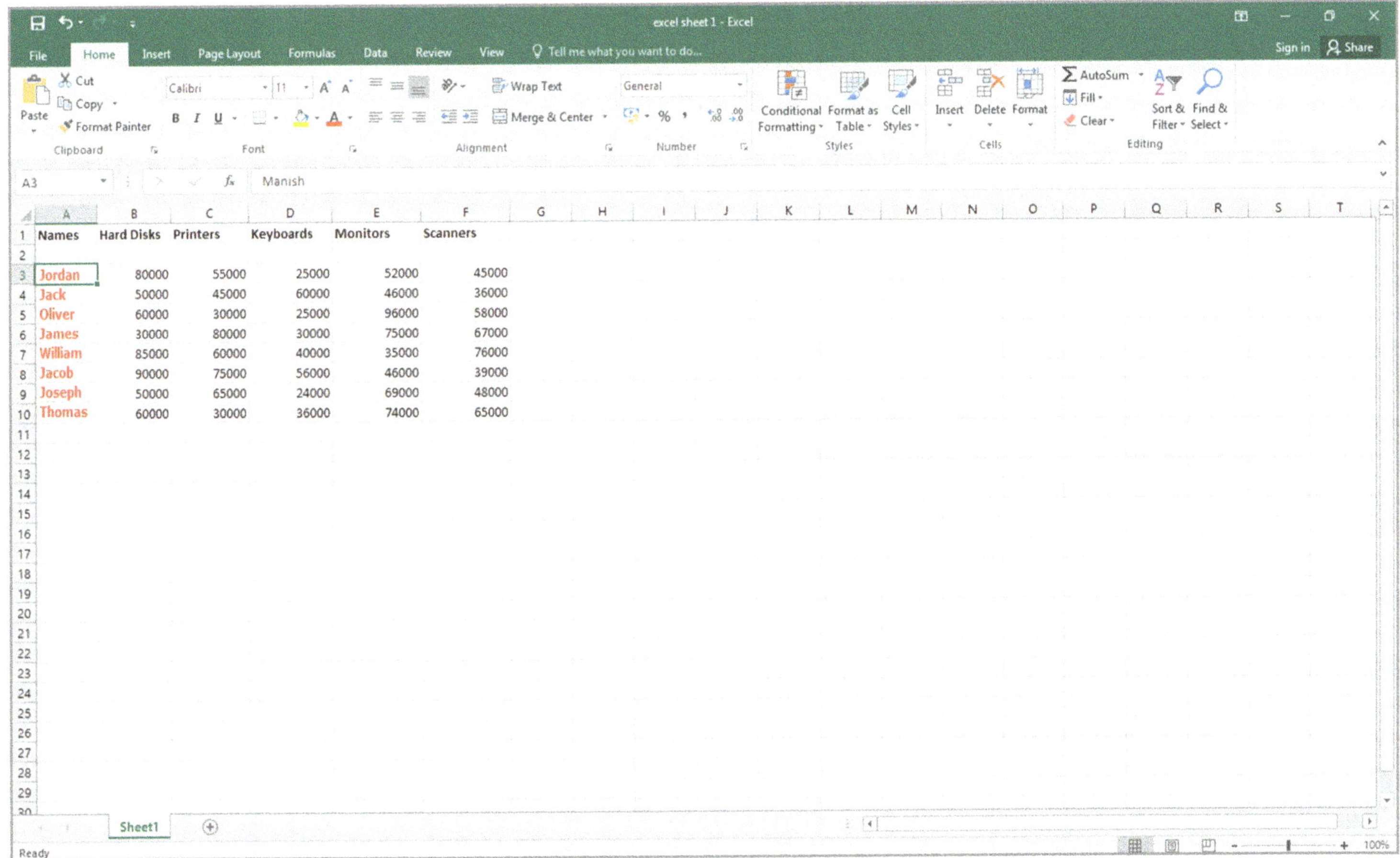

	A	B	C	D	E	F
1	Names	Hard Disks	Printers	Keyboards	Monitors	Scanners
2						
3	Jordan	80000	55000	25000	52000	45000
4	Jack	50000	45000	60000	46000	36000
5	Oliver	60000	30000	25000	96000	58000
6	James	30000	80000	30000	75000	67000
7	William	85000	60000	40000	35000	76000
8	Jacob	90000	75000	56000	46000	39000
9	Joseph	50000	65000	24000	69000	48000
10	Thomas	60000	30000	36000	74000	65000

a. Write the name of the workbook opened.

____

b. Name the activated cell.

____

c. Name the buttons present on the quick access toolbar.

____

d. Name the tabs present in Ribbon.

____

e. Where is worksheet tab located?

____

Summative Assessment
(Chapters 1-5)

1. Fill in the blanks:

a. The result you get after processing the data is known as ______________.
b. ______________ is the raw material for processing.
c. The process of starting or restarting a computer is called ______________.
d. ______________ is the multiprocessing operating system.
e. ______________ is any type of software that is designed to damage a computer.
f. The ______________ program is used to scan files from the hard drive.
g. A ______________ in MS-Word is used to design and style a character.
h. The address of an active cell is displayed in ______________.
i. ______________ is decorative text that you can add to a document as an eye-catching visual effect.

2. Write 'T' for True and 'F' for False in the boxes:

a. A collection of spreadsheets is called a workbook. ☐
b. The file extension of an Excel file is .xl. ☐
c. The Clip Art option is present in Insert tab. ☐
d. Adjusting the text around the picture is called text wrap. ☐
e. Embedded operating is used in Windows Mobile. ☐
f. A computer needs only external maintenance. ☐

3. Match Column A with Column B.

	Column A		Column B
a.	Keyboard	(i)	Horizontal and vertical lines
b.	Data	(ii)	Damage a computer
c.	Title Bar	(iii)	Hardware
d.	Quick Access Toolbar	(iv)	Ready-to-use text effects
e.	Gridlines	(v)	Top of the window
f.	WordArt	(vi)	Raw information
g.	Malware	(vii)	Save, Undo, Redo

4. Answer the following questions

(i) Answer each in a few lines:

a. Name the part of the computer that controls the working of all hardware.

b. Name the different kinds of printers.

c. Name any two types of operating systems.

d. Name the operating system that works on a desktop or laptop.

e. Name any two anti-virus programs.

f. Name some of the formatting options.

g. On which tab is the clipart feature present?

h. What different data types can be entered in MS-Excel?

(ii) Answer each comprehensively:

a. Explain the different features of MS-Excel.

b. Explain the different parts of a worksheet.

c. What is alignment? What are the different ways of alignment?

d. Give some tips to keep your computer case clean.

e. What are the internal maintenance techniques of the computer? Explain.

f. What are the different functions of an operating system?

g. Explain the working of the computer with a block diagram.

5. Differentiate between:

a. Hardware and Software

b. Data and Infomation

c. Workbook and worksheet

6. Define the following:

a. Computer

b. Spreadsheet

c. Formatting

d. Microsoft Windows

e. Operating System

f. Cell

6 Editing in MS-Excel

In this chapter, we will learn:

⇒ Selecting Cell and Range of Cells
⇒ Editing Data
⇒ Deleting Data
⇒ Moving or Copying Data
⇒ Changing Row Height and Column Width
⇒ Inserting Row/ Column
⇒ Deleting Row/ Column
⇒ Inserting Cells
⇒ Deleting a Worksheet

Hello friends, in your previous chapter, you learnt about Excel. You also learnt to enter text in the worksheet, saving text and closing the Excel program. Now in this chapter, you will learn to make changes in the given text.

But first, let us just recap what we learnt about Microsoft Excel.

MICROSOFT EXCEL

You have already learnt that Microsoft Excel is a powerful spreadsheet program that allows you to organise data, complete calculations, make decisions, graph data and develop reports.

Excel allows you to organise data in rows and columns. These rows and columns collectively are called a worksheet.

A spreadsheet file is similar to a notebook that can contain more than 1,000 related individual worksheets. Data is organized vertically in columns and horizontally in rows on each worksheet.

Each worksheet usually can have more than 16,000 columns and 1 million rows. One or more letters identify each column, and a number identifies each row. A cell is the intersection of a column and a row. Each worksheet has more than 17 billion cells in which you can enter data. The spreadsheet software identifies cells by the column and the row in which they are located. For example, the intersection of column B and row 4 is referred to as cell B4.

Selecting Cells

To perform editing, calculating and formatting tasks, you have to select cells. Selecting a single cell is quite simple: you just click the cell in excel. To select a group of cells, called a range, you can simply drag the mouse or hold the Shift key and press Arrow keys from the keyboard.

To Select a Cell

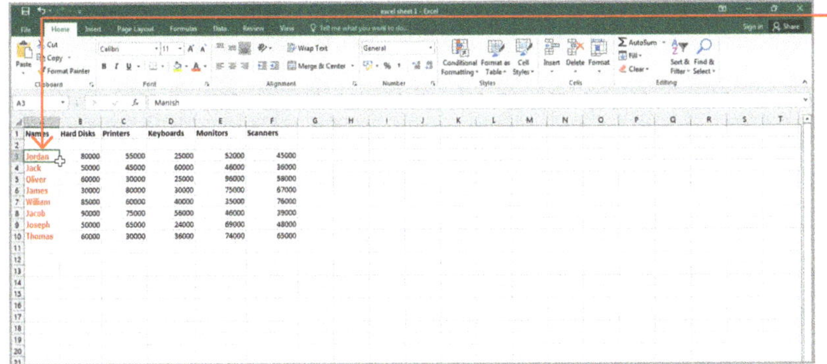

1. Click on the cell you want to select.

The cell becomes the active cell and displays a thick border.

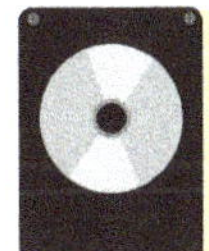

Remember
The selected cells appear to be highlighted in the worksheet.

To Select a Row

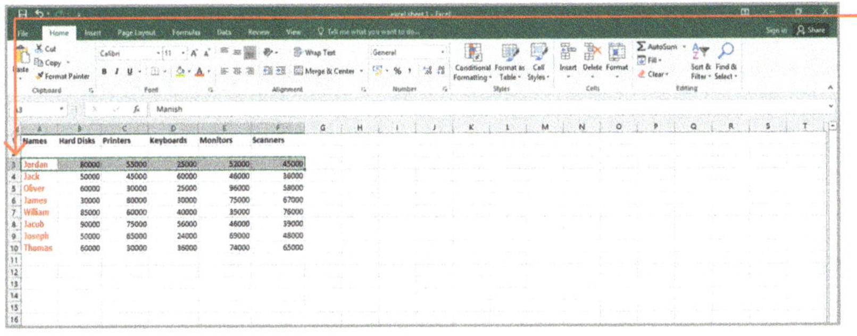

1. Click on the number of the row you want to select. The mouse pointer will change its shape into (➡).

To select multiple rows, drag the mouse pointer (➡) until you highlight all the rows you want to select.

To Select a Column

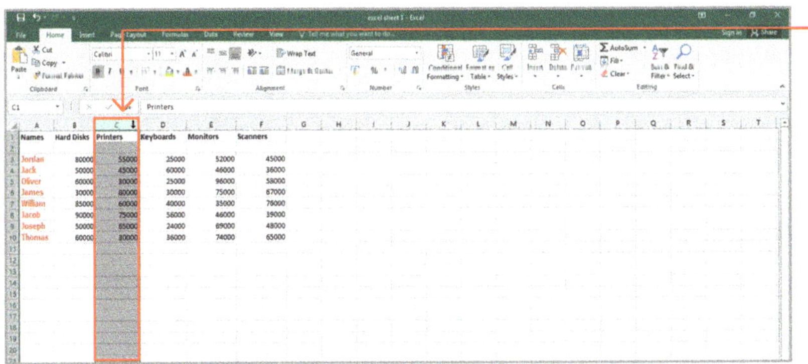

1. Click on the letter of the column you want to select. The mouse pointer will change its shape into (⬇).

To select multiple columns, drag the mouse pointer (⬇) until you highlight all the columns you want to select.

To Select a Group of Cells

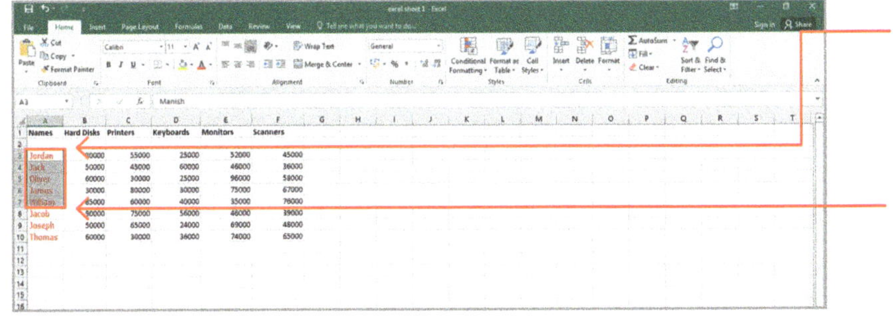

1. Place your mouse pointer (✚) over the first cell, you want to select.
2. Drag the mouse (✚) until you highlight all the cells, you want to select.

Editing Data in Worksheet

Making changes to the data in the worksheet is called editing. You can perform editing tasks to the data in your worksheets. To edit the data, follow the given steps:

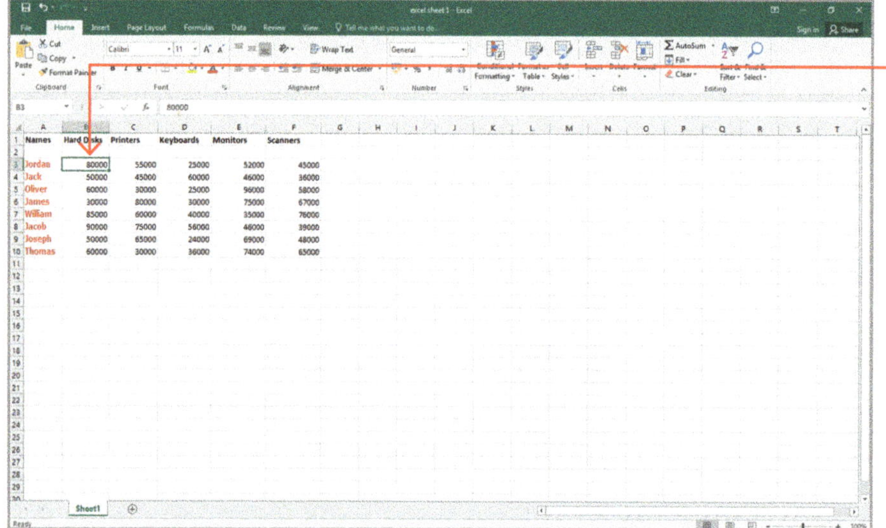

1. Double-click on the cell containing the data you want to edit.

   A flashing insertion point appears in the cell.

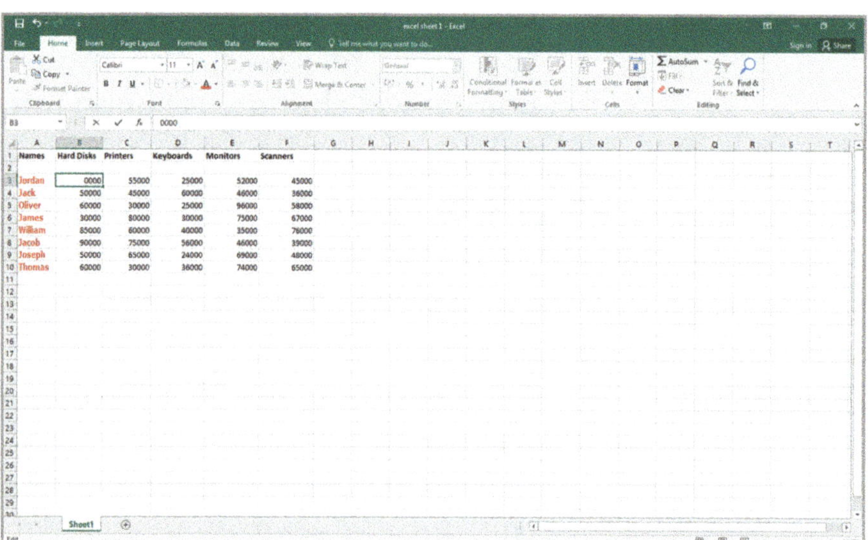

2. Press the arrow keys from the keyboard to move the insertion point from where you want to remove or add characters.
3. To remove the character to the left of the flashing insertion point, press the Backspace key.

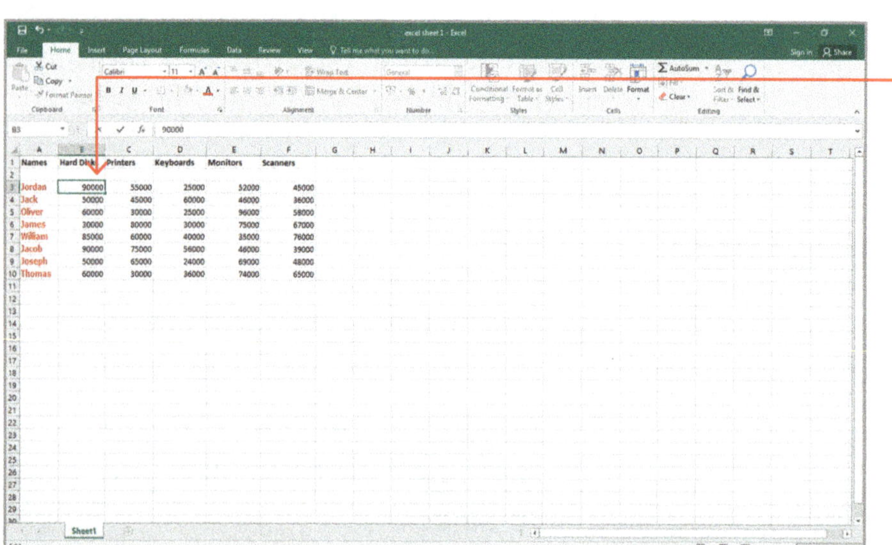

4. To add the data where the insertion point flashes on the screen, type the data.
5. When you have finished making changes to the data, press the Enter key.

Moving or Copying the Data

The data in Excel can be moved or copied by using Cut, Copy and Paste commands. The data can be moved or copied within Excel. You can move and share data between other Office programs. You can cut (move) a row/column and paste to another worksheet. You can even copy a formula from one cell to another cell in the same worksheet. You can also drag and drop data to move and copy it within a worksheet.

The Copy command makes a duplicate of the selected data, and the Cut command removes the data from the original file entirely.

You can follow the steps as given below to move or copy data:

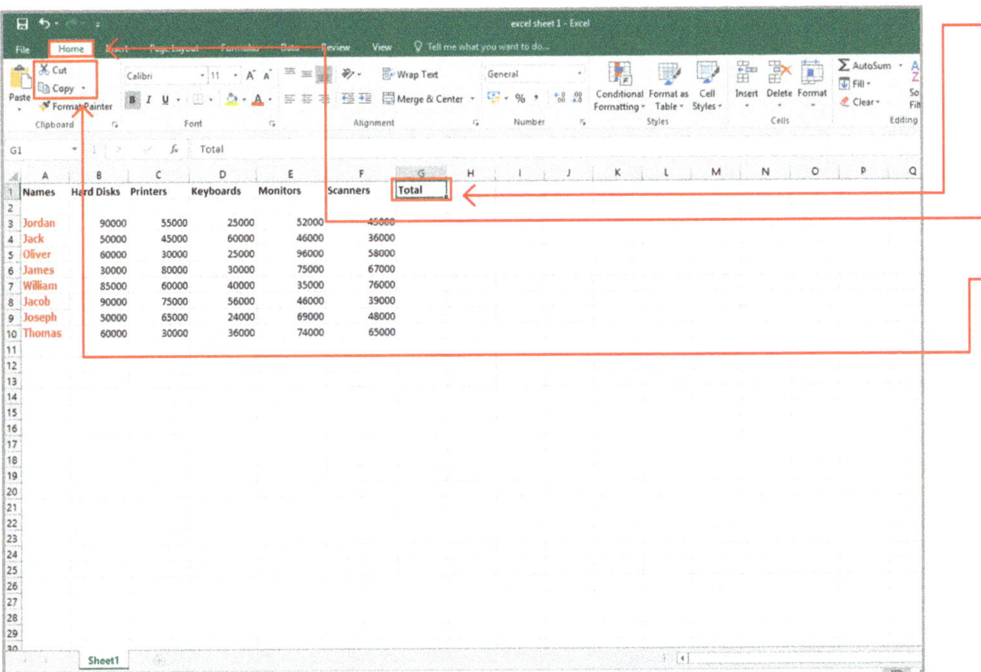

1. Select the cell or cells containing data you want to move or copy.
2. Click on Home tab.
3. Click on one of the following buttons:

   Move text (✂)

   Copy text ( )

In this example we choose Copy text, so the text will remain in its original location.

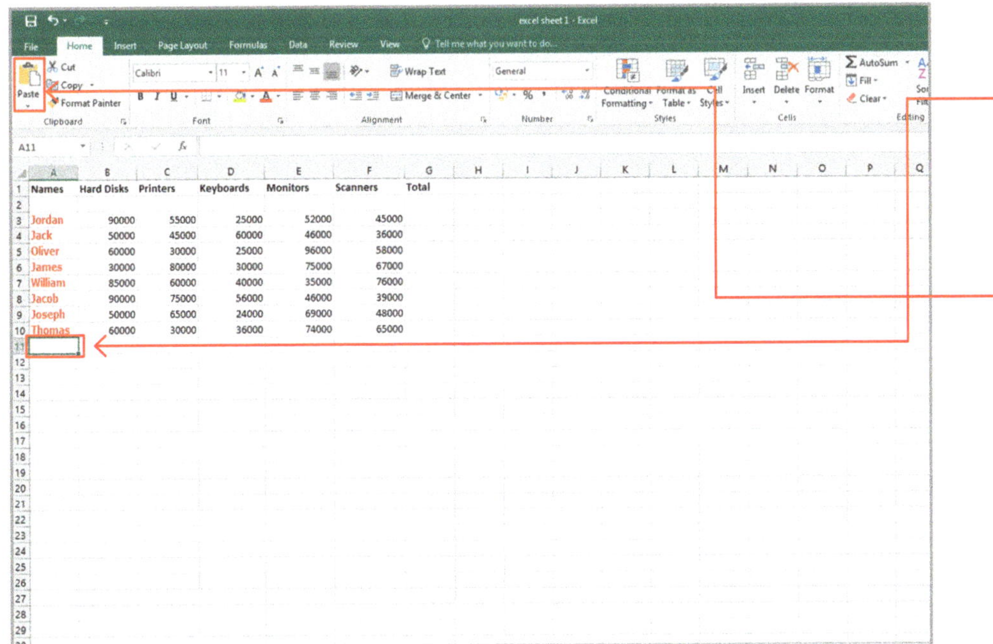

4. Click on the cell where you want to place the data.
5. Click on Paste ( ) button to the place data in a new location.

Data appears in the new location.

Changing Row Height and Column Width

The row heights or column widths in your worksheets can be increased or decreased if the data do not adjust in a particular cell.

By default row height is 12.75 points and the column width of a cell is 8.43 points.

Adjusting the Column Width

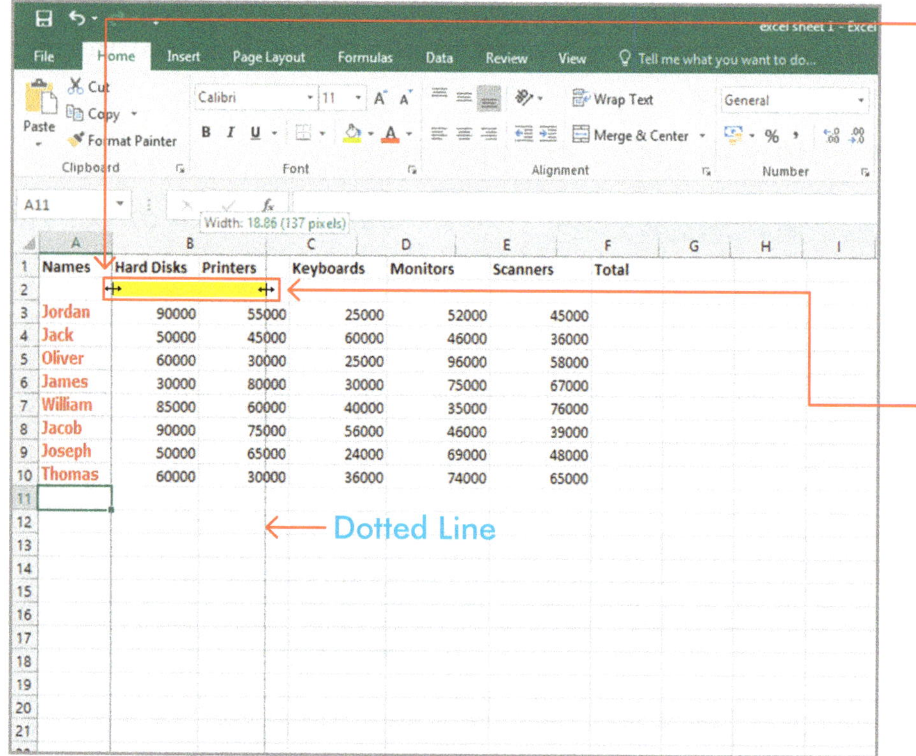

1. To change the width of a column, place the mouse over the right edge of the column heading.

The mouse pointer changes into (↔).

2. Drag the column edge until the dotted line displays the column width you want.

The column will display the new width.

Adjusting the Row Height

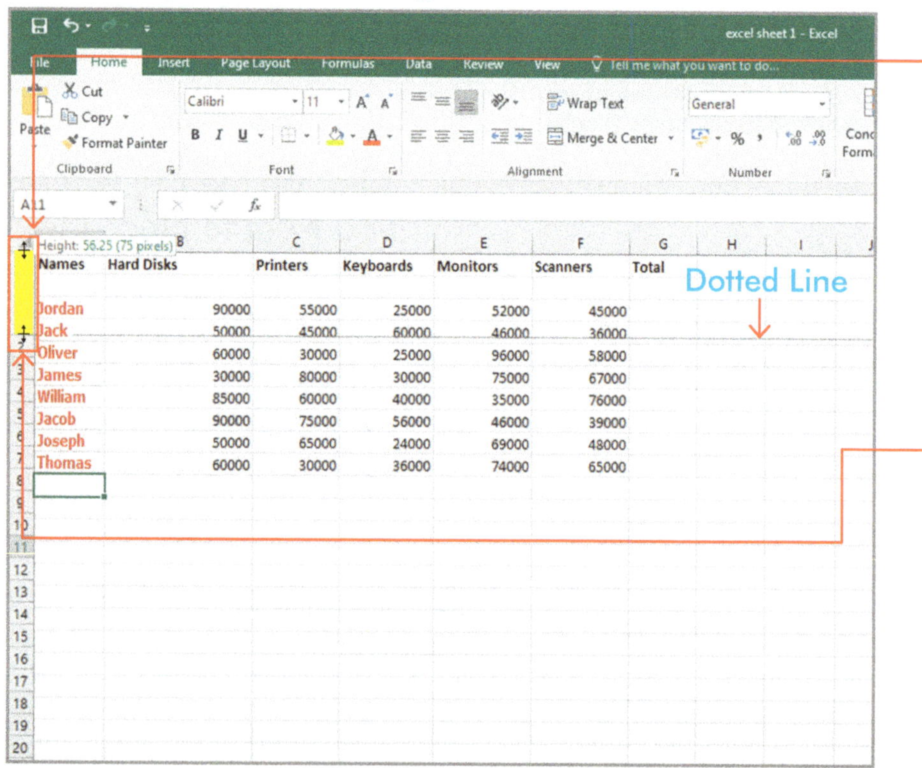

1. To change the height of a row, position the mouse pointer over the bottom edge of the row heading.

The mouse pointer changes into (↕).

2. Drag the row edge until the dotted line displays the desired row height.

The row will display the new height.

Adding Rows, Columns and Cells

To add more data within a worksheet in between the rows, columns or a cell, the new cells, columns or rows can be added in between without disturbing the entered data. For example, you might need to add a column in the middle of several existing columns. To add data you left out the first time, you enter data in the worksheet.

Inserting a Row

Excel will insert a row above the row you select. To insert a row, follow these steps:

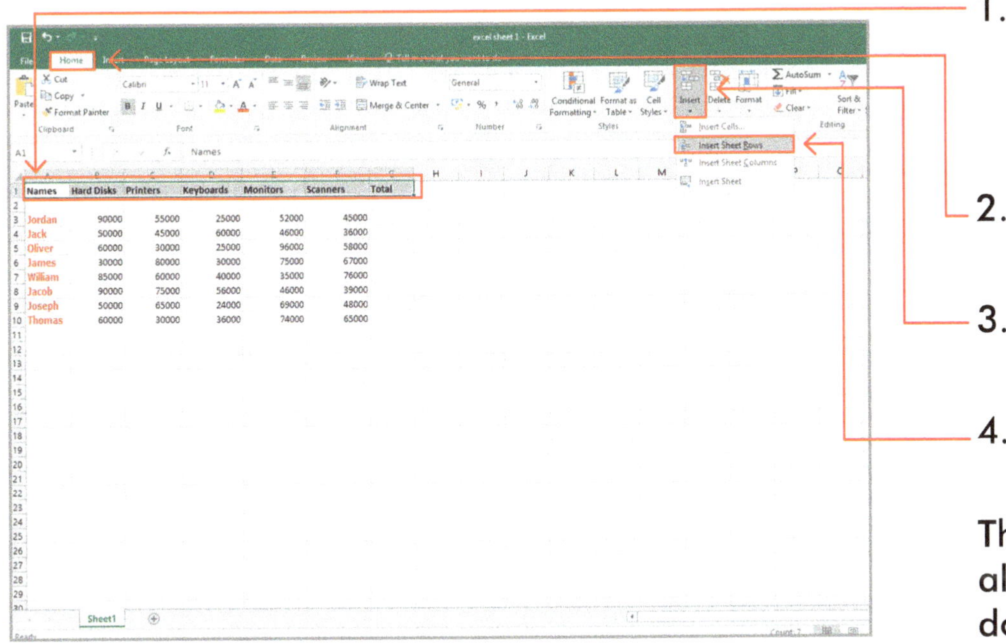

1. Click the heading of the row below where you want to insert a new row.
2. Click Home tab on the Ribbon.
3. Click on the down arrow of the Insert.
4. Click on Insert Sheet Rows.

The new row will appear and all the rows that follow, shift downward.

Inserting a Column

Excel will insert a column to the left of the column you select. To insert a column, follow these steps:

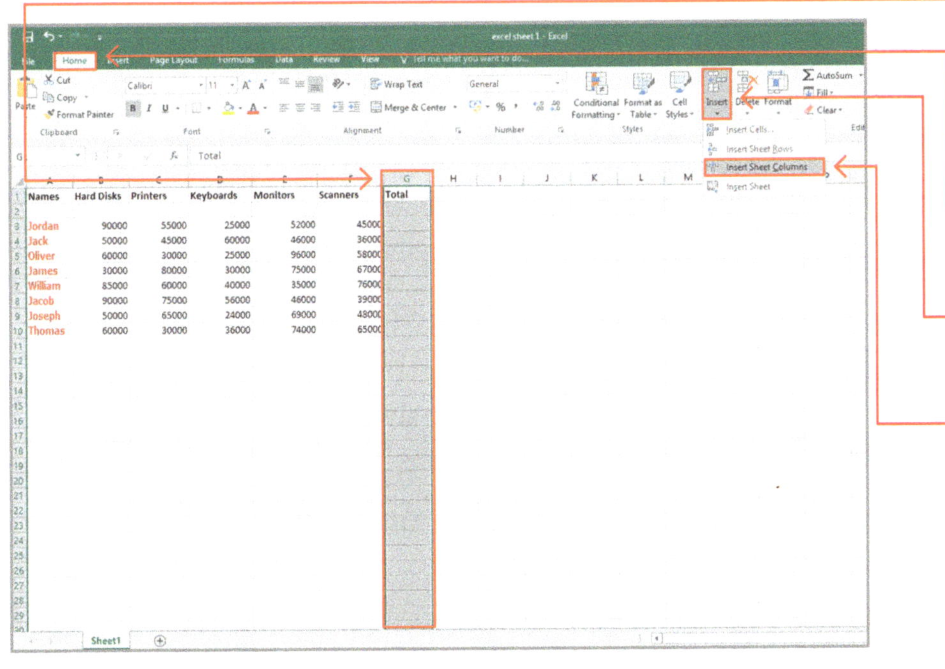

1. Click the heading of the column to the right where you want to insert a new column.
2. Click on Home tab on the Ribbon.
3. Click on the down arrow of the Insert.
4. Click on Insert Sheet Column.

The new column appears and all the columns that follow shift to the right.

Inserting Cells

The cells can be inserted by following these steps:

1. Select the cells where you want to insert the new cells.

Excel will insert the same number of cells as you select.

2. Click Home tab on the Ribbon.
3. Click on the down arrow of the Insert.
4. Click on Insert Cells. The Insert dialog box appears.

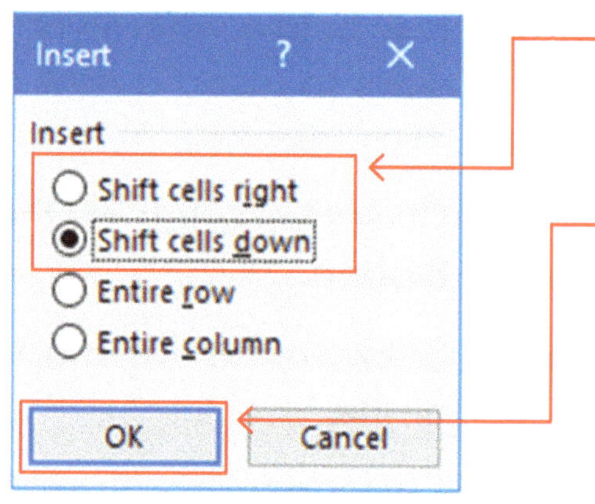

5. Click the radio button of an option to shift the surrounding cells right or downwards to make room for the new cells.
6. Click on OK to insert the cells.

Excel inserts the new cells and shifts the surrounding cells in the direction you specified.

To deselect cells, click any cell.

Deleting Cells, a Row, a Column or Data

You can delete cells, columns or rows you no longer need in the worksheet. When you delete an entire column or row, Excel deletes any existing data within the selected cells.

Clearing Cell data

Clearing cell data will delete or empty the cell contents without removing the cell from the worksheet.

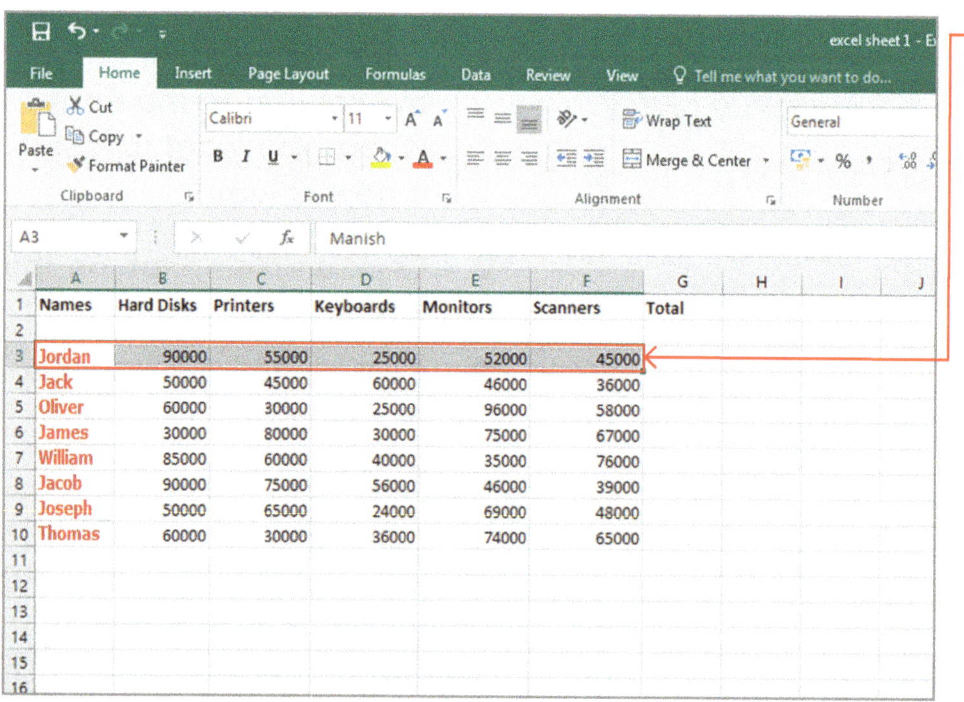

1. Select the cells containing the data you want to delete.
2. Press the Delete key from the keyboard.

The data in the cells that you have selected disappears.

To deselect cells, click any cell.

To delete cells

Deleting cells will clear the whole cell along with its data. When you delete the cell, the surrounding cells will move to fill the empty space.

1. Select the cells you want to delete.
2. Click on the Home tab on the Ribbon.
3. Click on the down arrow of the Delete.
4. Click on Delete Cells. The Delete dialog box appears.

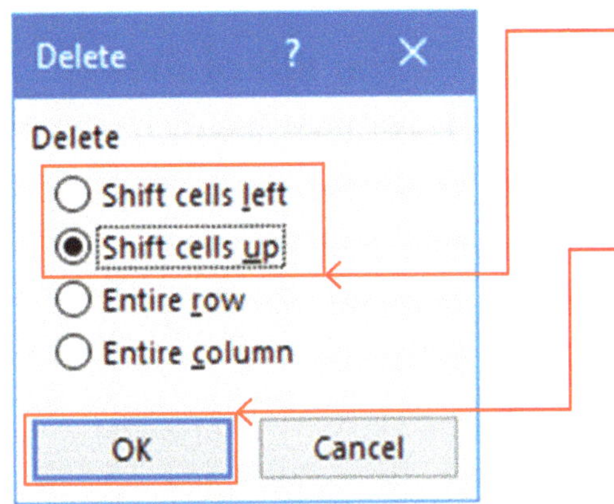

5. Click the radio button of an option to shift the surrounding cells to the left or up to fill the empty space.
6. Click on OK to delete the cells.

Excel removes the cells and shifts the surrounding cells in the direction you specified.

To deselect cells, click any cell.

To delete a Row

Follow these steps to delete an entire row:

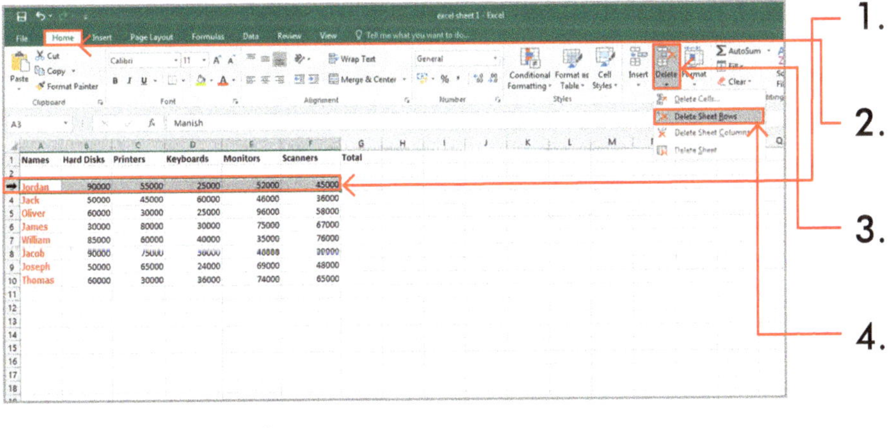

1. Click on the heading of the row that you want to delete.
2. Click on Home tab on the Ribbon.
3. Click on the down arrow of the Delete.
4. Click on Delete Sheet Row. Excel will delete the row.

To delete a Column

Follow these steps to delete an entire column:

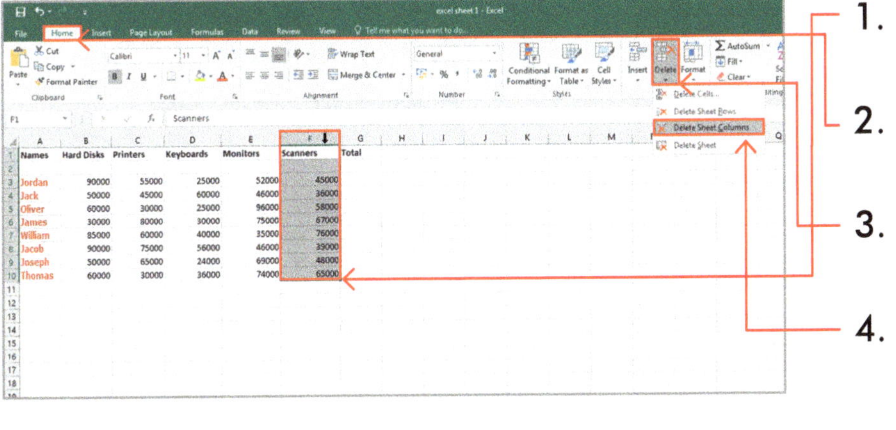

1. Click on the heading of the column that you want to delete.
2. Click on the Home tab on the Ribbon.
3. Click on the down arrow of the Delete.
4. Click on Delete Sheet Column. Excel will delete the column.

Switching Between Worksheet

As you know, a workbook consists of different worksheets. You can enter data in different worksheets by switching between them. You can just click on the worksheet tab present at the bottom of the worksheet.

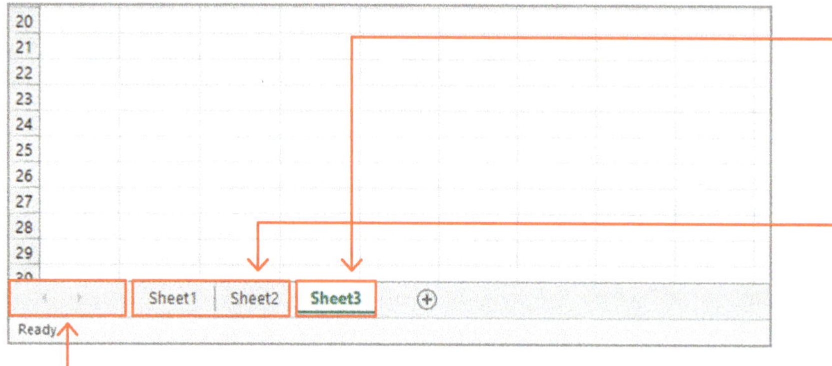

This area displays a tab for each worksheet in your workbook. The displayed worksheet has a white tab.

1. Click on the tab of the worksheet you want to display.

If you have many worksheets in your workbook, the worksheet tabs are not visible. Then click on one of the following buttons to move through the worksheet tabs:

(▶) Display next tab (◀) Display previous tab

Renaming a Worksheet

Worksheets are named as sheet 1, Sheet 2 and so on by default. You can add more worksheets in the workbook. You can change the names of these worksheets according to the data that helps to identify the content within the worksheet.

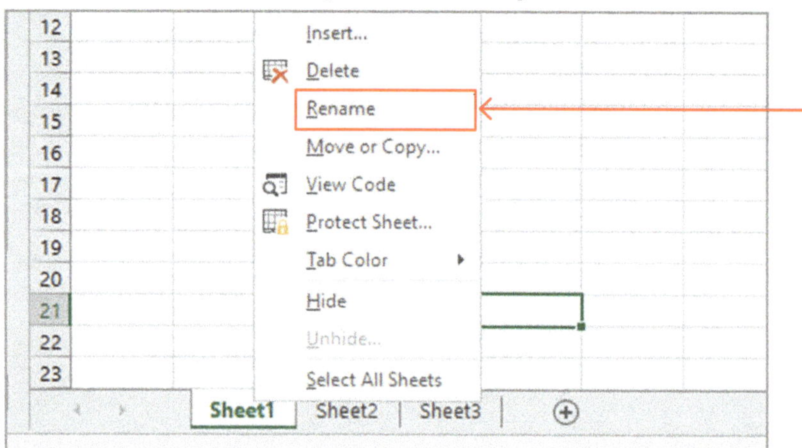

1. Right click on the worksheet you want to rename.
2. Click on the Rename.
3. Type a new name for the worksheet and then press the Enter key.

You can also double-click on the tab for selecting the name of the worksheet you want to rename.

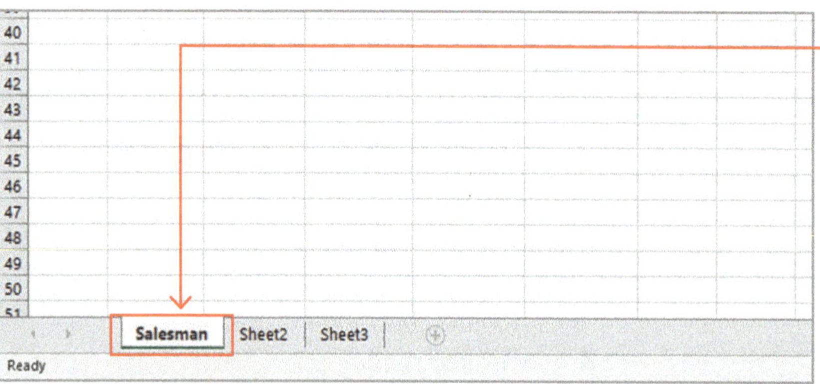

2. Type a new name for the worksheet and then press the Enter key

A worksheet name can contain up to 31 characters, including the spaces.

Adding a Worksheet

You can add/insert a new worksheet between the existing worksheets in which to enter more data. You can press the shortcut key (Shift+F11) to insert a new worksheet.

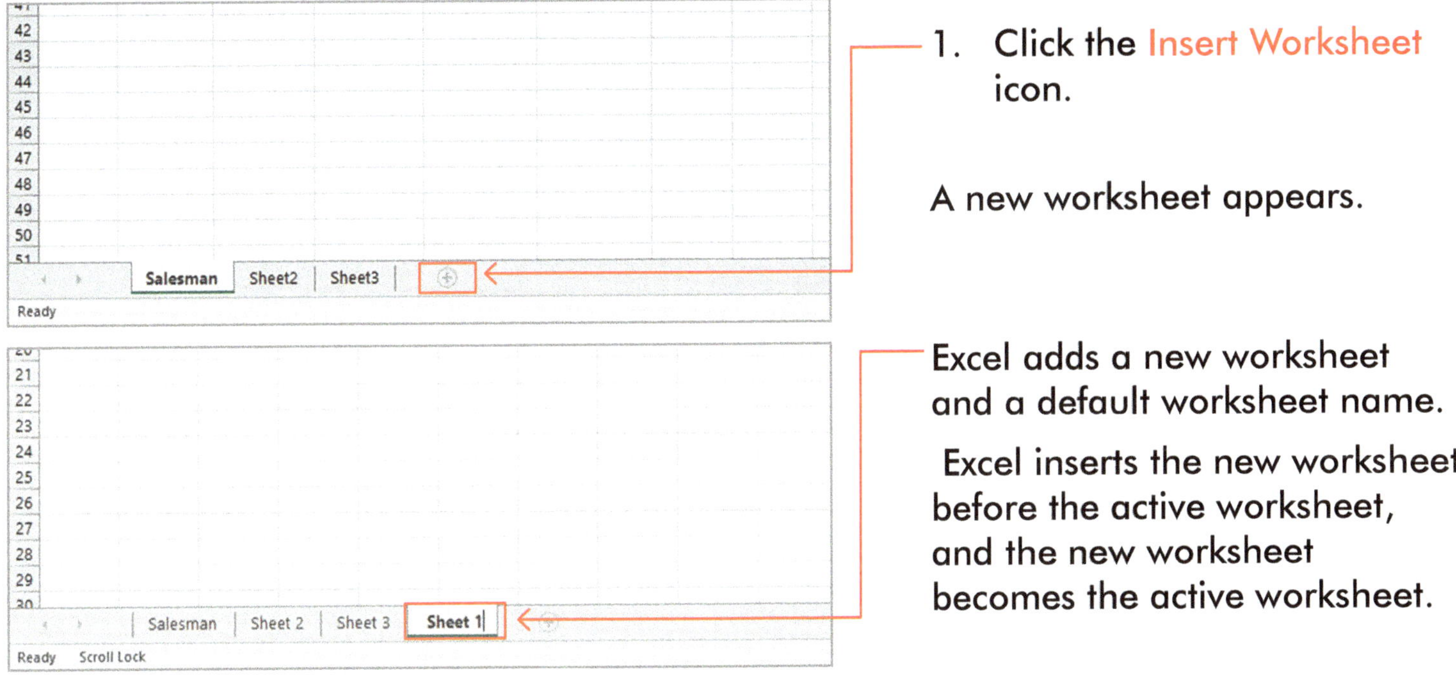

1. Click the Insert Worksheet icon.

A new worksheet appears.

Excel adds a new worksheet and a default worksheet name.

Excel inserts the new worksheet before the active worksheet, and the new worksheet becomes the active worksheet.

Deleting a Worksheet

The worksheet that is no more of use can also be deleted from the workbook. Always check the contents of the worksheet before deleting to avoid the loss of any important data. After you have deleted a worksheet, it is permanently removed from the workbook file.

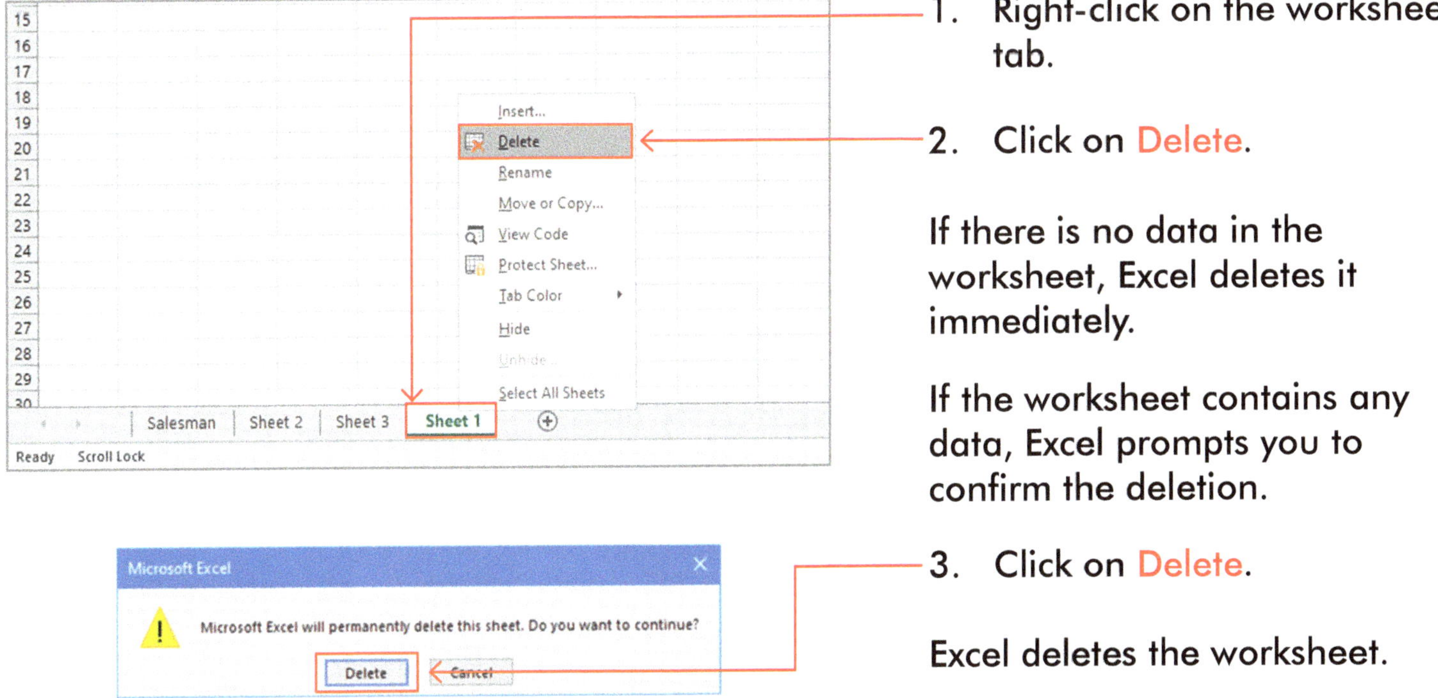

1. Right-click on the worksheet tab.
2. Click on Delete.

If there is no data in the worksheet, Excel deletes it immediately.

If the worksheet contains any data, Excel prompts you to confirm the deletion.

3. Click on Delete.

Excel deletes the worksheet.

LET'S HAVE A LOOK

- The cells are selected to make the editing and formatting of data.
- The selected cells appear to be highlighted with the dark border around it.
- Making changes to the data in the worksheet is called Editing.
- Drag and Drop method can also be used to move or copy a data.
- The Row height and Column width in the worksheet can be increased and decreased.
- You can move from one sheet to another by clicking on a worksheet tab.

SHORTCUT KEYS

Opening a saved file	:	Ctrl+O	Copying	:	Ctrl+C
Selecting a current row	:	Shift+spacebar	Pasting	:	Ctrl+V
Selecting a current column	:	Ctrl+spacebar	Cutting	:	Ctrl+X
Moving one page up	:	page up	Selecting all	:	Ctrl+A
Moving one page down	:	page down			
Moving one column right	:	Shift+tab			

BRAIN TEASER

1. Multiple Choice Questions

Tick (✓) the correct answer:

a. The shortcut key to open a workbook:

i. Ctrl + O ☐ ii. Ctrl + N ☐ iii. Alt + O ☐

b. To select the group of cells, hold the ____________ key and press arrow keys:

i. Range ☐ ii. Grouping ☐ iii. Shift ☐

c. The default column width:

i. 12.75 points ☐ ii. 8.43 points ☐ iii. 8.34 points ☐

d. The simple method used to move or copy data:

i. Double-click ☐ ii. Right-click ☐ iii. Drag and Drop ☐

e. The shortcut key to copy the data:

i. Ctrl+C ☐ ii. Ctrl+N ☐ iii. Alt+O ☐

f. The intersection of rows and columns:

i. Cell ☐ ii. Data ☐ iii. Sheet ☐

2. Fill in the blanks:

a. The cells are selected to make the ____________ and ____________ of data.

b. Making changes to data in the worksheet is called ____________.

c. The selected cells appear to be ____________ in the worksheet.

d. By default the row height is ____________ and the column width is ____________.

e. Deleting a cell will clear the whole ____________.

f. The intersection of rows and columns is called ____________.

3. Write 'T' for True and 'F' for False in the boxes:

a. You cannot select a group of cells together. ☐

b. The formula can also be copied in the other worksheet. ☐

c. You cannot add a row in the worksheet. ☐

d. By default, Excel contains 3 worksheets. ☐

e. You cannot change the row height and the column width in Excel. ☐

f. You cannot change the name of a worksheet. ☐

4. Answer the following questions

(i) Answer each in a few lines:

a. What is Excel?

b. Where is Cut/Copy button present?

c. What is a selected group of cells called?

d. How can you identify selected cells?

e. Where are you required to click to switch between worksheets?

f. What is the row height and column width by default?

(ii) Answer each comprehensively:

a. Why do you select cells in Excel? How can you select a range of cells?

b. What do you mean by editing?

c. How is moving different from copying?

d. Why do you need to adjust column width and row height?

e. Why do you need to switch between the different worksheets?

5. **Write the procedure of each for the following:**

a. Inserting a Column

b. Renaming a Worksheet

c. Changing a Row Height

d. Deleting a Row

Open Microsoft Excel 2016 and enter the following cell values in sheet 1.

Month	Income	Expenses	Balance Amount	Profit / Loss
JANUARY	90000	95000	— 5000	LOSS
FEBRUARY	85000	81000	4000	PROFIT
MARCH	70000	65000	5000	PROFIT
APRIL	80000	72000	8000	PROFIT
MAY	95000	88000	7000	PROFIT
JUNE	70000	67000	3000	PROFIT
JULY	80000	71000	9000	PROFIT
AUGUST	70000	65000	5000	PROFIT
SEPTEMBER	90000	98000	— 8000	LOSS
OCTOBER	65000	68000	— 3000	LOSS
NOVEMBER	70000	67000	3000	PROFIT
DECEMBER	60000	56000	4000	PROFIT

- Give the title at the top of this worksheet as Account Balance.
- Rename the worksheet as 'Account'.
- Save the workbook as 'Balance Sheet'.
- Using the name box, locate the cell B6 and change its value to 90,000 and balance amount to 2,000.
- Locate the cell B10 and change its value to 95,000. Modify the rest of the values in the row accordingly.
- Save the workbook and close it.

7 Formatting In Ms-Excel

In this chapter, we will learn:

⇒ Formatting
⇒ Changing the Font, Font Size
⇒ Alignment
⇒ Changing Cell Colour
⇒ Adding Border
⇒ Changing Number, Formats
⇒ Applying Workbook Themes
⇒ Adding a Background
⇒ Format with Style

FORMATTING

Formatting refers to the appearance or presentation of your worksheet. You can make your worksheets more presentable by applying one or several formatting features of excel.

The different formatting features, like changing the font, font size, adding colours and shading make your worksheet more presentable. Let's have a look on some of the formatting features, such as:

Changing the Font

You can change the font of data to make your worksheet more presentable. Follow the steps to change the fonts.

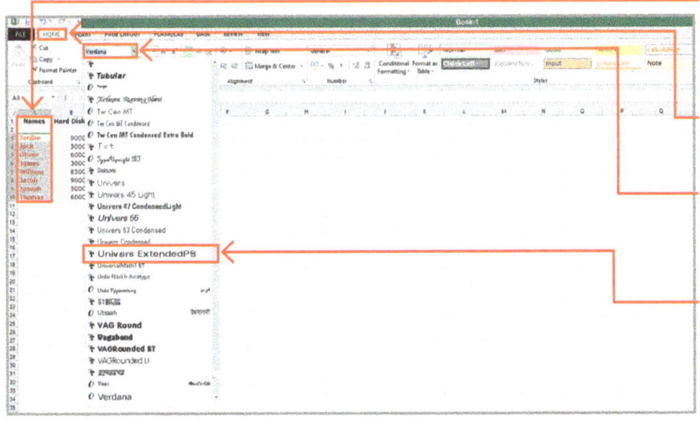

1. Select the cells containing data you want to change to a different font.
2. Click on Home tab on the ribbon.
3. Click on the down arrow button of Font to display a list of the available fonts.
4. Click on the font you want to use.

Excel immediately applies the font.

To deselect cells, click on any cell.

Changing the Font Size

You can also increase or decrease the size of the data to make it easier to read. For example, you can make the worksheet title larger than the rest of the data or you can resize the font of the entire worksheet.

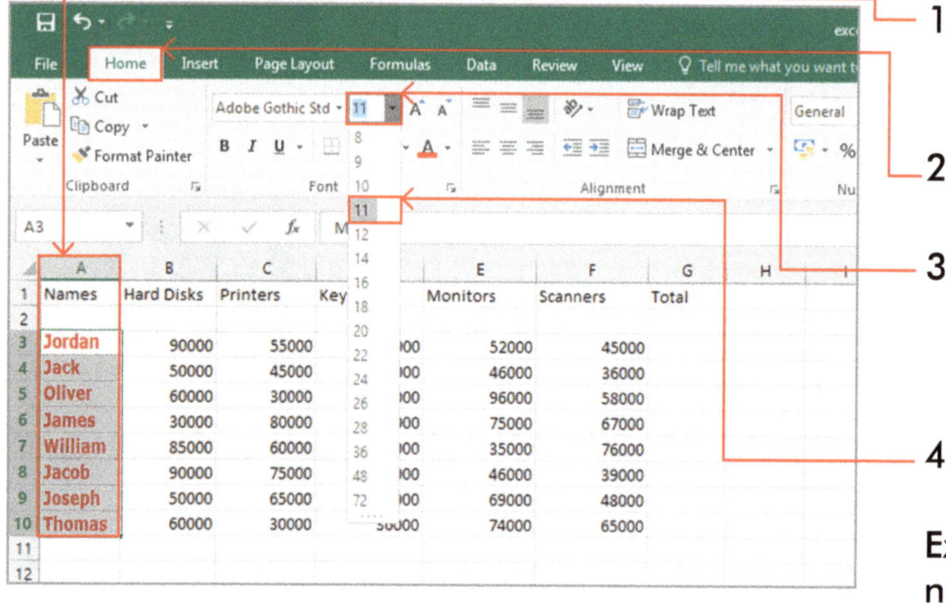

1. Select the cells containing data you want to change into a different font size.
2. Click on Home tab on the ribbon.
3. Click on the down arrow button of Font size to display a list of the available sizes.
4. Click on the size you want to use.

Excel immediately applies the new size.

Bold, Italic and Underline

To format the worksheet, the data can be made **Bold**, *Italic* and <u>Underline</u>. For example, you might underline a column heading or bold a title in a worksheet.

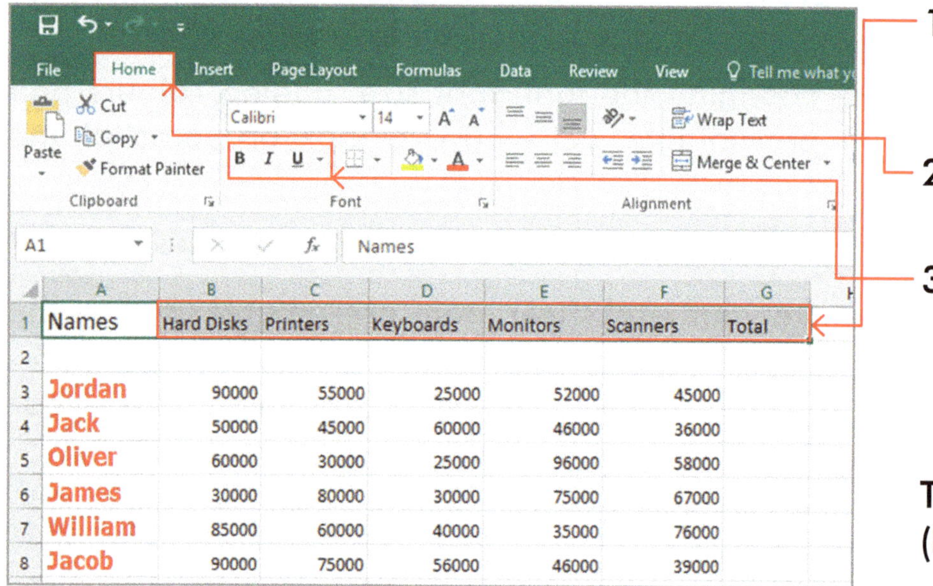

1. Select the cells containing data you want to bold, italicize or underline.
2. Click on Home tab on the ribbon.
3. Click on one of the following buttons.

   (**B**) **Bold** (*I*) *Italic*

   (<u>U</u>) <u>Underline</u>

The data appears in the style (Bold) you selected.

To remove a bold, italic or underline style, repeat steps 1 to 3.

MS-Excel is a spreadsheet program.	**MS-Excel is a spreadsheet program.**	*MS-Excel is a spreadsheet program.*	<u>MS-Excel is a spreadsheet program.</u>
Normal	Bold	Italic	Underline

Changing the Alignment

Alignment is a way in which the data is settled within the boundary of a cell. You can align the data within the cell in three different ways, such as left align, centre align, right align. To align the data, you have to:

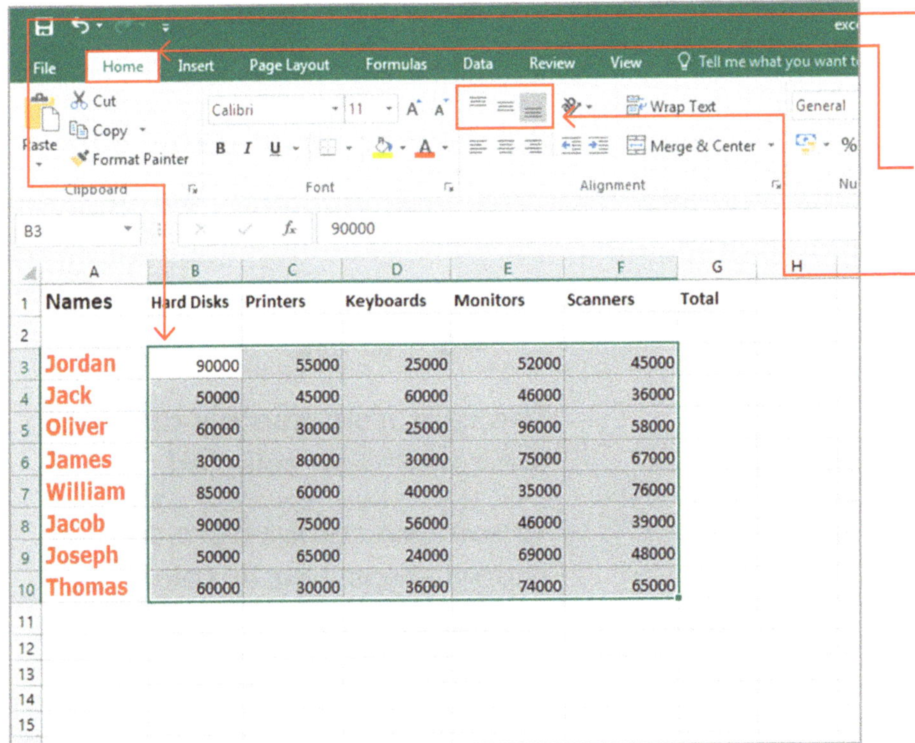

1. Select the cells containing the data you want to align differently.
2. Click on Home tab on the ribbon.
3. Click on one of the following buttons.

( ) Left align

( ) Center

( ) Right align

The data appears in the new alignment. In this example we have chosen Right alignment.

Centre Text Across the Column

You can centre a title or heading across a range of cells in your worksheet. The Merge and Center command is used to centre data across several columns in your worksheet.

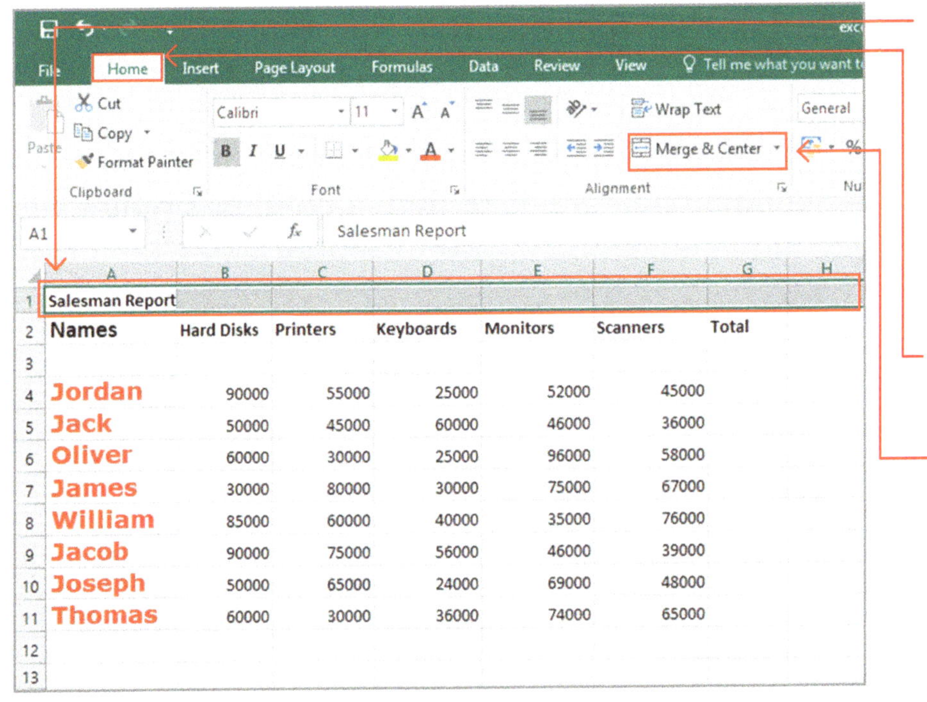

1. Select the cells you want to centre the data across.

The first cell you select should contain the data you want to centre.

2. Click on Home tab.
3. Click on Merge & Center button ( ) to centre data across the columns.

Excel centres data across the columns.

Changing the Colour of the Cell

The background colour of cells can be changed to help draw attention to the cell data.

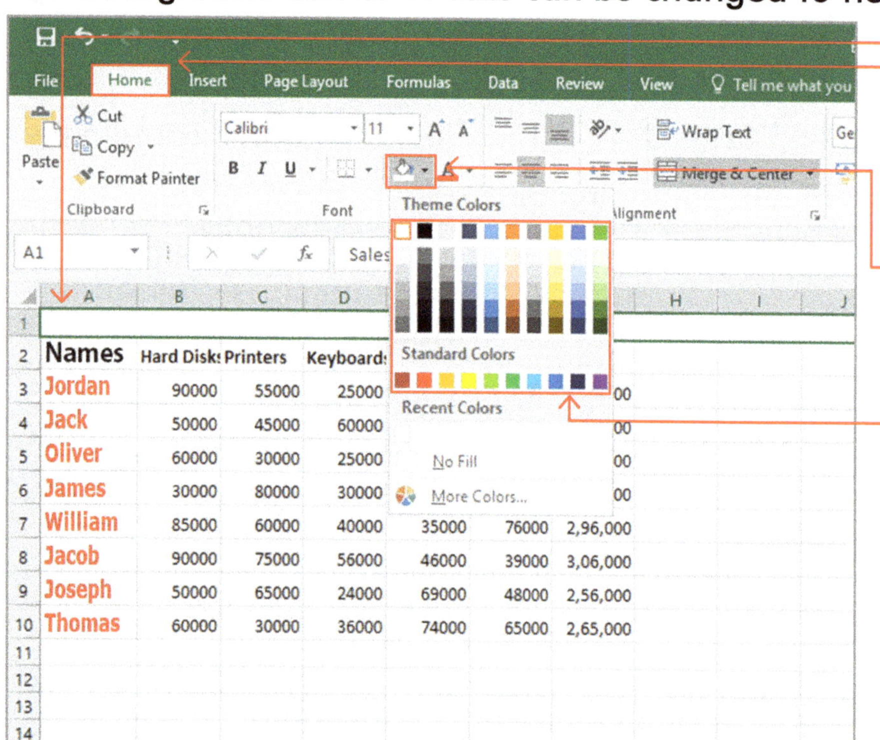

1. Select the cell or cells you want to change into a different colour.
2. Click on Home tab.
3. Click on down arrow button of Fill Colour to display the available colours.
4. Click on the colour you want to use.

The cells immediately appear in the colour you selected.

To remove colour from cells, repeat steps 1 to 4, selecting No Fill in step 4.

Changing the Colour of Font

You can give the different colours to different types of data to give it a colourful look. For example, you can use a different colour for the column headers in your worksheet.

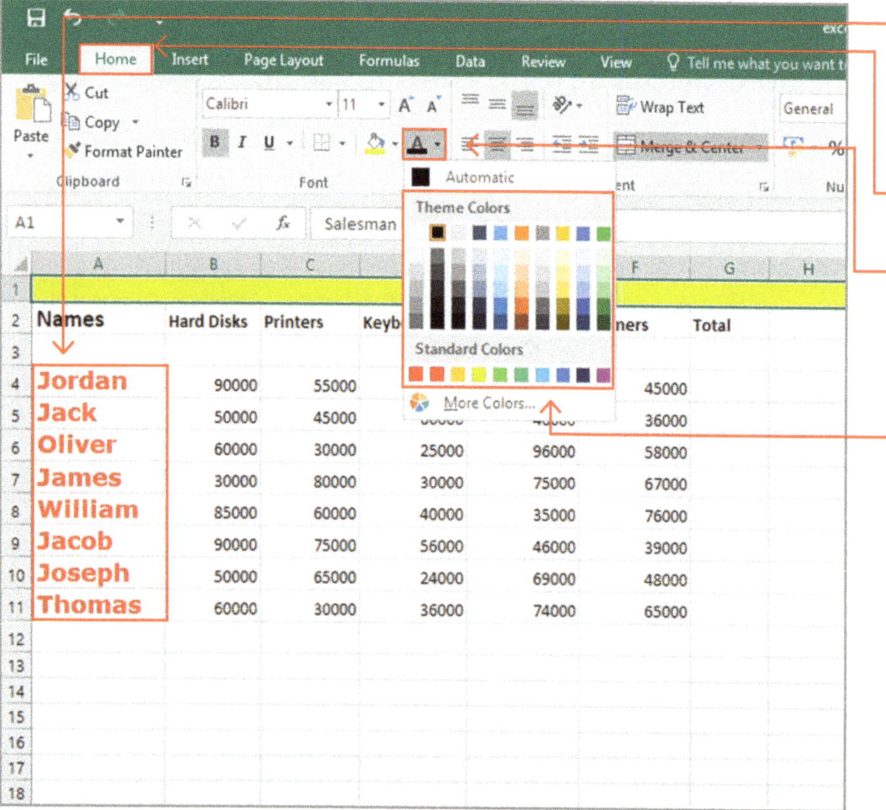

1. Select the cells containing data you want to change into a different colour.
2. Click on Home tab.
3. Click on down arrow button of Font Colour to display the available colours.
4. Click on the colour you want to use.

The data immediately appears in the colour you selected.

To return data to its original colour, repeat steps 1 to 4, selecting Automatic in step 4.

Adding Border

You can give different border patterns around the cells in the worksheet to get the clear look of the table. Border helps define the contents more clearly or separate the data from surrounding cells.

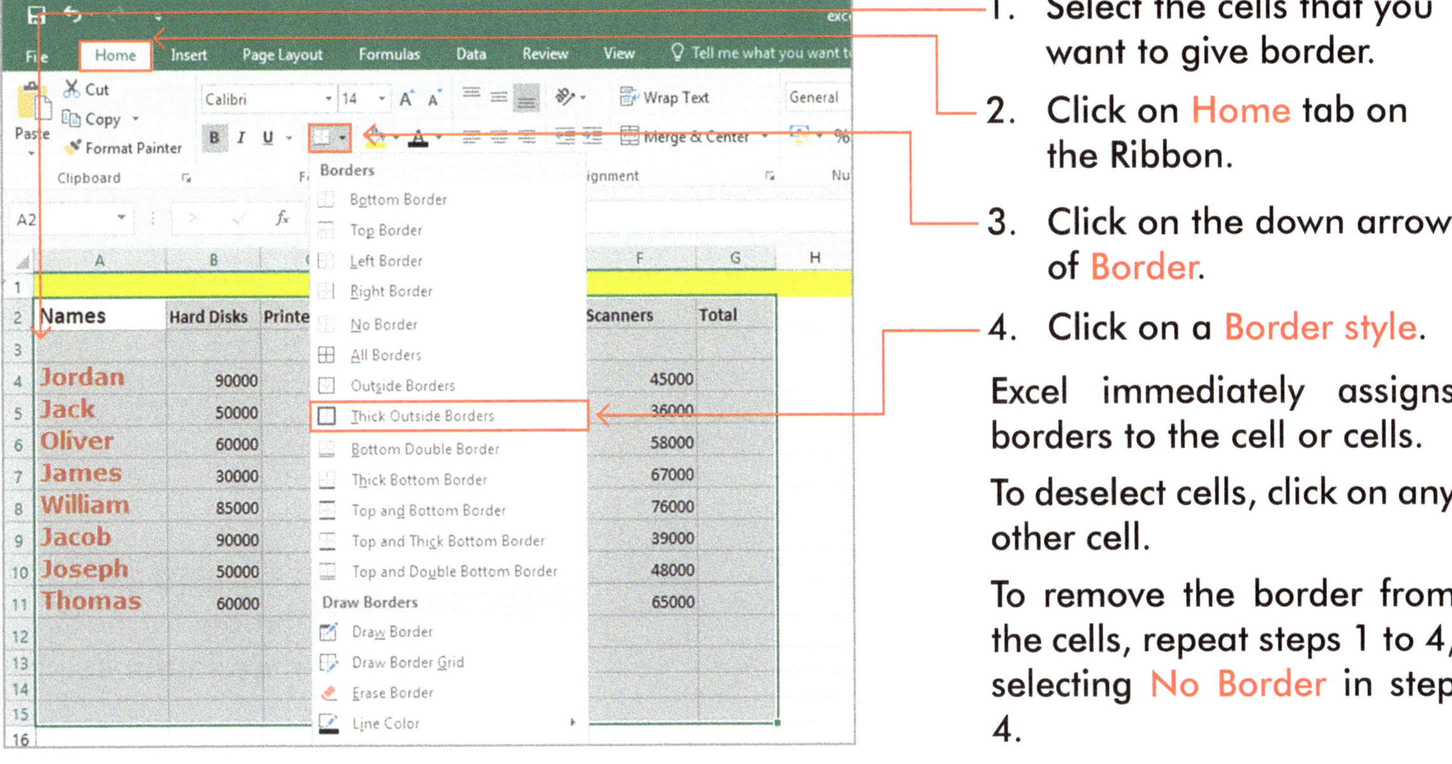

1. Select the cells that you want to give border.
2. Click on Home tab on the Ribbon.
3. Click on the down arrow of Border.
4. Click on a Border style.

Excel immediately assigns borders to the cell or cells.

To deselect cells, click on any other cell.

To remove the border from the cells, repeat steps 1 to 4, selecting No Border in step 4.

Changing Number Format

Number formatting is used to control the look of numerical data. For example, if there is a data that shows prices, you can apply the currency format to it. There are 12 such number formats to be chosen from.

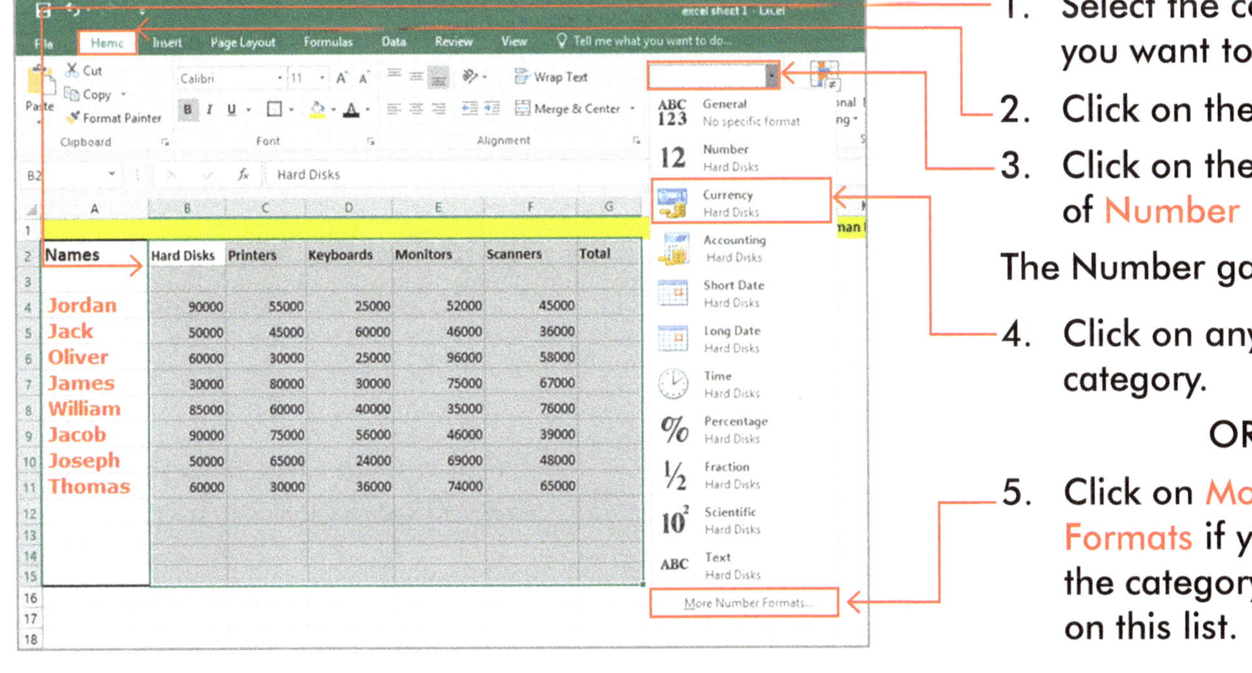

1. Select the cell or data you want to format.
2. Click on the Home tab.
3. Click on the down arrow of Number Format.

The Number gallery opens.

4. Click on any number category.

OR

5. Click on More Number Formats if you don't see the category you want on this list.

The Format Cells dialog box will open.

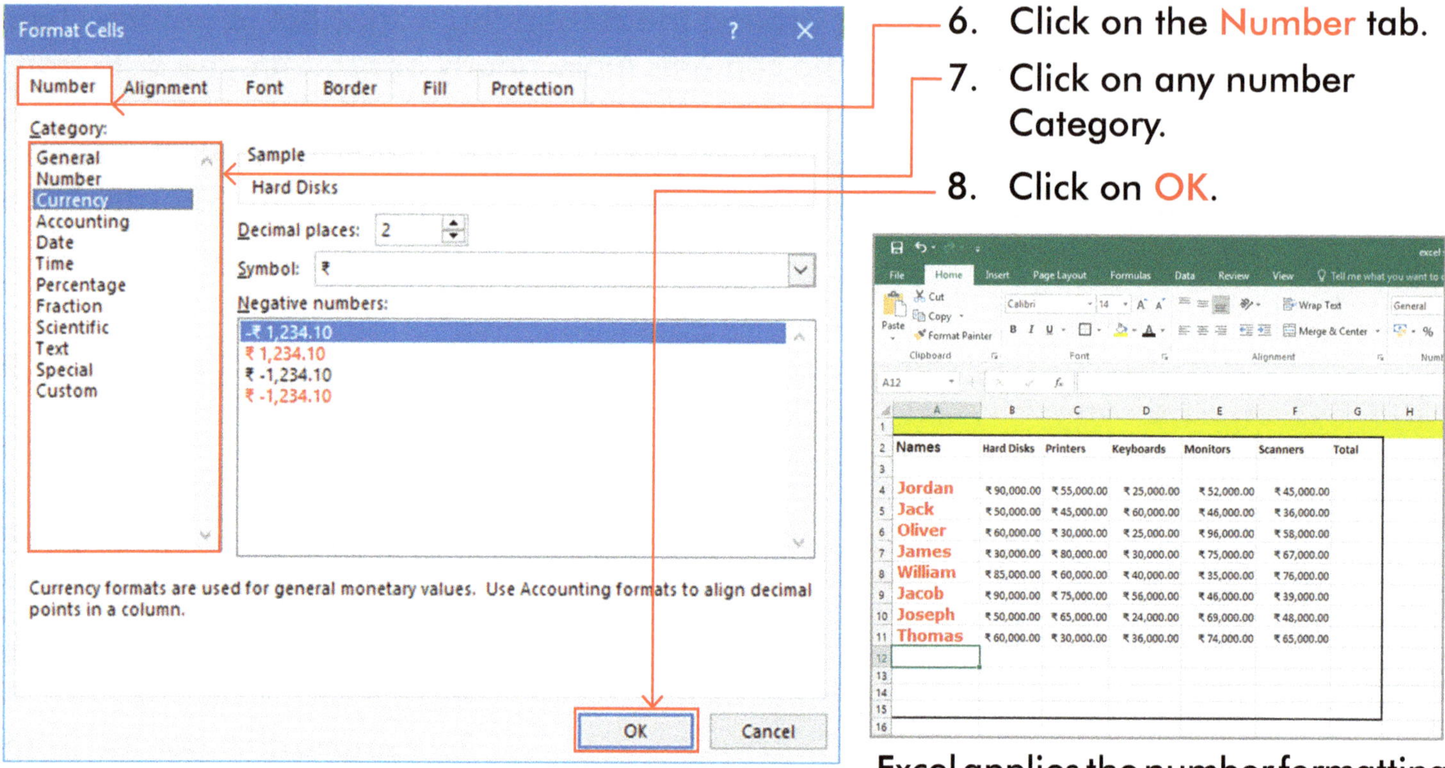

6. Click on the Number tab.
7. Click on any number Category.
8. Click on OK.

Excel applies the number formatting to the numerical data in the cell or range.

Applying Background

You can give background to a worksheet to add interest. For example, if your worksheet relates to the computer, you might add a picture of a computer.

1. Click on the Page Layout tab.
2. Click on Background. The Sheet Background dialog box opens.

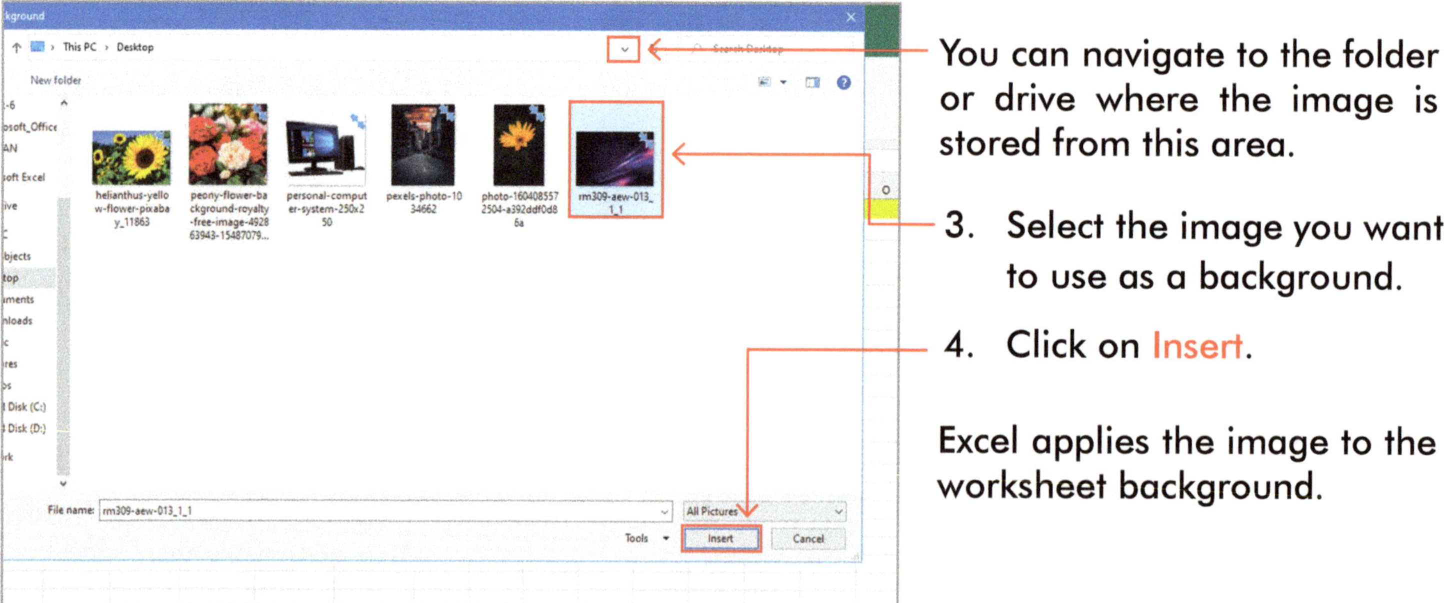

You can navigate to the folder or drive where the image is stored from this area.

3. Select the image you want to use as a background.
4. Click on Insert.

Excel applies the image to the worksheet background.

Applying Workbook Theme

Theme Gallery is provided by Excel that shows the combinations of different formattings (colours, fonts and effects) at once. It gives a more attractive look to your data. To apply the themes to the data, follow these steps.

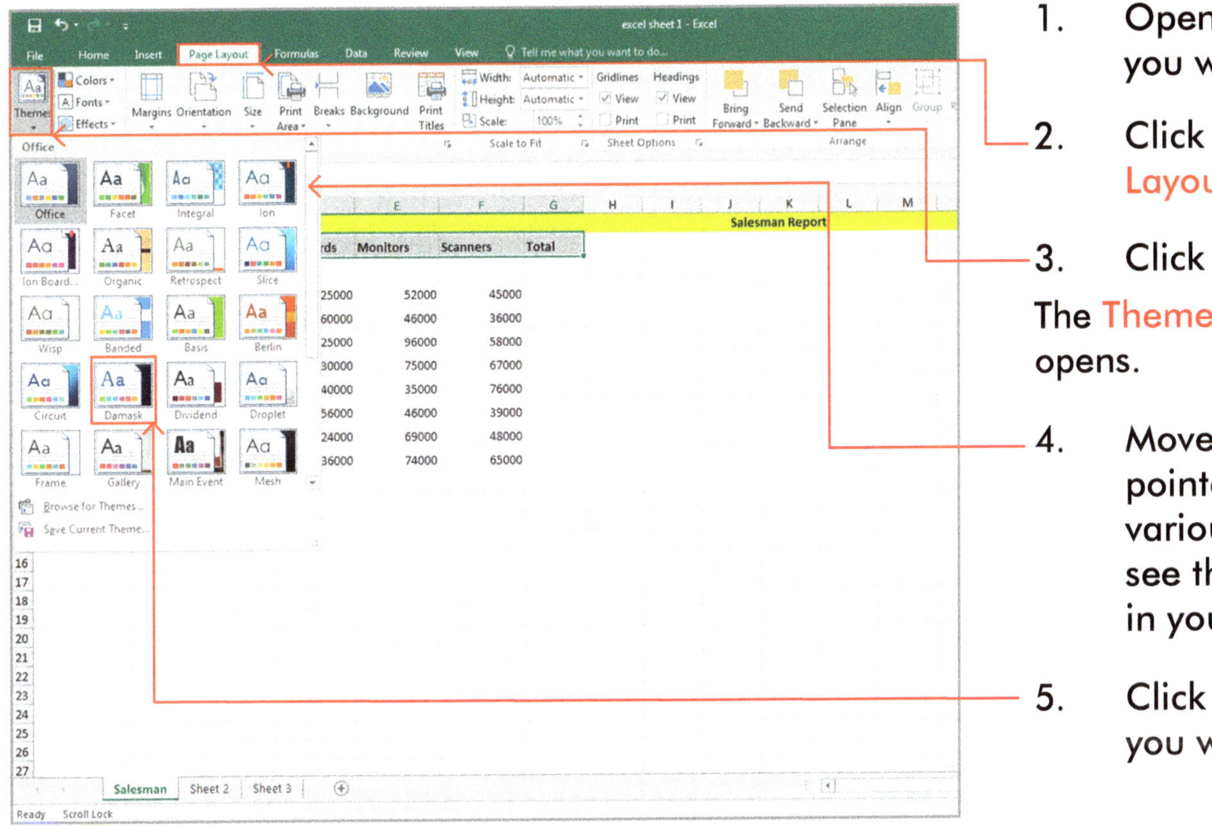

1. Open the workbook you want to format.
2. Click on the Page Layout tab.
3. Click on Themes.

The Themes Gallery opens.

4. Move your mouse pointer over the various themes to see them previewed in your worksheet.
5. Click on the Theme you want to apply.

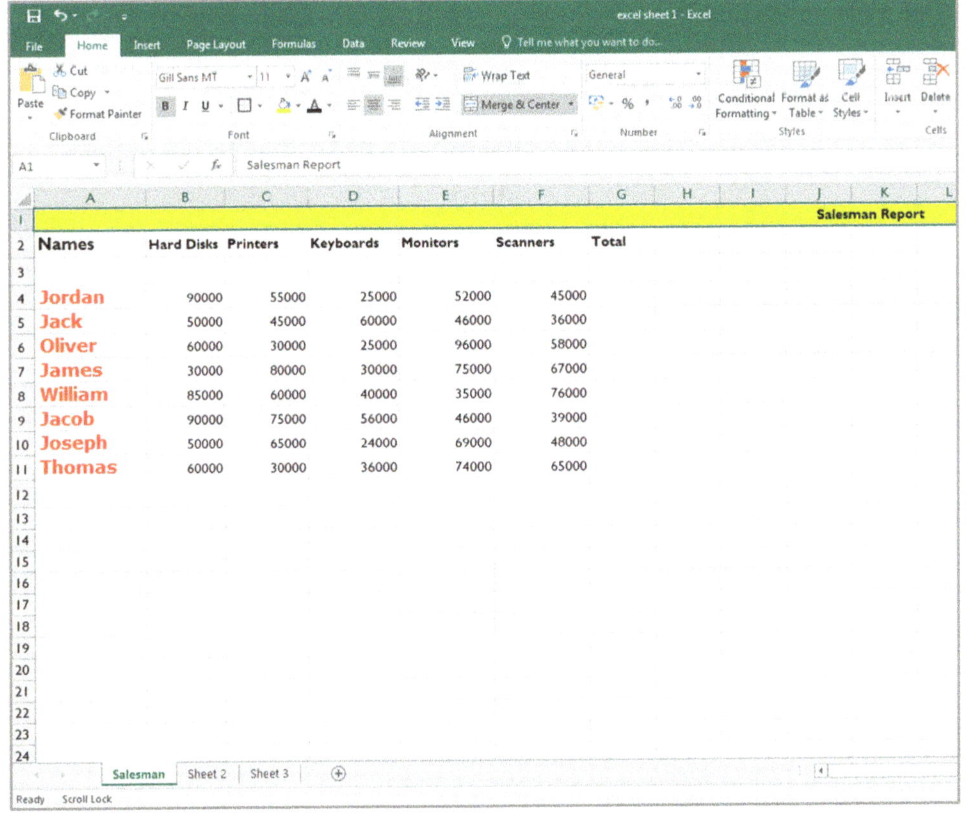

Salesman Report

Names	Hard Disks	Printers	Keyboards	Monitors	Scanners	Total
Jordan	90000	55000	25000	52000	45000	
Jack	50000	45000	60000	46000	36000	
Oliver	60000	30000	25000	96000	58000	
James	30000	80000	30000	75000	67000	
William	85000	60000	40000	35000	76000	
Jacob	90000	75000	56000	46000	39000	
Joseph	50000	65000	24000	69000	48000	
Thomas	60000	30000	36000	74000	65000	

Excel applies the formatting to the workbook.

You can see that the font style has changed in the worksheet.

Format With Styles

Ready-made table styles are also provided in Excel which have preset formatting designs. A style is a collection of formatting, whether you define a font and size or a background colour. To apply the format styles, the steps are:

FORMAT AS A TABLE

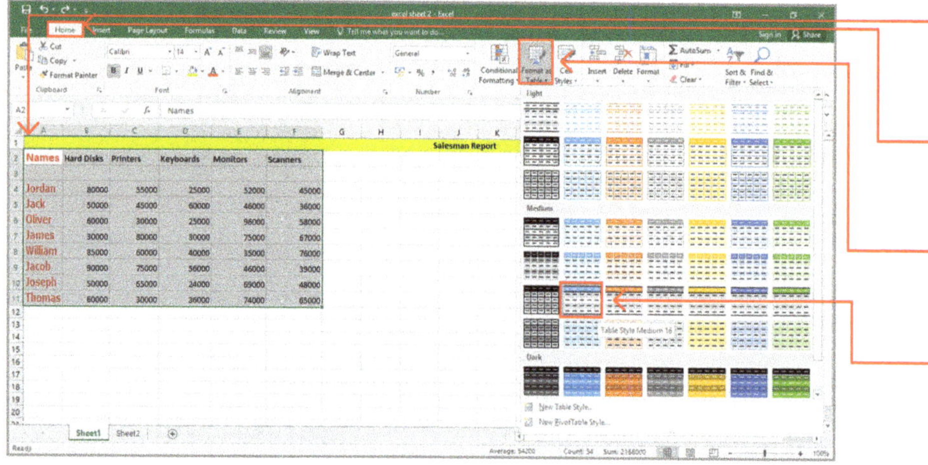

1. Select the cells that you want to format.
2. Click on Home tab on the Ribbon.
3. Click on the Format as Table button.
4. Click on a table style.

APPLY A CELL STYLE

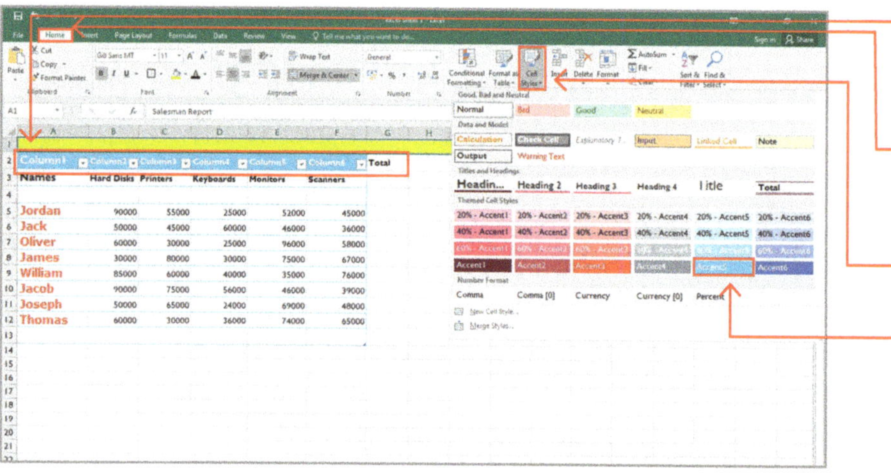

1. Select the cell or cells that you want to format.
2. Click on Home tab on the Ribbon.
3. Click on Cell Styles button.
4. Click on a style.

Excel applies the formatting style.

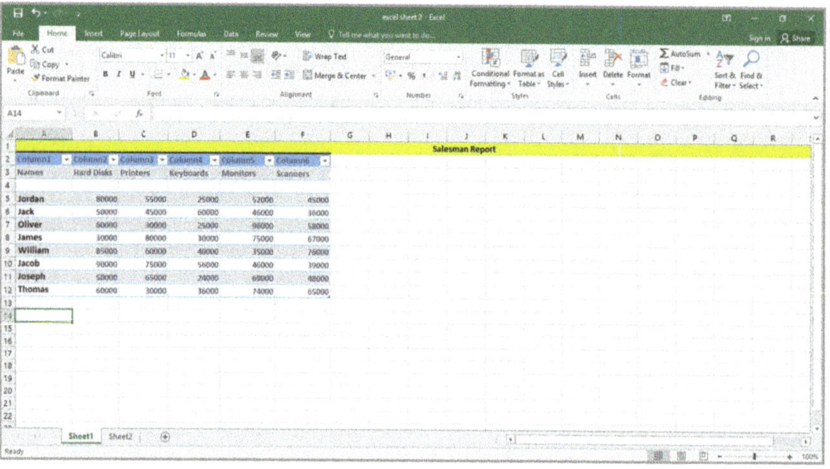

Excel applies the formatting to the selected cell.

To deselect cells, click on any cell.

LET'S HAVE A LOOK

- Formatting refers to the appearance and presentation of the worksheet.
- Alignment is the way in which the data is settled within the boundary of the cell.
- Merge and Center command is used to centre the data across several columns in a worksheet.
- Excel provides a Theme Gallery in which the combinations of different formatting are given.
- Number format is given to make the look of data in a similar manner.

SHORTCUT KEYS

Bold	:	Ctrl+B	Left Align	:	Ctrl+L
Italic	:	Ctrl+I	Center Align	:	Ctrl+E
Underline	:	Ctrl+U	Right Align	:	Ctrl+R
Increase font size	:	Ctrl+]	Justification	:	Ctrl+J
Decrease font Size	:	Ctrl+[			

BRAIN TEASER

1. Multiple Choice Questions

Tick (✓) the correct answer:

a. The appearance or presentation of your worksheet:
   i. Formatting ☐ ii. Editing ☐ iii. Creating ☐

b. The Alignment buttons are present in:
   i. Insert tab ☐ ii. Home tab ☐ iii. Data tab ☐

c. The feature used for centring title over the data:
   i. Spacing ☐ ii. Center align ☐
   iii. Center data across column ☐

d. Theme Gallery is located in:
   i. Data tab ☐ ii. View tab ☐
   iii. Page Layout tab ☐

2. Fill in the blanks:

a. Formatting feature is used to give your worksheet an ____________ and ____________ outlook.

b. The font size can also be ____________ or ____________.

c. Different ways of alignments are ____________, ____________ and ____________.

d. There are ______________ number formats to be chosen from.

e. ______________ command is used to centre the data across several columns.

3. Write 'T' for True and 'F' for False in the boxes:

a. Bold, Italic and Underline are the formatting features in Excel. ☐

b. You cannot background an image in the worksheet. ☐

c. Theme Gallery gives the pictorial background to the worksheet. ☐

d. There are 15 number formats to be chosen from. ☐

4. Answer the following questions

(i) Answer each in a few lines:

a. Name the different formatting options.

b. What are the different number formats?

c. Name the three different ways of alignment.

d. On which tab are the formatting buttons present?

e. Name the tab where Cut, Copy and Paste buttons are located.

f. Where is Theme Gallery located?

g. Which feature is used to give a combinations of different formattings?

(ii) Answer each comprehensively:

a. How is formatting useful?

b. What is the use of alignment options?

c. What is the use of 'Center across the column' feature?

d. What is the use of Number formatting?

e. What is the use of applying border to the cells?

f. What is Theme Gallery?

Open the Worksheet you made in the previous chapter.

Month	Income	Expenses	Balance Amount	Profit / Loss
JANUARY	90000	95000	– 5000	LOSS

FEBRUARY	85000	81000	4000	PROFIT
MARCH	70000	65000	5000	PROFIT
APRIL	80000	72000	8000	PROFIT
MAY	95000	88000	7000	PROFIT
JUNE	70000	67000	3000	PROFIT
JULY	80000	71000	9000	PROFIT
AUGUST	70000	65000	5000	PROFIT
SEPTEMBER	90000	98000	– 8000	LOSS
OCTOBER	65000	68000	– 3000	LOSS
NOVEMBER	70000	67000	3000	PROFIT
DECEMBER	60000	56000	4000	PROFIT

1. Choose the proper font size and style for title.
2. Centre Align the Month and Profit / Loss.
3. Change the heading colour into green.
4. Change the font style of Month into bold italic.
5. Change the colour of Income cells into yellow and Expenses cells into blue.
6. Apply a border to the table.

8 Advanced Features in MS-Excel

In this chapter, we will learn:

⇒ Generating a series
⇒ Sorting data
⇒ Filtering data
⇒ Removing filter

GENERATING A SERIES

Dear children, now you are much familiar with MS-Excel and can work well by using different features of it. After practising the features learnt in previous chapter, let's learn about some advanced features provided by Excel to make your work faster and easier. The advanced features like generating a series of numbers, names of days, months, etc. automatically, sorting the data in increasing or decreasing order alphabetically or numerically or filtering the data will be discussed in this chapter.

Generating a Text Series

You can use AutoFill feature to help you automate data-entry tasks. This feature lets you generate a series, like of excel days of the week or names of months, etc. automatically. Using AutoFill feature you can quickly fill cells with a series of numbers or add duplicate entries. To generate a text series, follow these steps:

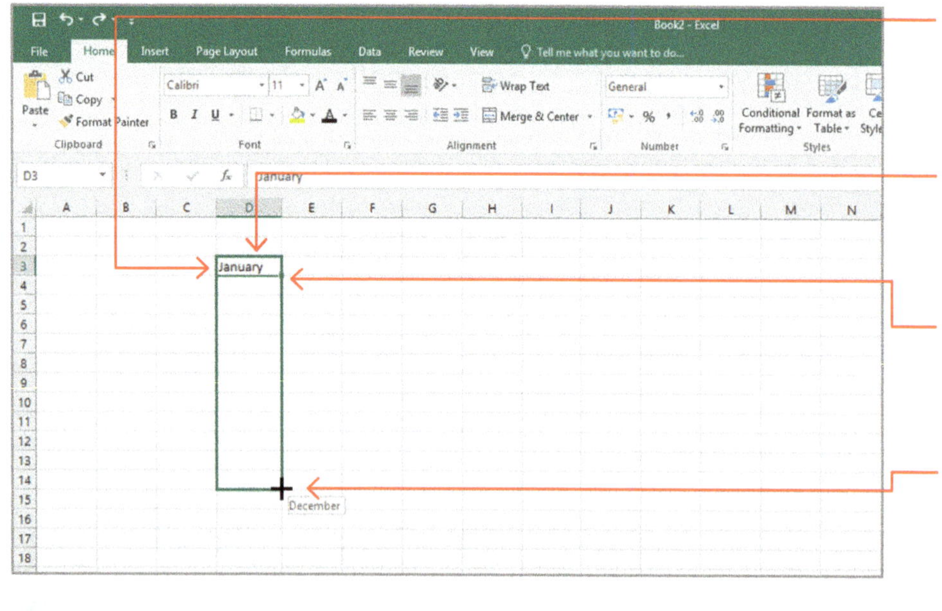

1. Enter the text you want to start the series with, e.g., January.
2. Click on the cell containing the text you entered.
3. Position the mouse over the bottom right corner of the cell.
4. Drag the mouse (+) over the cells you want to include in the series.

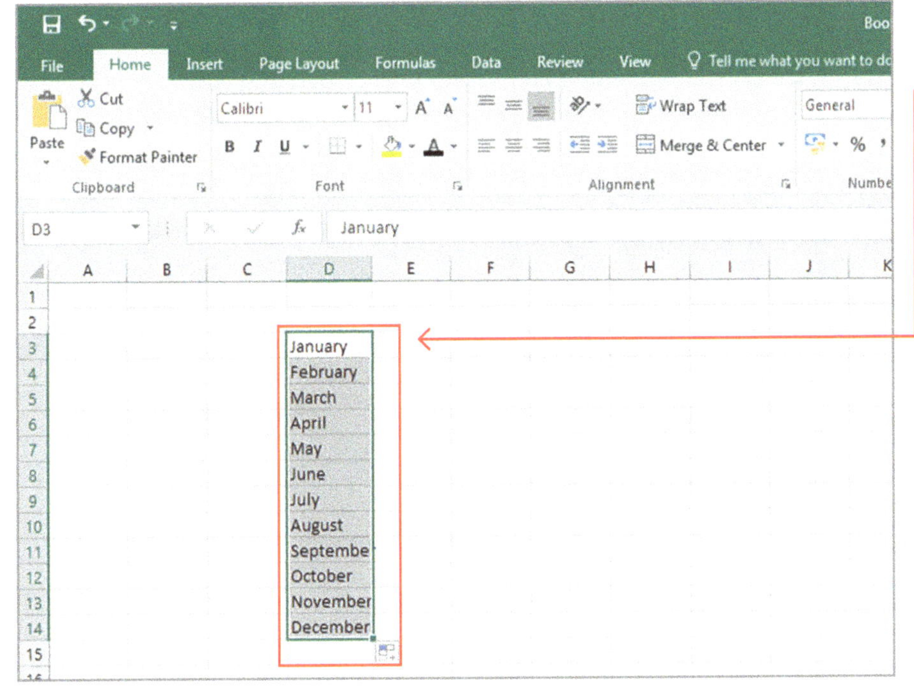

The cells display the text series.

If Excel cannot determine the text series you want to complete, it will copy the text in the first cell to all the cells you have selected.

To deselect the cells, click any cell.

Generating a Number Series

Just like a text series, you can generate a number series, as:

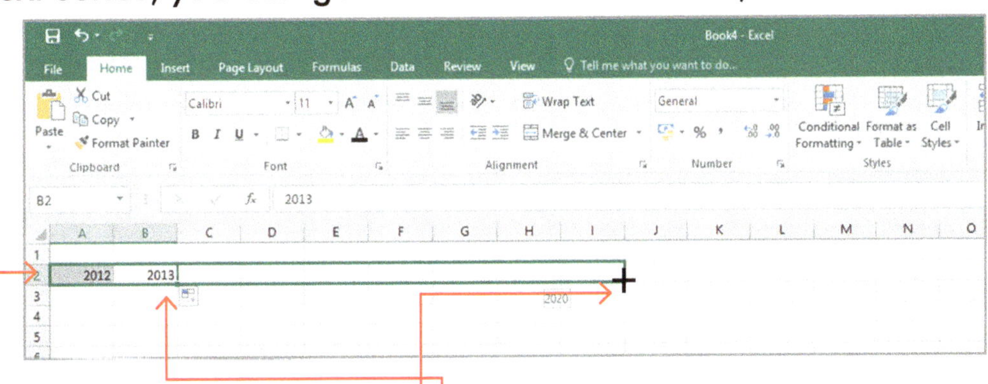

1. Enter the first two numbers you want to start the series with.
2. Select the cells containing the numbers you have entered.
3. Position the mouse pointer over the bottom right corner of the selected cells. The mouse pointer changes into (+).
4. Drag the mouse over the cells you want to include in the series.

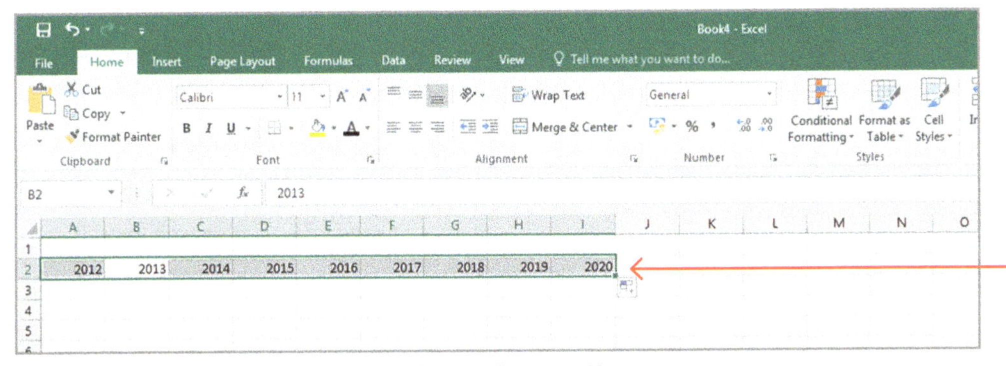

The cells display the number series.

Click on any cell to deselect the cells.

Generating a Date Series

Just like text series and number series, the Date series can also be created, as:

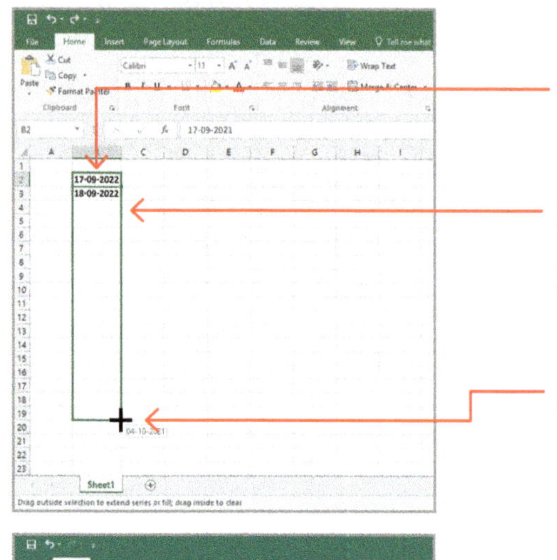

1. Enter the first two dates you want to start the series with in mm/dd/yy style.
2. Select the cells containing the dates you entered.
3. Position the mouse pointer, over the bottom right corner of the selected cells.
4. Drag the mouse over the cells you want to include in the series.

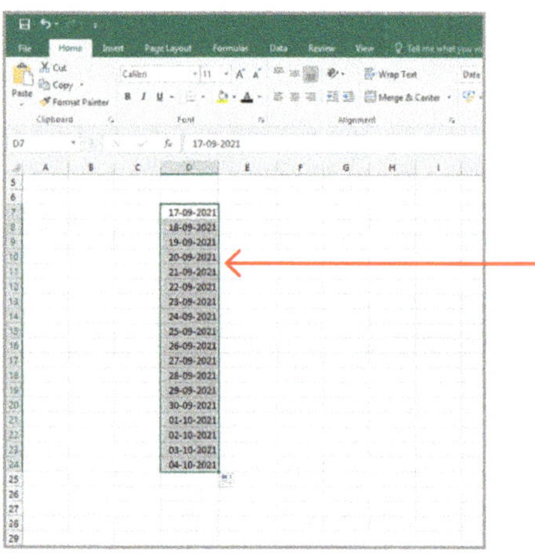

The cells display the date series.

Click on any cell to deselect the cells.

Generating a Custom Series

You can also generate your own series for the values you enter frequently by using a Custom AutoFill series option. To create a custom AutoFill series, follow these steps:

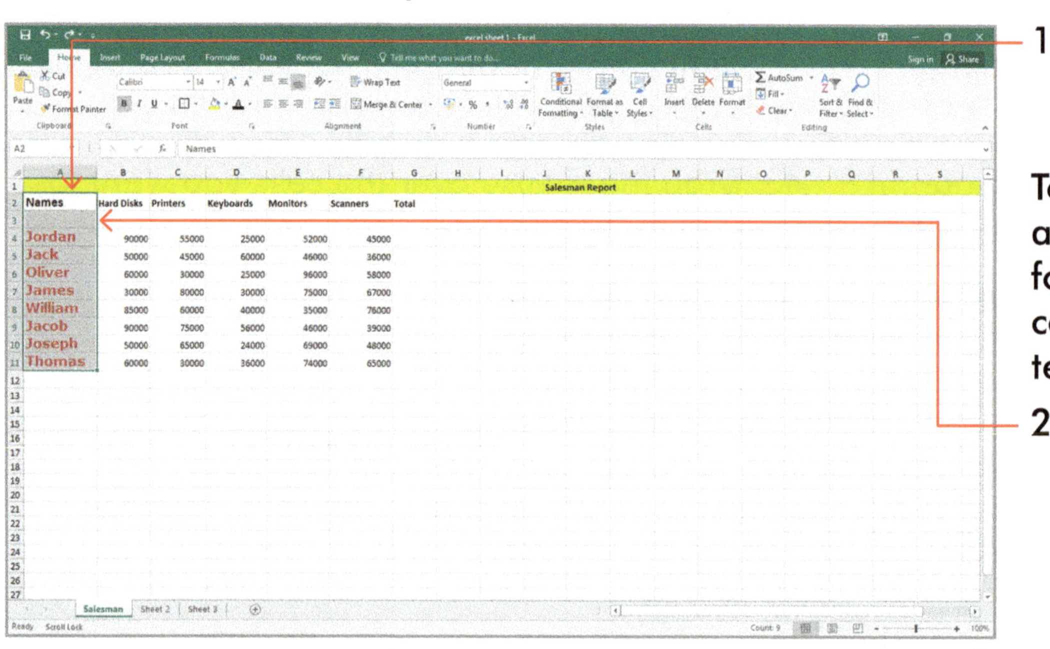

1. Enter the text you want to save as a series.

To include numbers in a series, you must first format the cells that will contain the numbers as text.

2. Select the cells containing the text you have entered.

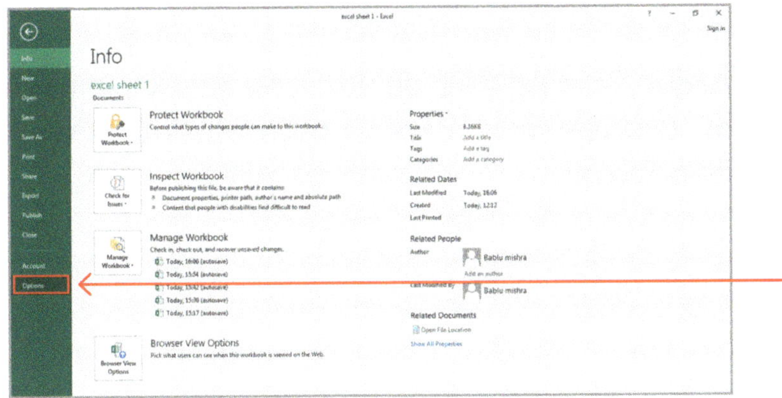

3. Click on the File button.

4. Click on Options button.

The Excel Options dialog box appears.

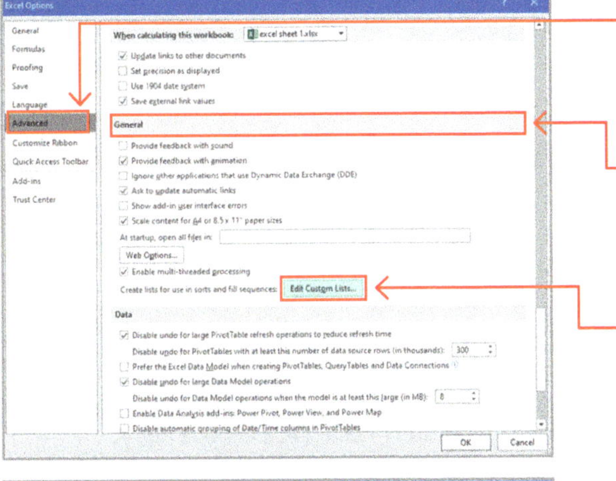

5. Click on Advance tab.

6. Use the scroll bar and bring the General section in view.

7. Click on Edit Custom list. Custom List dialog box will appear.

8. Click Import to create the custom series.

This area displays the text in the series.

9. Click on OK.

Excel Option menu will appear.

10. Click on OK.

Complete a Custom Series

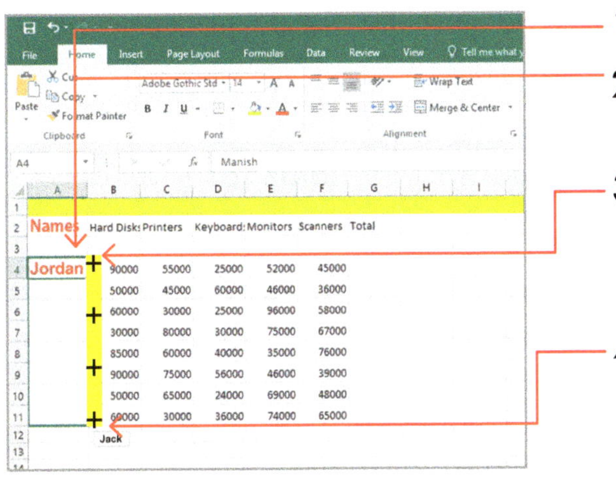

1. Enter the text which starts your custom series.
2. Click the cell containing the text you have entered.
3. Position the mouse (✣) over the bottom right corner of the cell.

   (✣) changes to (+).
4. Drag the mouse (+) over the cells you want to include in the series.

   The cells display your custom series.

SORTING

Sorting means to arrange the data in a given order. Sorting in Excel lets you easily reorder your data based on the type of sorting that you choose. You can sort out numeric as well as character data. The data can be sorted in two ways:

Ascending Order

Numeric data - (1, 2, 3, 4, 5, 6, ...)

Character data - (A, B, C, D, E, F, ...)

Descending Order

Numeric data - (9, 8, 7, 6, 5, 4, ...)

Character data - (Z, Y, X, W, V, U, ...)

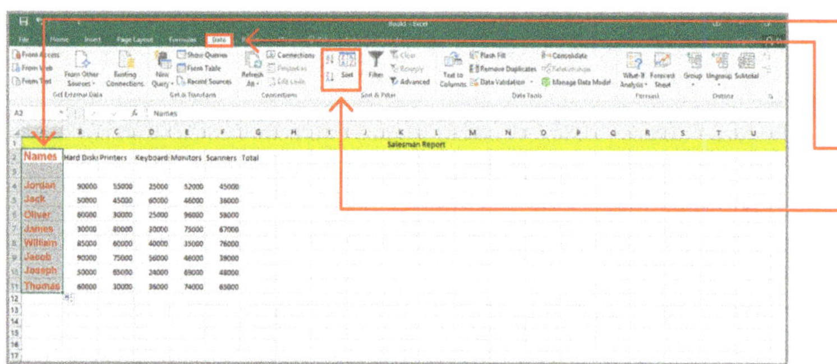

1. Select the column data you want to sort.
2. Click on Data tab.
3. Click on Ascending or Descending button.

The data will be sorted accordingly.

Sort with the Sort Dialog Box

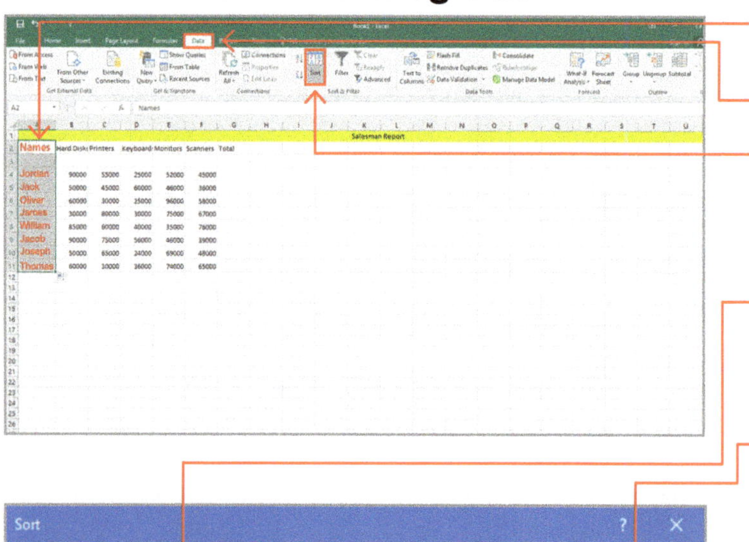

1. Select any cell in the data list.
2. Click on Data tab.
3. Click on Sort.

The Sort dialog box appears.

4. Click on the drop-down menu and then select the primary field to be sorted.
5. Click on the drop-down menu and choose to sort the field in ascending order (A to Z).

   Click on the drop-down menu to specify additional fields for the sort and choose criteria.
6. Click on Add Level to add additional sort levels.
7. Click on OK to sort the data.

The data will get rearranged as per the selection option in the worksheet.

FILTERING THE DATA

With the help of Filter option, you can view only the portions of your data. Filter data displays only the rows that meet criteria that you specify and hides those rows that you do not want to be displayed.

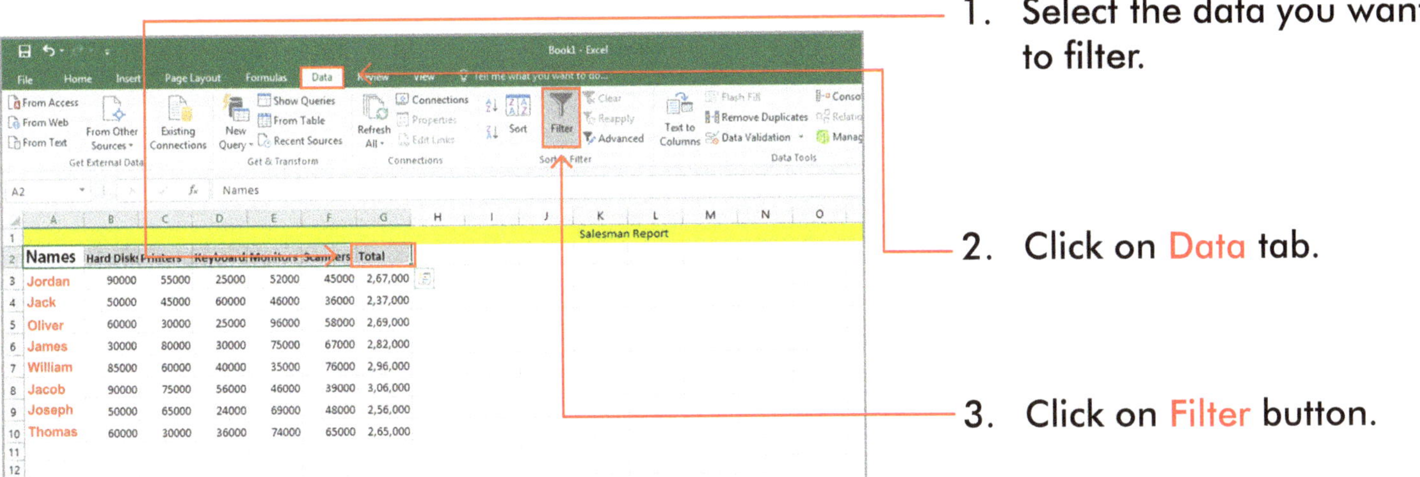

1. Select the data you want to filter.
2. Click on Data tab.
3. Click on Filter button.

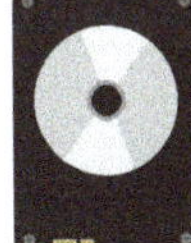

Remember

When you have a large amount of data then filter option helps you to view only that data which you want.

AutoFilter drop-down button will appear to the right of the column labels in the filtered range.

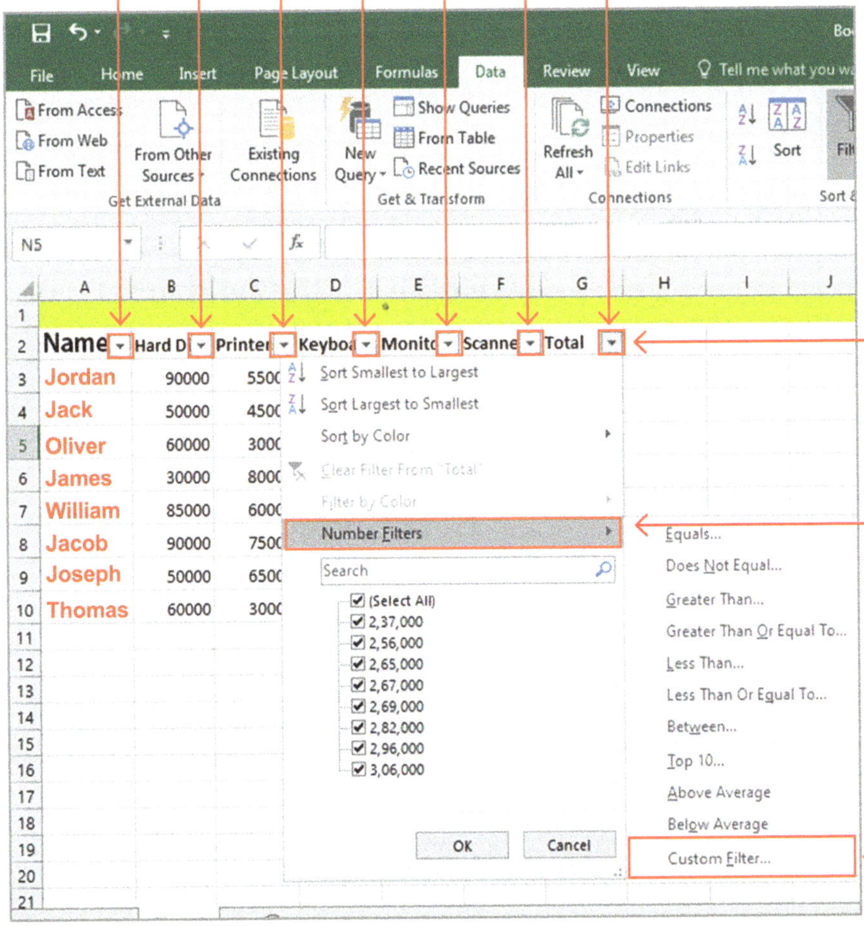

4. Click on the drop-down arrow of the field on which you want to apply the filter. In this example, we have clicked on the down arrow of Total.

A menu will appear.

5. Click on Number Filters.

A popup menu appears.

6. Click on the Custom Filter.

Custom AutoFilter dialog box will appear.

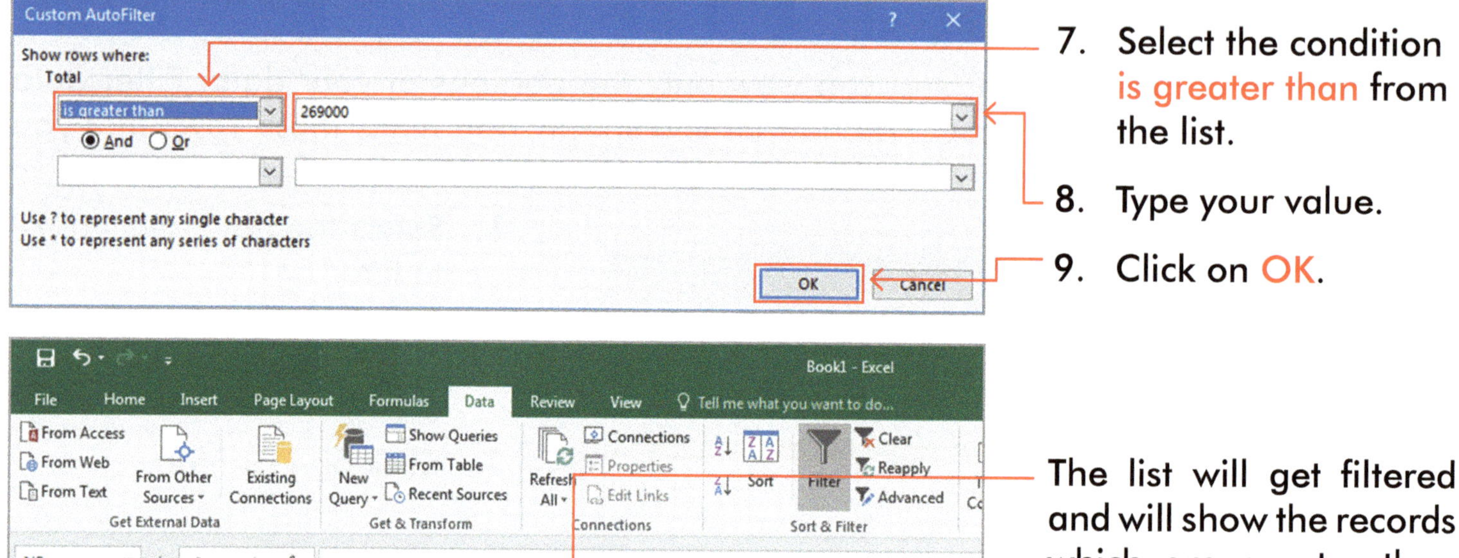

7. Select the condition is greater than from the list.
8. Type your value.
9. Click on OK.

The list will get filtered and will show the records which are greater than 269000.

Filter arrow has changed with a filter icon

Auto Filter

Through Auto Filter option, you can manage the long list of items easily, efficiently and quickly. The following are the steps that can help you to set up an auto filter and display just the information you required.

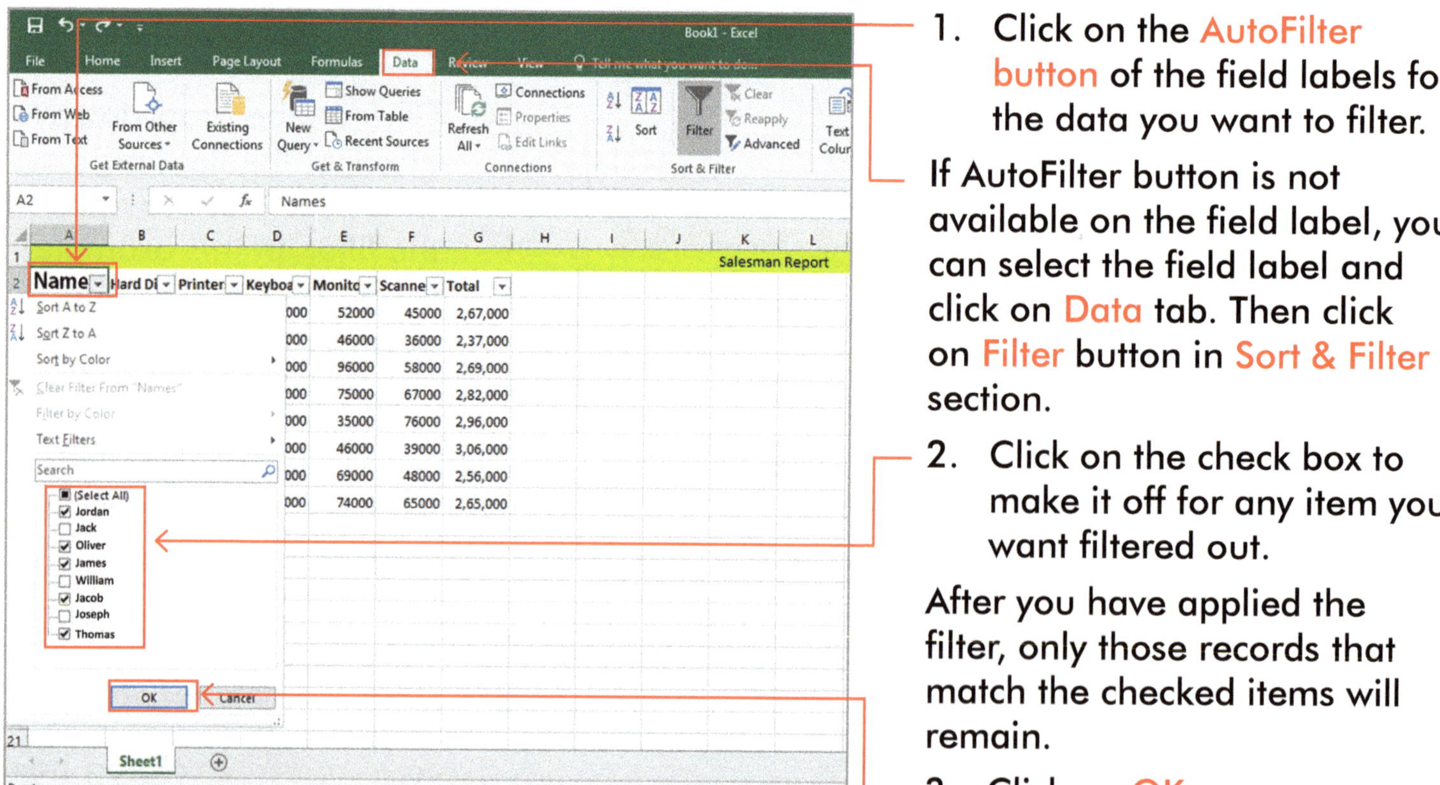

1. Click on the AutoFilter button of the field labels for the data you want to filter.

If AutoFilter button is not available on the field label, you can select the field label and click on Data tab. Then click on Filter button in Sort & Filter section.

2. Click on the check box to make it off for any item you want filtered out.

After you have applied the filter, only those records that match the checked items will remain.

3. Click on OK.

Excel filters the table and shows only those records which were not checked OFF.

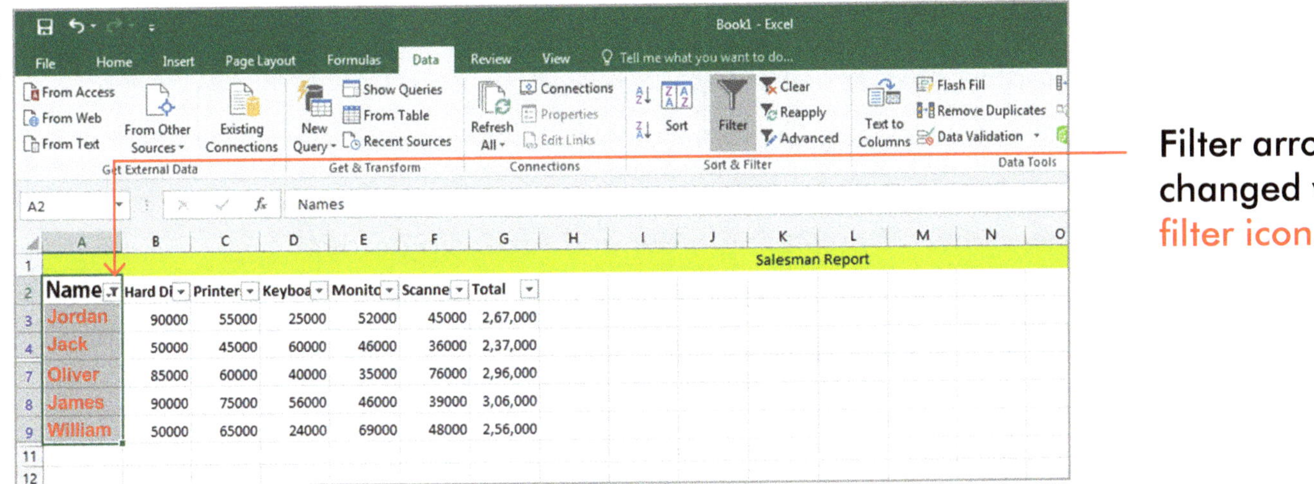

Filter arrow has changed with a filter icon.

Showing the Hidden Records Again

You can display the hidden record after filtering by following these steps:

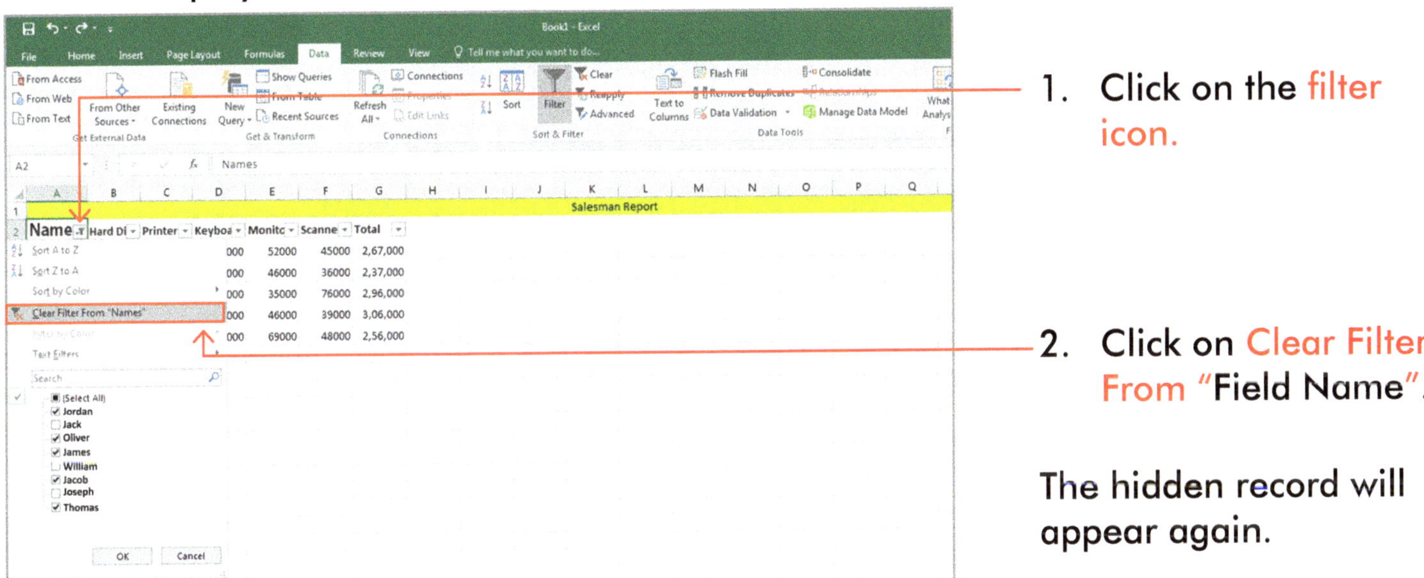

1. Click on the filter icon.
2. Click on Clear Filter From "Field Name".

The hidden record will appear again.

Removing the Filter

You can remove the filter option to display again the complete data by following these steps:

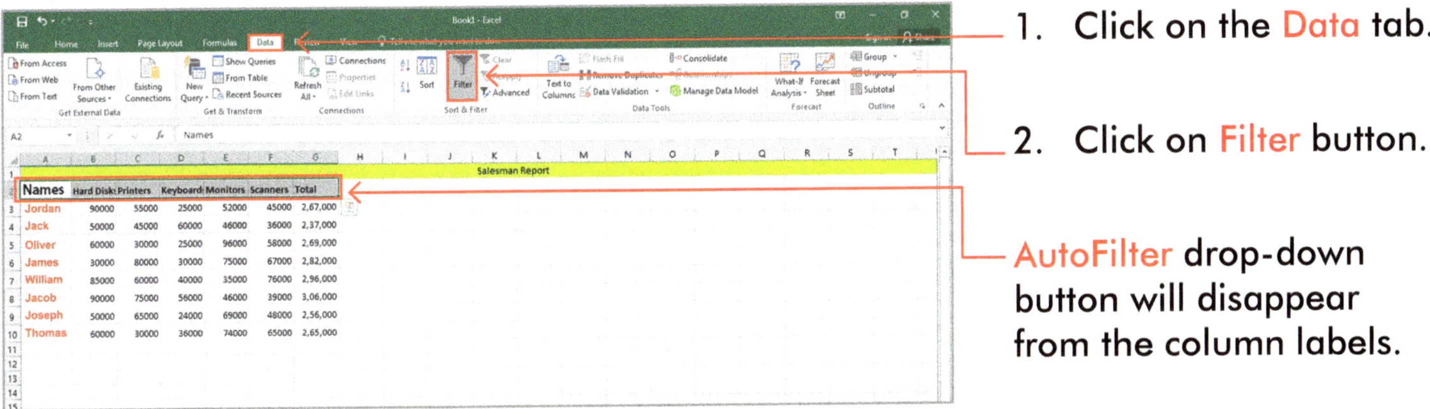

1. Click on the Data tab.
2. Click on Filter button.

AutoFilter drop-down button will disappear from the column labels.

LET'S HAVE A LOOK

- You can create the different types of series in Excel.
- You can generate your own series using Custom AutoFill Series.
- Sorting means to arrange data in a given order.
- Sorting can be done in two ways - Descending order and Ascending order.
- The filter option is used to view only required data from a large amount.
- By removing the filter option you can again view computer data.

BRAIN TEASER

1. Write 'T' for True and 'F' for False in the boxes:

a. You cannot generate your own series. ☐

b. Sorting feature is used to view only required data. ☐

c. Sorting can be done in two ways, *i.e.* smallest and biggest. ☐

d. Through Filter option you can hide the rows you do not want. ☐

e. Auto filter option can manage long lists very easily. ☐

2. Match Column A with Column B :

Column A		Column B
a. Filter	(i)	Ascending order
b. A - Z	(ii)	Advanced tab
c. Sort	(iii)	List of values you enter frequently
d. Custom AutoFill	(iv)	Data tab
e. Edit Custom List button	(v)	Option for analyzing a large amount of data
f. Descending order	(vi)	Z - A

3. Answer the following questions.

(i) Answer in a few lines:

a. Name the different types of series that can be generated in a worksheet.

b. On which tab is the Filter option present?

c. Name the two advanced features provided in Excel.

d. On which tab is the Sort option present?

e. Can you generate your own list you frequently require?

f. What is descending order?

g. Can you remove the filter that you have applied?

(ii) Answer comprehensively

a. How is sorting different from filtering?

b. What are the two ways of sorting data?

c. Explain the different types of series created in Excel.

d. How is filter feature useful?

4. Write the procedure of:

a. Generating series : Weekdays, names of months

b. Sorting the data in ascending/descending order

c. Filtering the data

LAB ACTIVITY

1. Visit your computer lab and create a date series from 01/11/2013 to the next 30 days.

2. Create the following worksheet:

S. No.	Name	Age	Department	Salary	Sex
1	Richard	30	Science	26,000	M
2	Oliver	25	Maths	33,000	F
3	Michel	35	Computer	34,000	M
4	John	28	English	30,000	M
5	Walker	32	EVS	33,000	F

a. Filter records of male teachers.

b. Filter records in which age is more than 30 yrs.

c. Filter records whose salary is more than ₹ 30,000.

Formative Assessment-3
(Chapters 6-8)

1. Prepare a small chart of different editing features and formatting features provided in MS-Excel.

2. Write the steps for:

a. Changing a column width

b. Generating a series (week days)

3. Write the two differences between

a. Cut/Paste | Copy/Paste

b. Sorting | Filtering

E-Mail

In this chapter, we will learn:

- ⇒ Introduction to E-Mail
- ⇒ E-Mail Vs Ordinary Post
- ⇒ Advantages of E-Mail
- ⇒ E-Mail programs
- ⇒ E-Mail Address
- ⇒ How E-Mail travels
- ⇒ Exchange information through Computers
- ⇒ Components of an E-Mail message
- ⇒ Receiving and sending E-Mails
- ⇒ Some common E-Mail terms
- ⇒ E-Mail etiquettes

Dear Children, in the previous class, you learnt about the Internet and working on it. On the Internet, you have one of the most important features, *i.e.* E-mail. In this chapter, you will study about the features of E-mail in detail.

E-MAIL

E-mail is also known as Electronic Mail which is used to send or receive messages from one computer to another anywhere in the world. It is one of the fastest and appropriate methods to communicate with people. You can send text data, images, audio and video through an e-mail. It allows users to communicate with one another in less time and at a nominal cost.

In order to use the e-mail facility on the Internet, you need to create an e-mail account on a mail server, such as Gmail, Yahoo Mail, Rediff Mail, etc.

Advantages of an E-mail

There are numerous benefits of using an e-mail service. Some of the benefits are as follows:

Easy to use : When you send a message through an e-mail the person you send it to does not have to be online at that time to receive it. Mail can be collected whenever the person chooses to Log In to his/her computer network or mail server.

Speed : E-mail is extremely fast. One can receive a message in a matter of seconds after it has been sent, irrespective of the geographic location of the sender and the recipient. For sending messages you cannot find a better medium than e-mail.

Reliable and Secure : It is a reliable mode of communication, *i.e.* once the message is sent from a source computer, it will definitely be delivered. It is a secure medium of communication. No one can access anybody's e-mail account without knowing the password.

Cost-Effective : There is no charge for sending and receiving e-mail; the only charge you need to pay is to your Internet Service Provider. There is no extra payment even if a long message is sent or the message has to travel to the remotest corner of the world.

Environment Friendly : Postal mails use paper as a medium to send letters. Electronic mail, therefore, prevents a large number of trees from getting axed. It also saves fuel needed in transport.

Data Storage : You can send documents, graphics, sound files or any file as an attachment along with your e-mail. An e-mail service like Gmail offers enough space for data storage.

Disadvantages of an E-mail

⇒ A slight error in the e-mail address of the recipient can prevent the delivery of the message. There is always a chance of the failure of sending and receiving an e-mail.

⇒ Sometimes viruses can enter into your system through the attachments received in e-mails.

⇒ E-mails are not checked regularly. As a result, sometimes the recipient may not read an important message in time.

E-Mail Address

Just as you address a letter while using the postal system, you address an e-mail message with the e-mail address of your intended recipient. Likewise, when someone sends you a message, he or she must have your e-mail address.

An e-mail address is a unique address that identifies the sender.

An e-mail address is a combination of two parts – a user name and a domain name. These parts identify the user, so he or she can receive messages.

The user name is a unique combination of characters that identify you. It must differ from the other user names located on the same mail server.

Domain name is the location of the person's account on the Internet.

These two parts (User name or Domain name) are separated by the @ symbol. @ means at the rate.

Getting an E-mail Account

By creating your e-mail account you can get an e-mail address. There are different e-mail service providers, such as Gmail, Hotmail, AOL, Yahoo mail, etc., through which you can create an e-mail account.

For creating an e-mail account you simply have to fill an online form provided by the service provider. Your e-mail account will be ready to use once you have filled in the form and agreed to the terms and conditions for the services.

How E-mail travels

Computers have to be linked together via a network (Internet) so that the e-mail message may travel. The message has an address so that it may be sent directly to the right destination.

When you have sent the message, it is sent to a mail server which is connected to the Internet. A program on the mail server determines how to route the message through the Internet and then sends the message in packets. Packets are the small chunks which are broken by the Internet while sending the e-mail message from one computer to another. Each packet contains the address of the destination computer. The messages are put back together from the packets to form the e-mail message, when this message reaches the recipient's mail server. Then the message transfers to a POP or POP3 server. POP (Post Office Protocol) server is a communications technology for retrieving e-mail from a mail server. The POP server holds the message until the recipient retrieves it with his or her e-mail software.

When you receive the message, it is placed in your mailbox. A mailbox is a storage location usually residing on the computer that connects you to the Internet, such as the server operated by your Internet Service Provider (ISP). The server often is called a mail server that contains mailboxes. A mailbox contains your messages until you use your e-mail program to retrieve them.

E-MAIL AND POSTAL MAIL

E-mail is a method used to send and receive electronically small files, letters, music and video almost instantly. Anything sent using e-mail methods is broken down into small packets and sent out into many different directions towards the receiver's address. E-mail can be accessed through most computers, smartphones and other devices.

Postal mail is a method of sending and receiving physical mails, like letters, packages and anything imaginable items. Postal mail is carried by aeroplanes, mail trucks, mail carriers, trains and boats. Postal mail takes many days to reach its destination.

E-mail

Postal mail

Similarities between E-mail and Postal Mail

⇒ Both forms of mailing (electronic mail and postal mail) are used to send and receive messages even through one slightly takes more time than the other. But they both get the job done.

⇒ They both have a mailbox.

⇒ There are many stops along the way to the destination.

⇒ Both have rules and regulations.

⇒ In both cases, one has to write the receiver's address in order to send the mail.

Differences between E-mail and Postal Mail

⇒ E-mail is sent electronically and postal mail is sent physically.

⇒ A person cannot send a package through e-mail. Packages can only be sent through postal mail.

⇒ E-mail uses an electronic address while postal mail uses a physical address.

⇒ E-mail does not need stamps.

⇒ Postal mail has specific routes.

E-mail Program

An e-mail program is required to create, send, receive, forward and print messages. The received or sent messages are placed in your personal mailbox provided by the service provider. There are many service providers of e-mail programs, such as Yahoo mail, Outlook, Hotmail, Gmail, etc.

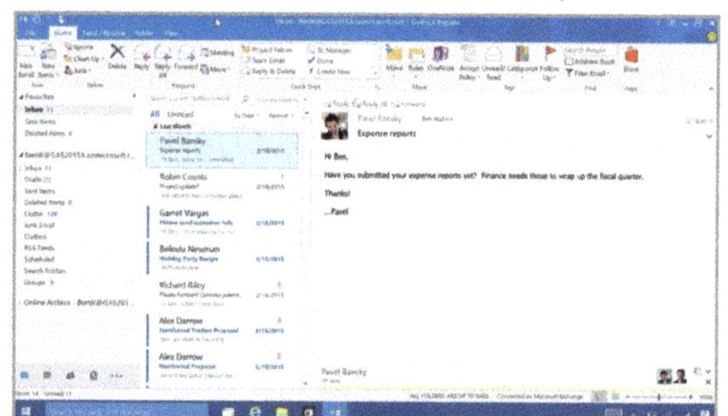

Outlook

Hotmail

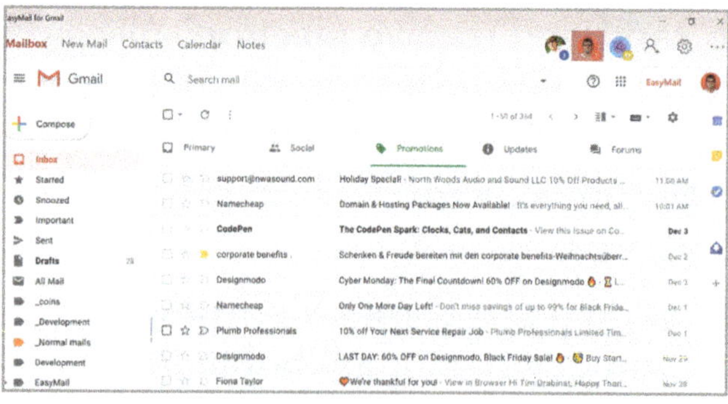

Gmail

An e-mail program provides various facilities through different features, such as:

Inbox : It is a folder or directory, which stores all incoming mails.

Compose : This feature is used to write a new e-mail message to someone.

Send : Pressing this button will send the message to the recepient that you have written in the mail box.

Reply : This button helps you to reply to the incoming e-mail.

Reply to All : Sometimes you will receive an e-mail of which you are not the only recipient. Pressing this button allows you to reply to all of the e-mail addresses from that e-mail.

Forward : This button helps you to forward an incoming message to someone else.

Delete : This button is used to delete the message.

Print : This button is used to take a hard copy (printout) of your e-mail message.

Attachment : This button helps you to attach the document or files with an e-mail message to be sent.

Address book : You can store the person's e-mail address and other information in it.

E-mail Window

Whenever you open an e-mail program, the window appears on the screen as shown below.

An e-mail window is divided into two parts, *i.e.* header part and body part.

Header : It is a part that contains the information about the sender and the recipient:

Sender (From) : Here you will find an e-mail address of the sender.

Recipient (To) : Here you will type the e-mail address of the recipient, *i.e.* where the message is actually to be sent.

Cc : Cc stands for Carbon Copy. It is an exact copy of the message. A person who is not directly involved, but you would like the message to be known to him/her; his e-mail address is written in this section.

Bcc : Bcc stands for Blind Carbon Copy. If you want to send the same message to several people, without knowing them that others have also received the same message, you can take the help of the Bcc.

Subject : A very short content of your message is written in this section. For example, if you are sending a resume in your e-mail, you can write Resume in the Subject section.

Send : This button is used to send the e-mail message to the recipient.

Body : The body of a message contains the content of the message.

Signature : It is place where you can give information about yourself at the end of every message you send in an e-mail program. This is called signature.

CREATING AN E-MAIL ACCOUNT IN GMAIL

Electronic mail or e-mail is used to send messages electronically from one place to another. But to use this facility, we need to get registered with an e-mail service provider to get our e-mail ID.

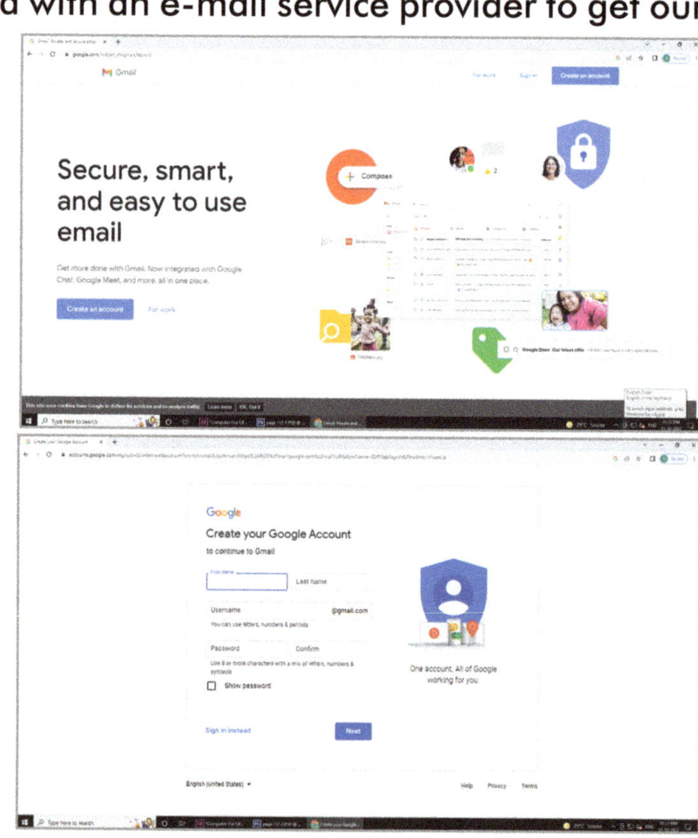

⇒ Lauch your browser (i.e. Chrome) and enter the web address www.gmail.com in the address bar.

⇒ Gmail Home Page will appear on the screen.

⇒ Click on the link 'Create account' in the Home Page to open Gmail registration form.

⇒ Firstly, enter your first name and the last name in the form and after that, enter the desired login name.

⇒ If someone else has taken the same login name, a message will appear 'Someone already has that username. Try another?'. and show you the choices from where you can select the new user name.

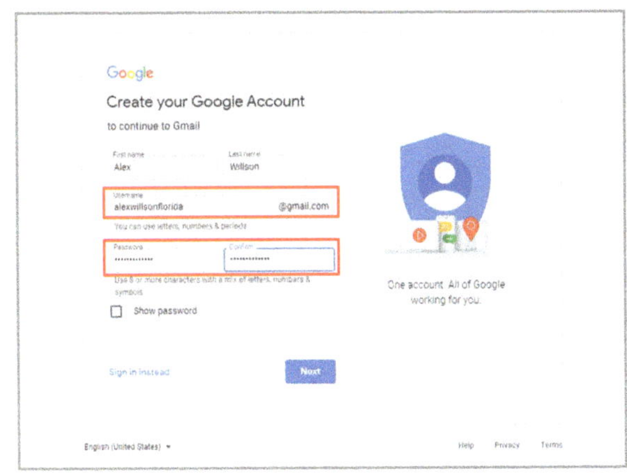

- ⇒ Once your login name is selected, enter a password of minimum 8 characters. Repeat the same password in the box called 'Re-enter password'.
- ⇒ Fill up the rest of the entries in the form as they are asked and finally click the button 'I accept' or 'Continue to Gmail'.
- ⇒ If all the entries are correctly added by you, you will get a confirmation for your new account and now your new e-mail address is <login name>@gmail.com.

SENDING AND RECEIVING E-MAIL

After creating the e-mail account, you can give it to your friends or relatives to send you e-mail and you can read your incoming mails or can send mail messages to others using your login ID and password.

- ⇒ Launch your browser once again and enter the Web address 'www.gmail.com' in the address box.
- ⇒ Click on Go button or press Enter key to open Gmail login page.
- ⇒ Click in the 'Username' box and type your login ID. Make sure that letters are typed in the same case (uppercase and lowercase) as they were typed while creating the account.
- ⇒ Enter the password in the 'Password' text box, which appears in the form of black dots.
- ⇒ Click 'Sign in' button to open your mail box.
- ⇒ It will show you the list of all your incoming mails. You can now click any one of them to open and read the contents of that mail.
- ⇒ You can click 'Inbox' button for coming back to your mail box.
- ⇒ To send the mail, click the 'Compose' button to open compose mail Web page.
- ⇒ In the To: box, write the e-mail address of your friend to whom you want to send the mail. Write the subject and then type the message in the space provided.
- ⇒ Click on 'Send' button. Your mail will be sent to the recipient.
- ⇒ Close your mail box by clicking the 'Sign out' link at the top.

ATTACHING FILES TO E-MAILS

Sometimes, you may need to send files, such as pictures, audios or other documents along with the text message through e-mail. This can be accomplished by attaching the files to your text message. The file you attach to the message is known as an attachment. To attach file(s) with your e-mail, follow these steps.

Open your e-mail account.

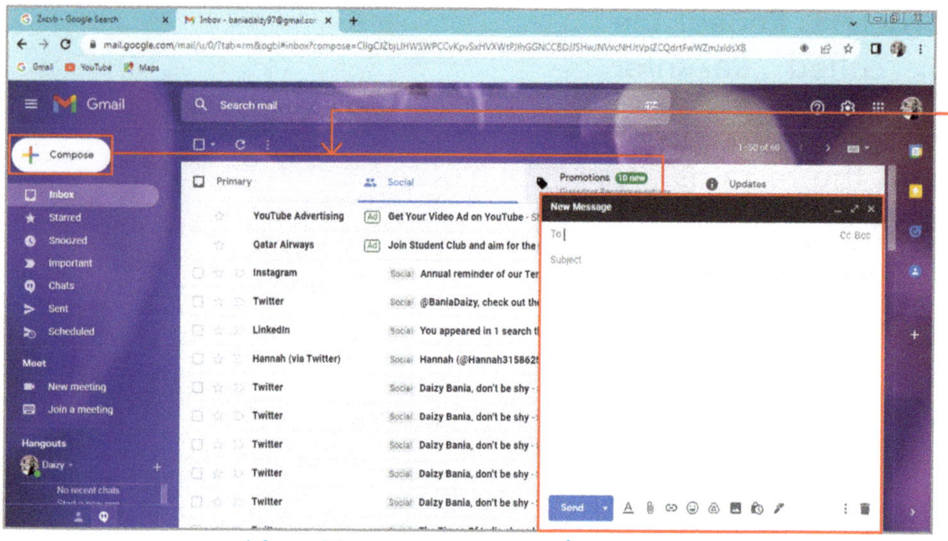

New Message pop-up box

1. Click the Compose button on the left side of the Gmail window.
2. A small New Message window appears at the bottom-right side of the screen.

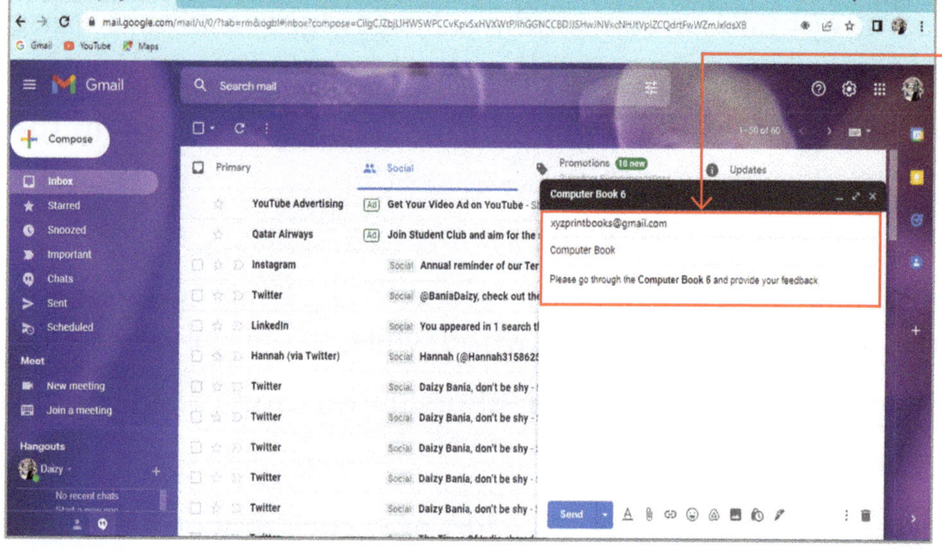

3. Type the recipient's e-mail address, subject of message and the message in the respective boxes.

4. Click the Attach files (📎) button at the bottom of the New Message window.
5. The Open dialog box appears.

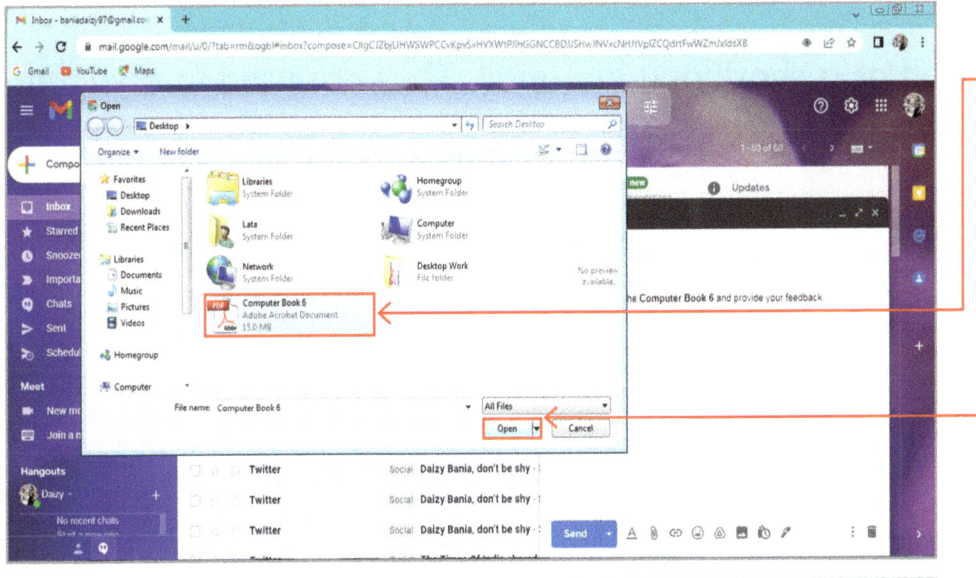

6. Locate and select the file to be attached.

7. Click the Open button.

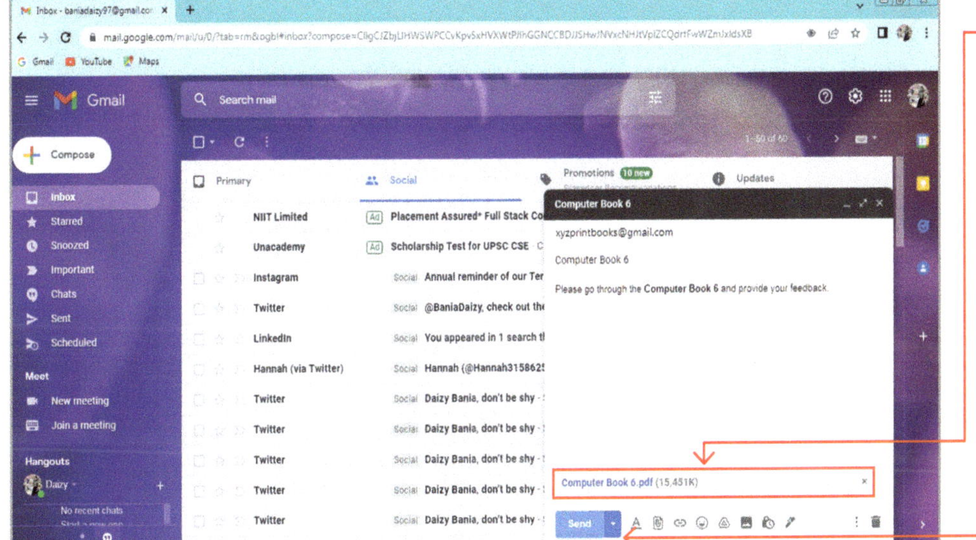

8. The selected file name appears in the compose window. Repeat step 4 and step 5 to attach more files.

9. Click the Send (Send) button to send the e-mail with attachment(s).

E-MAIL TERMINOLOGY

Here are some of the most commonly used terms while using e-mail.

Smileys

A smiley, also called an emoticon, is an expression of emotion typed into a message using standard keyboard characters. These characters look like human faces when you turn them sideways.

Cry	→ :'-(	Great!	→ :^D
Smile	→ :-)	Screaming	→ :-@
Laugh	→ :-D	Tongue out	→ :-&
Sad	→ :-(	Kissing	→ :*
Wow	→ :-o	Angel	→ O:-)
Wink	→ ;-)	Clowning	→ :*)

Abbreviation

Abbreviations are commonly used as a shorthand in e-mail. They are used to save time while typing message in an e-mail.

AISI	As I See It	**AS**	Another Subject
ASAP	As Soon As Possible	**B4N**	Bye For Now
BAK	Back At Keyboard	**BBIAB**	Be Back In A Bit
BBL	Be Back Later	**CU**	See You
BTW	By The Way	**IC**	I See
DK	Don't Know	**LOL**	Laughing Out Loud
SYS	See You Soon	**Gr8**	Great

Shouting

To use ALL CAPITAL LETTERS in e-mail is annoying and very hard to read. This is called shouting. E-mail messages should always use letters in uppercase and lowercase.

Please Don't Shout

Bounce Messages

Bounce message is a message informing the user that e-mail could not be delivered to its intended recipient. The failure may be due to an incorrectly typed e-mail address or a network problem.

E-MAIL ETIQUETTES

E-mail etiquettes are the guidelines that will help you to avoid mistakes and misunderstanding. These code rules of e-mail etiquettes help you to communicate better via e-mail.

⇒ Be formal, not sloppy - You can use abbreviations in the message that you are sending to your colleagues or friends but while communicating with an external person, you should follow the standard and formal writing.

⇒ Always try to keep your message short and focused.

⇒ USING ALL CAPS LOOKS LOOK LIKE AS IF YOU'RE SHOUTING-Using all lowercase letters looks lazy. So, always use sentence case while typing messages.

⇒ Don't send junk mails.

⇒ Use smileys to make sure that something is not misunderstood. They can support your statement.

⇒ Use a signature that includes contact information.

⇒ Summarize long discussions.

LET'S HAVE A LOOK

- E-mail is the way of sending or receiving the message electronically from one computer to another.
- E-mail saves a lot of time and is very cost-effective.
- Postal mail is the method used to send/receive physical mail.
- An e-mail address identifies the address of mail, where the message is to be sent/received.

BRAIN TEASER

1. Multiple Choice Questions

Tick (✓) the correct answer:

a. The electronic tool of communication is:

i. Sorting ☐ ii. E-mail ☐ iii. Browsing ☐

b. Which of these is not an e-mail program?

i. Gmail ☐ ii. Hotmail ☐ iii. Amazon ☐

c. The user name and the domain name all separated by:

i. At ☐ ii. @ ☐ iii. # ☐

d. The feature used to write new messages:

i. Compose ☐ ii. Inbox ☐ iii. Send ☐

e. The part of the e-mail window where contents are written

i. Header ☐ ii. Body ☐ iii. Signature ☐

f. A message written in CAPITAL LETTERS is like:

i. Smileys ☐ ii. Shouting ☐ iii. Bounced message ☐

g. A message that is not delivered to the destination and comes back:

i. Browsing ☐ ii. Shouting ☐ iii. Bounced message ☐

2. Fill in the blanks:

a. E-mail is the quickest way of ______________.

b. E-mail is sent ______________ and postal mail is sent ______________.

c. In the e-mail address, the user name and the domain name are separated by ______________.

d. An e-mail address can be got by creating an ____________.

e. E-mail when sent is converted into a ____________ of data.

f. In ____________ area, you give the description of the topic of the given message.

g. You can get an e-mail ____________ by creating an e-mail account.

3. Write 'T' for True and 'F' for False in the boxes:

a. E-mail is also known as physical mail. ☐

b. E-mail is the quickest way of communication. ☐

c. An E-mail address is a unique address that identifies the sender. ☐

d. The user name and the domain name are separated by #. ☐

e. Packets are small chunks which are broken while sending e-mail. ☐

f. Postal mail is a method to send and receive mail electronically. ☐

g. Inbox is a folder or directory, which stores all incoming mails. ☐

h. Send button is used to send an e-mail message to the recipient. ☐

4. Write the abbreviations of the following:

a. By The Way ____________

b. Laughing Out Loud ____________

c. I See ____________

d. See You soon ____________

e. Be Back In A Bit ____________

f. Back At Key board ____________

g. Be Back Later ____________

5. Make the smiley for each of the following:

a. Sad [ ]

b. Great [ ]

c. Smile [ ]

d. Clowning [ ]

e. Wink [ ]

f. Angel [ ]

6. Answer the following questions

(i) Answer each in a few lines:

a. What does e-mail stand for?

b. Name some commonly used e-mail programs.

c. What are the two parts of an e-mail address?

d. What does @ stand for in an e-mail address?

e. Give the full forms of Cc and Bcc.

f. What are the two parts of an e-mail window?

(ii) Answer each comprehensively:

a. How is e-mail a useful tool of communication?

b. What are the differences between e-mail and postal mail?

c. What are the different advantages of e-mail?

d. What is an e-mail address? How can you get it?

e. How does e-mail travel from one computer to another?

f. Explain the different features of an e-mail program.

g. Write the different e-mail etiquettes to be followed while sending an e-mail.

Go to your Computer Lab and write an e-mail to your causin inviting him/her in your school's annual function.

10 The Computer Virus

In this chapter, we will learn:

⇒ About computer virus

⇒ How a computer gets viruses

⇒ The way to protect our computer from viruses

⇒ About the anti-virus software

Dear children, in Chapter 3, you have studied about malware. Malware is any type of software that is designed to damage your computer or gain unauthorised access to your personal information. It includes viruses, worms, Trojan horses, spyware and other types of viruses. In this chapter, we will study about some more about computer viruses.

COMPUTER VIRUS

A program that can copy itself is called the computer virus. It can harm a computer without permission or knowledge of the user. Computer viruses are computer programs that have been intentionally created by some people to infect other users' work in the computer.

A computer system cannot develop a virus on its own. A virus can spread from one computer to another through a medium such as an infected floppy disk, a CD or pen drive.

If your computer acts differently from usual, it may be infected with a virus. When a virus infects the computer, it causes the reduced performance of the computer, data loss, reduced hard disk space, program crashes, unusual messages, computer lockups, etc.

Sources of Virus

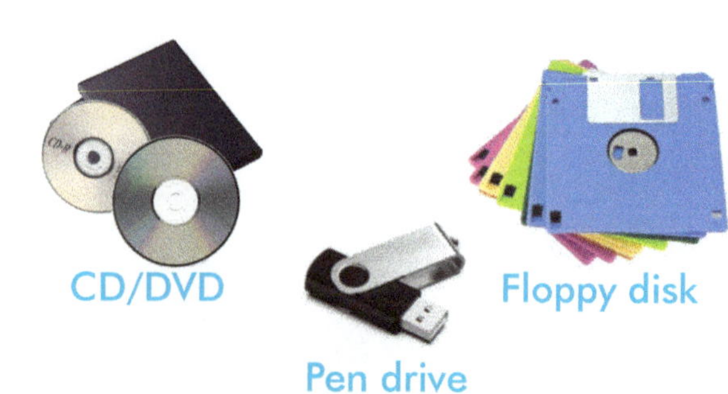
CD/DVD Pen drive Floppy disk

Storage mediums like floppy disks, CDs, DVDs and pen drives are the most common sources that spread viruses among computers. When you put an infected file on the CD or floppy, the virus that was with the file goes with it. When you insert that floppy or CD to another computer to run the program, the virus goes into the new computer. So do not use any of these storage devices received from another person unless you are certain that the device does not contain a virus or is free from infection.

These days, the Internet has also become a source that spreads viruses. People take advantage of it to spread viruses quickly to many computers. You should download programs or other information only from reputed sources on the Internet. You should also be careful of files and messages you receive attached to e-mail messages. Remember, always download and open only those files which are sent by trusted people.

E-mail viruses are spread by files attached to e-mail messages. As e-mail attachments become more common, the number of e-mail viruses may also increase. You cannot get an e-mail virus from a message that contains only text. When you open an e-mail attachment that contains a virus, the virus spreads to your computer. If you forward the attachment to other people, their computers will also be affected when they open the attachment. Many e-mail viruses can also access your address book and automatically send themselves to the e-mail addresses stored there.

Examples of Viruses

Worm : It is a quite harmless virus that simply replicates itself. But in the long run, it takes over all the resources of the system and the PC becomes useless. Worms have the capacity to travel from system to system very easily.

Trojan Horse : This virus comes as a friendly program (as a game, etc.). But it is very dangerous as it destroys all data. Trojan horses do not replicate themselves but they can be destructive. The Trojan horse can spread in a number of ways but the common means of infection is the attachment of mail.

Rootkit : Rootkit is a program that hides in a computer and allows someone from a remote location to take full control of the computer. Once the rootkit is installed, the rootkit author can execute programs, change settings, monitor activity, and access files on the remote computer.

Logic Bomb : A logic bomb is a program or portion of a program, which lies dormant until a specific piece of program logic is activated. In this way, a logic bomb is very analogous to a real-world landmine. The most common activator for a logic bomb is a date. The logic bomb checks the system date and does nothing until a pre-programmed date and time is reached. At that point, the logic bomb activates and executes its code in the computer.

Virus Warning Signs

Viruses can cause all sorts of damage from deleting a file to using your computer as a source to hack a bank and steal a lot of money. It is good to know the warning signs.

⇒ If your computer starts working slow, it could be the result of a number of mischief happening on your computer. Malware infections like viruses and spyware, however, are widely considered to be a primary reason for a computer suddenly becoming slow.

⇒ If your computer starts doing some strange activity, for example, showing strange messages on your computer, it could indicate a virus.

⇒ If the computer will not boot, it could mean a virus has corrupted your computer. Though as always, there are other possibilities like hardware failure.

⇒ If your computer crashes or freezes such as program not responding, showing errors or the computer just shuts down without warning, it could indicate a virus.

⇒ If some strange characters appear on the screen, it is also a sign of a computer virus.

HOW TO PROTECT YOUR COMPUTER

A computer can be protected from viruses by installing anti-virus software. In the modern age of the Internet, it is essential to have anti-virus software to keep your computer free from viruses.

Anti-Virus Software

You must have an anti-virus software installed on your computer; it detects the presence of the virus in the external memory device attached to the computer. It does not let the virus copy itself on your computer system.

Anti-virus software can also be used to check files or folders on your computer for viruses. You can run this anti-virus software as a preventive measure or if you find the symptoms of a virus in the computer. There are many anti-virus programs available in the market. Norton and McAfee are the most common anti-virus programs.

Norton AntiVirus : Norton antivirus is developed and distributed by Symantec Corporation. It protects your computer from various viruses and Internet threats.

McAfee : McAfee anti-virus delivers complete virus protection and Internet security. So, you can protect your computer.

Prevention is better than cure. So, always keep your anti-virus software updated.

Today, it is the age of the Internet. Hundreds of new viruses are developed every hour.

Anti- virus software developers regularly release updates on the Internet that allow their programs to detect the latest known viruses. You can update your copy of anti-virus only through the Internet. So, it is essential to have an Internet connection to update anti-virus software. You should make sure that the anti-virus program you use is updated regularly.

Let us know some measures to keep the computer free from virus infection.

⇒ Check the secondary memory devices for viruses by running an anti-virus software.

⇒ Install an anti-virus software on your computer before it gets infected.

⇒ Do not copy data from secondary memory devices until they are checked by the anti-virus software.

⇒ Check all your hard drives for viruses regularly.

⇒ Use the Internet under the supervision of your elders. Open only those sites which are free from viruses.

⇒ Do not open messages or files sent by unknown persons through e-mail. They may contain viruses.

⇒ Do not send messages to unknown people.

Follow the above measures to keep your computer free from trouble.

LET'S HAVE A LOOK

- Viruses are programs which are written deliberately to damage data.
- If your computer has a virus, files or operating system may get damaged.
- Viruses attach themselves to program files and move with them from disk to disk.
- A computer can be protected from viruses by installing an anti-virus software.
- Infected floppy disks, CDs, pen drives, e-mail attachments, downloading from the Internet, etc. are some of the sources of viruses.
- An anti-virus program protects a computer against viruses by identifying and removing them from the memory.
- Nortan, McAfee are some kinds of the anti-virus software.
- We should follow safety measures to keep our computer free from viruses.

BRAIN TEASER

1. Multiple Choice Questions

Tick (✓) the correct answer:

a. A computer program that harms your computer is:

i. Virus ☐ ii. Fever ☐ iii. LOGO ☐

b. Sources of virues are:

i. Input Devices ☐ ii. Storage Devices ☐ iii. Output Devices ☐

c. Source that spreads a virus is:

i. Keyboard ☐ ii. Scanner ☐ iii. Internet ☐

d. Prevention from virus:

i. Medicine ☐ ii. Anti-virus ☐ iii. Internet ☐

e. A quite harmless virus that simply replicates itself:

i. Worm ☐ ii. Anti-virus ☐ iii. Rootkit ☐

2. Fill in the blanks:

a. A computer ______________ copies itself.

b. A computer system cannot ______________ a virus.

c. A computer can be protected from viruses by installing an ______________.

d. Storage devices and the ______________ are sources that spread viruses.

e. Check all of your ______________ for viruses regularly.

3. Write 'T' for True and 'F' for False in the boxes:

a. A computer system develops a virus itself.

b. A virus can harm your computer.

c. Floppy disks, CDs, DVDs and pen drives are the sources of viruses.

d. Viruses do not spread through the Internet.

e. An anti-virus software protects your computer from viruses.

f. McAfee is an anti-virus software.

4. Answer the following questions

(i) Answer each in a few lines:

a. Define malware.

b. What is a worm?

c. Which software helps to prevent, detect and remove viruses?

d. Which virus comes as a friendly program?

e. Write the names of some anti-virus programs.

(ii) Answer each comprehensively:

a. What is a virus?

b. Write a short note on the Trojan horse.

c. How can a virus harm your computer?

d. What are the different sources of viruses?

e. List any four warning signs that show that your computer is infected with viruses.

f. What is an anti-virus software and how is it helpful?

g. List some of the popular anti-virus software available in the market.

Formative Assessment-4
(Chapters 9-10)

1. Label the different components of an e-mail box:

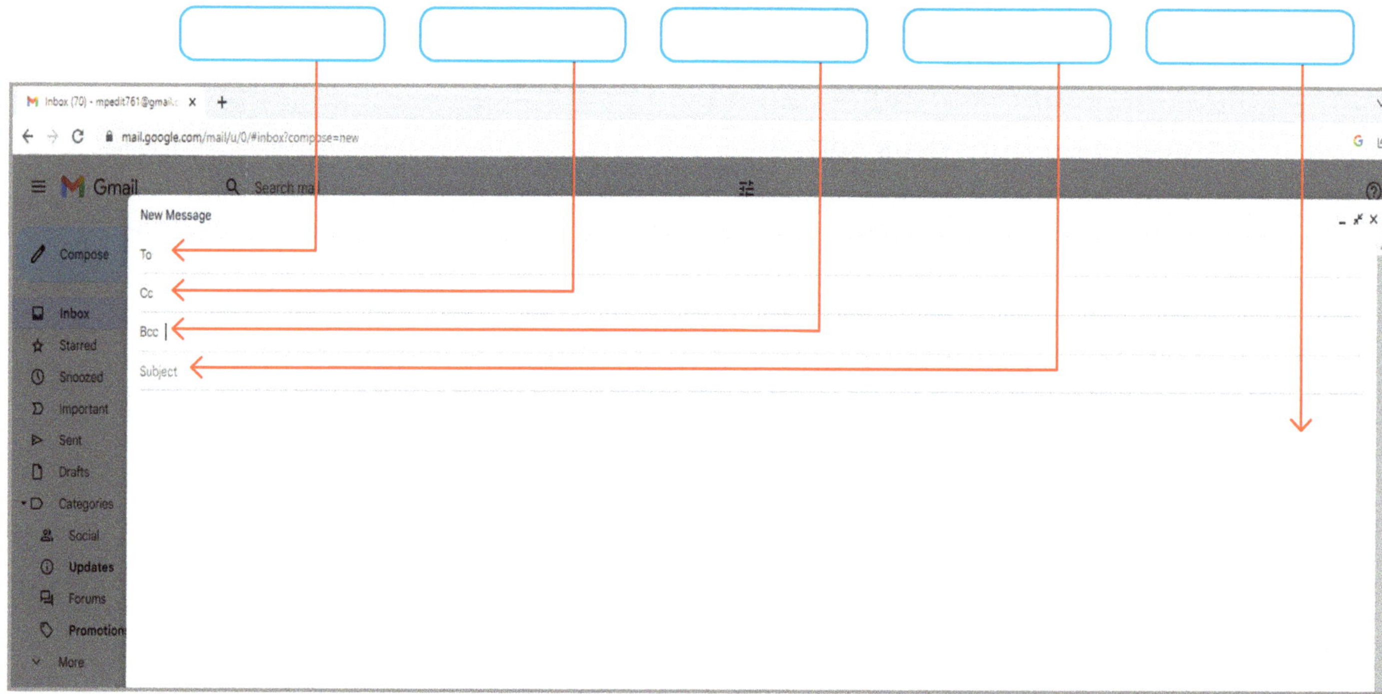

2. Explore the Internet and make a list of different:

E-mail Programs	Viruses	Anti-virus programs
______________	______________	______________
______________	______________	______________
______________	______________	______________
______________	______________	______________
______________	______________	______________
______________	______________	______________
______________	______________	______________
______________	______________	______________
______________	______________	______________
______________	______________	______________

Summative Assessment-2
(Chapters 6-10)

1. Fill in the blanks:

a. The selected cells appear to be ________________ in the worksheet.

b. The range of the cell can be selected by ________________ the mouse.

c. You can also ________________ or ________________ the size of data.

d. ________________ is the way in which data is settled.

e. Sorting feature is used to sort data in ________________ or ________________ order.

f. ________________ feature is used for centring titles over the data.

g. ________________ is a selected group of cells.

h. ________________ is the default row height in a worksheet.

i. You can get an e-mail address by creating an e-mail ________________.

j. Two parts of the e-mail address are ________________ and ________________.

2. Write 'T' for True and 'F' for False in the boxes:

a. Send feature is used to write a new e-mail message. ☐

b. E-mail is the quickest way of communication. ☐

c. You cannot use smileys in an e-mail address. ☐

d. The vertical and horizontal lines in a worksheet are called gridlines. ☐

e. Cut, Copy and Paste are the editing features in Excel. ☐

f. Excel is a word processing software. ☐

g. Through sorting data is arranged in a particular order. ☐

h. Filter option is used to arrange data in ascending or descending order. ☐

i. The alignment buttons are present on the Home tab. ☐

j. The default row height is 8.43 point. ☐

3. Answer each in a few lines:

a. Name the electronic tools of communication.

b. Name the feature used to write a new message.

c. Name two types of data filtration.
d. Name the tab on which Sort option is present.
e. Name the different Number formats in Excel.
f. Name the feature used to give the combinations of different formattings.
g. How are selected cells identified?
h. What is the simple method to move or copy?

4. Answer each comprehensively:

a. What is the need for selecting a cell? Write the different methods of selecting cells.
b. Explain the use of Theme gallery.
c. Explain the different types of series created in Excel.
d. What are the different advantages of e-mail?
e. Write a short note on e-mail.
f. What are the causes of viruses?
g. What is the use of an anti-virus programme?

5. Define the following:

a. Editing
b. Formatting
c. Sorting
d. Alignment
e. E-mail
f. E-mail address
g. Smileys
h. Bounced message

PROJECT WORK

MS-WORD

Creating tables in MS-Word to store tabular data:

- Start MS-Word and open a blank document in MS-Word.
- In this document, Insert a table that contains 11 rows and 6 columns.
- Enter the following values in the table:

Customer ID	Customer's Name	Product	Quantity	Amount (in $)	Total (in $)
001	Steven	Keyboard	4	400	1600
002	Robert	Monitor	8	5000	40000
003	Matthew	Mouse	4	200	800
004	Michael	Hard Disk	10	3000	30000
005	Ronald	Laptop	1	35000	35000
006	William	Scanner	9	1200	10800
007	Richard	Laser Printer	2	12000	24000
008	Joseph	Inkjet Printer	4	4000	16000
009	Larry	LED Monitor	2	8000	16000
010	Christopher	Pen Drive	30	500	15000

- Insert the other column after Total; give the heading 'Mode of Payment' to this column.
- Enter the mode of payment 'Cash' whose total is less than $ 15000 and enter the mode of payment 'Credit card' whose total is more than $15000.
- Add a new row to the table and store the following record in it.

011	Philip	UPS	4	2000	8000	Cash

- Apply Table style to all the lines of the table.
- Align all the cell values in the middle of the cell using Table and Border toolbar.
- Apply suitable font formatting to the header and the cell values in the table.
- Save the document as 'Computer hardware'.

1. Create the following worksheet:

a. Choose the proper font size and style for heading.

b. Centre Align the Deposit, Withdraw and Balance.

c. Change the heading colour into green.

d. Change the font style of Name column into bold italic.

e. Change the colour of Depost cells into yellow and Withdraw cells into blue.

f. Apply a border to a table.

Sr. No.	Name	Deposit	Withdraw	Balance
1	Russell	50000	20000	30000
2	Albert	45000	15000	30000
3	Julia	60000	15000	45000
4	Arthur	40000	30000	10000
5	Roger	25000	20000	5000
6	Christina	60000	50000	10000
7	Victoria	10000	9000	1000
8	Peter	30000	22000	8000
9	Jack	70000	50000	20000

2. Create a worksheet in Excel and make the following entries:

	A	B	C	D	E	F	G	H	I
1		1	2	3	4	5	6	7	8
2	MON	Maths	English	History/Civics	Science	EVS	Computer	Maths	Music
3	TUE	Maths	English	History/Civics	Science	EVS	Computer	Science	Dance
4	WED	Maths	English	History/Civics	Science	EVS	Computer	Maths	Sports
5	THU	Computer	EVS	Geo	Science	Maths	Computer	English	Library
6	FRI	Computer	Computer	Geo	Science	Maths	Games	English	Sports
7	SAT	Computer	English	Art	Library	Maths			

- Rename of 'Sheet 1' to 'School'.
- Change the cell H2 as Chemistry and H3 as Physics.
- Partially modify the cells G2, G3 and G5 with 'Computer Lab' by adding word 'Lab' to the contents 'Computer'.
- Change the Cell C6 as Maths.
- Change the last period of SAT as Games.
- Save the workbook as 'Timetable of class 6' and close the Excel worksheet.

3. **Create the following worksheet:**

a. Choose the proper font size and style for title.

b. Centre Align the Max and Min temperature.

c. Change the heading color into green.

d. Change the font style of cities into bold italic.

e. Change the colour of Max cells into yellow and Min cells into blue.

f. Apply a border to a table.

	CITY	MAX	MIN
1	Brasilia	33	28
2	Ottawa	38	29
3	Santiago	40	30
4	Havana	35	24
5	Belmopan	32	21
6	Quito	37	26
7	Guatemala	31	20
8	Nassau	30	19

4. **Create a worksheet showing the Olympic medals:**

S. No.	Country	Gold	Silver	Bronze	Total
1	People's Republic of China	46	31	35	112
2	Great Britain	19	25	19	63
3	Russian Federation	16	20	13	49
4	Australia	16	13	19	48
5	Ukraine	15	12	15	42
6	United States of America	12	11	17	40
7	Germany	8	11	10	29
8	Brazil	7	4	3	14
9	France	5	9	8	22
10	Poland	5	4	2	11
11	Cuba	5	3	2	10
12	Ireland	5	2	1	8
13	Nigeria	4	5	1	10
14	Republic of Korea	4	3	4	11
14	New Zealand	4	3	4	11
16	Islamic Republic of Iran	4	2	1	7
17	Spain	3	9	7	19
18	Canada	3	7	3	13
19	Netherlands	3	4	9	16
20	Italy	3	3	2	8

Now do the following adjustments:

a. Use the AutoFill feature to generate the S.No. column.

b. Format the data list using one of Auto Format options.

c. Give a name to the sheet as "Medals".

d. Save the workbook as "Olympic".

11 Python Turtle the Programmer

In this chapter, we will learn:

⇒ What is Python
⇒ Uses of Python Language
⇒ Code to draw basic geometrical shapes using turtle: Square, Triangle, Rectangle, Circle
⇒ Saving the Program
⇒ Changing the Screen Colour
⇒ Changing the Pen Size
⇒ Changing the Turtle Shape

Python is a popular programming language. It works on different platforms (Windows, Mac, Linux, Raspberry Pi, etc.). This language has a simple syntax similar to the English language.

Python runs on an interpreter system, meaning that code can be executed as soon as it is written. This means that prototyping can be very quick.

Python can be treated in a procedural way, an object-oriented way or a functional way.

USES OF PYTHON LANGUAGE

This language can be used on a server to create web applications. It can be used along with software to create workflows. Python can connect to database systems. It can also read and modify files.

Python can be used to handle big data and perform complex mathematics. It can be used for rapid prototyping, or for production-ready software development.

The most recent major version of Python is Python 3, which we shall be using in this lesson.

Python Syntax compared to other programming languages

Python was designed for readability, and has some similarities to the English language with influence from mathematics.

It uses new lines to complete a command, as opposed to other programming languages which often use semicolons or parentheses.

This language relies on indentation, using whitespace, to define scope, such as the scope of loops, functions and classes. Other programming languages often use curly brackets { }, for this purpose.

Knowing the Python Turtle Library

Turtle is a pre-installed Python library that enables users to create pictures and shapes by providing them with a virtual canvas. The onscreen pen that you use for drawing is called the turtle and this is what gives the library its name. The turtle is mainly used to introduce children to the world of computers. It's a straightforward yet versatile way to understand the concepts of Python. This makes it a great avenue for kids to take their first steps in Python programming.

With the Python turtle library, you can draw and create various types of shapes and images.

STARTING PYTHON

Let's open Python on your computer.

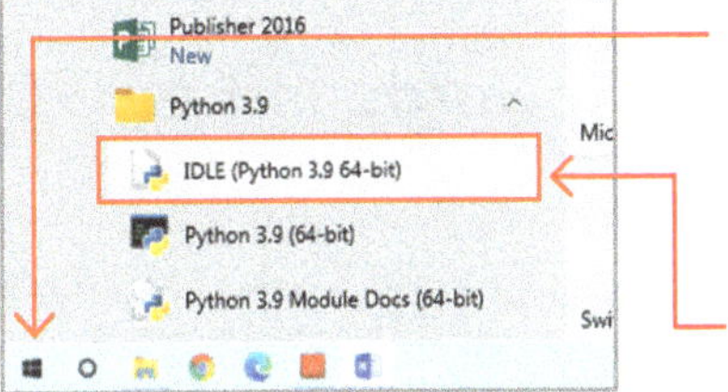

1. Click on the Start button.
2. Click on IDLE (Python 3.X 64-bit).

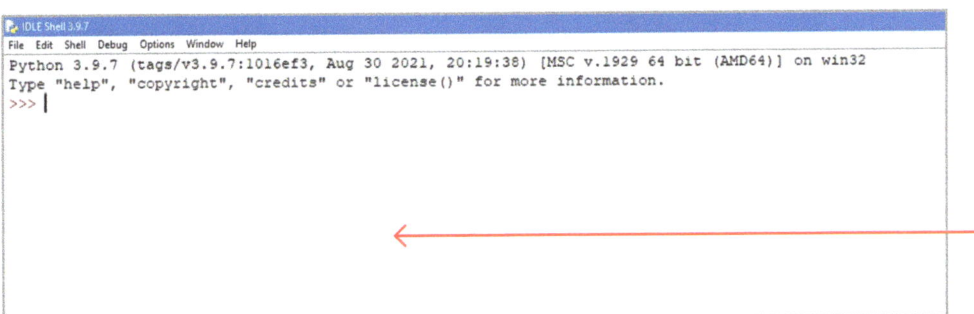

This is the Python Shell

CREATE A NEW FILE IN PYTHON

In the Python Shell, click on File menu select New File to create a file in Python.

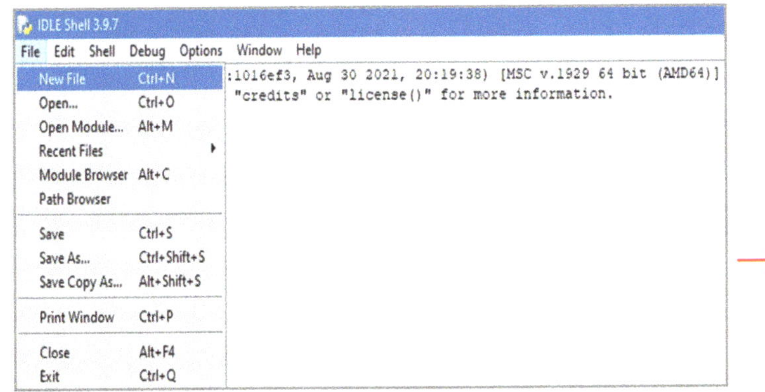

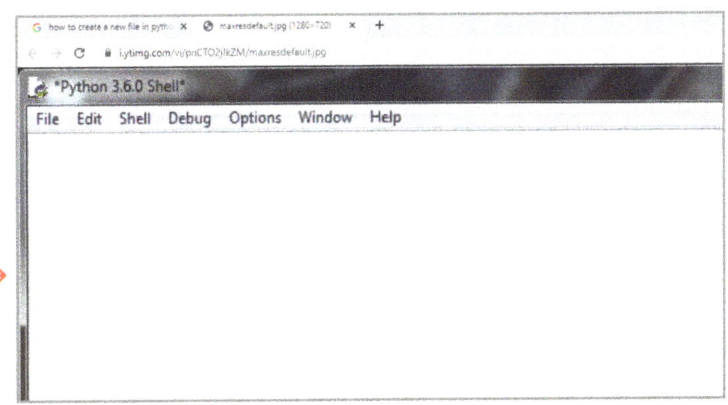

PROGRAMMING WITH TURTLE

You need to import the python library to access all its functions and methods in the program.

Import turtle as 't'

The above statement would import the turtle library and would give it the name 't'. With the help of 't' you can access all its functions.

Moving the Turtle

Turtle can move in four directions *i.e.* forward, backward, left and right. The functions for the same are as follows:

⇒ **To move Forward :** t. forward (100) or t. fd (100) would move the turtle in forward direction by 100 units.

⇒ **To move Backward :** t. backward (100) or t. bk (100) would move the turtle in backward direction by 100 units.

⇒ **To turn Left :** t. left (90) or t. lt (90) would turn the turtle towards left by 90 degrees.

⇒ **To turn Right :** t. right (90) or t. rt (90) would turn the turtle towards right by 90 degrees.

DRAWING A SQUARE

In a square all the sides are equal; therefore, we need to move the turtle in forward direction by the same units 4 times. As a square has 4 sides, we need to change the direction of the turtle 3 times.

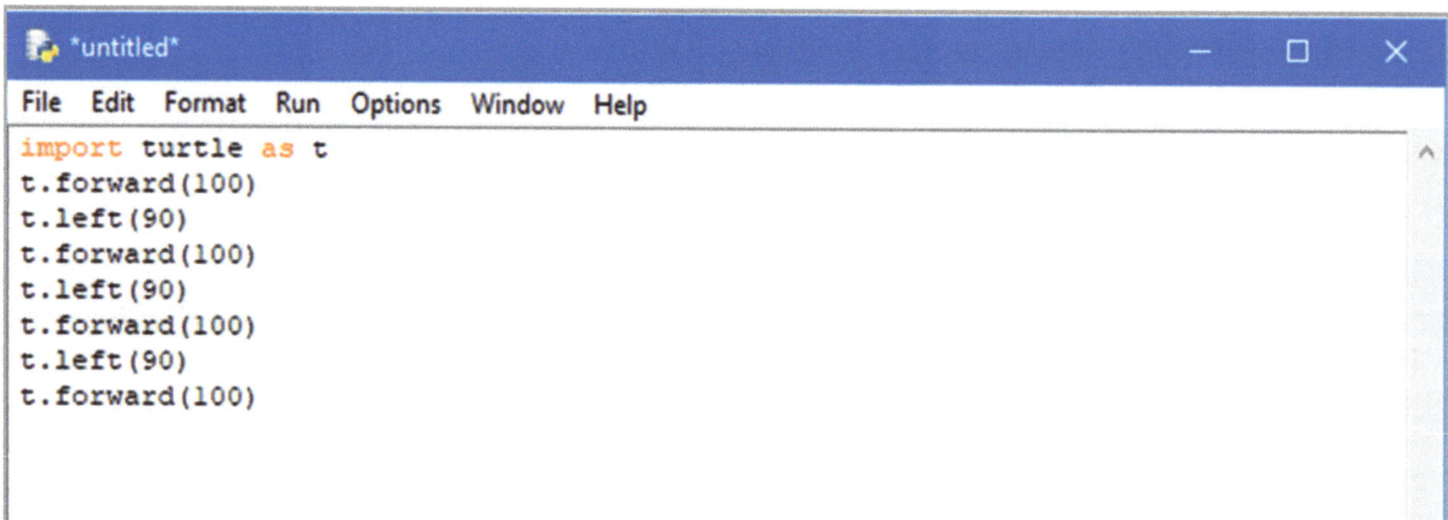


```
import turtle as t
t.forward(100)
t.left(90)
t.forward(100)
t.left(90)
t.forward(100)
t.left(90)
t.forward(100)
```

We have written the code (program) to draw a square. To check the coding we need to turn (execute) it. But you can run the program only when it is saved.

SAVING THE PROGRAM

Let us save the program in Python so that we may run it.

To save any program,

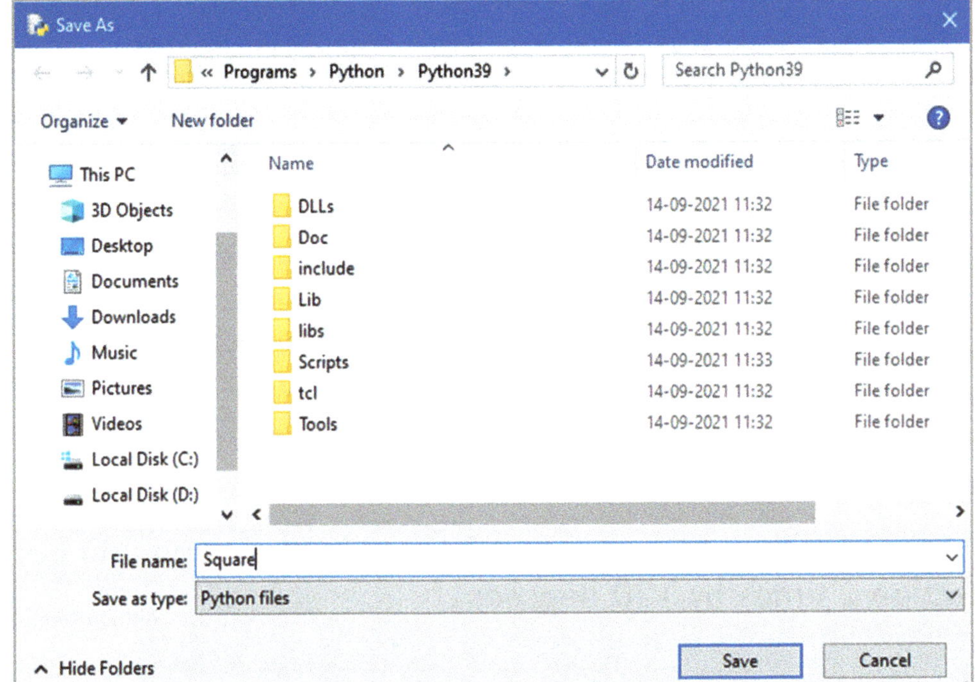

1. Click on File menu.
2. Select Save As option.

   The Save As dialog box appears.
3. In the Save As dialog box type the name of the program and click on Save button.

RUN THE FIRST PROGRAM

As you saved the program, you can see the result by running the program now.

1. Click on Run menu.
2. Select Run Module to run the code which you have written and generate the output.

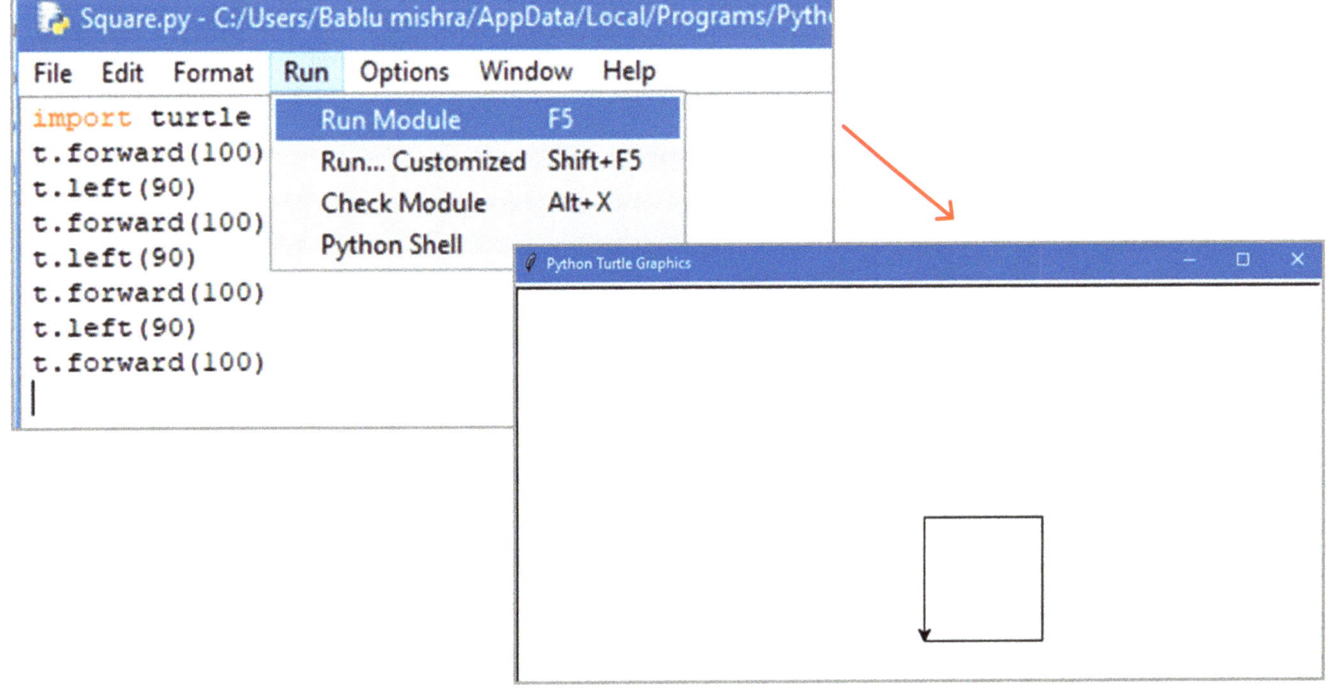

DRAWING A RECTANGLE

A Rectangle has 4 sides, but 2 opposite sides are equal. Therefore, you need to move the turtle in forward direction by the same unit 2 times, alternately. But you need to change the direction 3 times, as you have done while drawing a square.

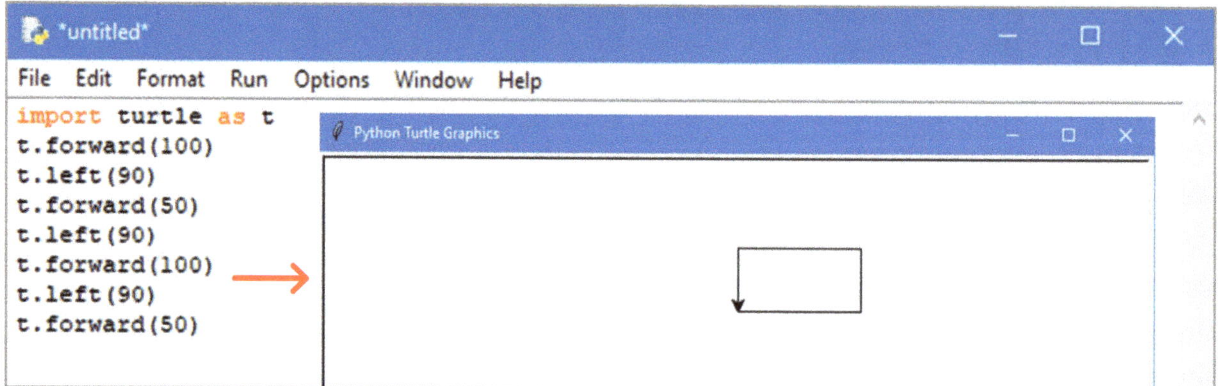

DRAWING A TRIANGLE

A triangle has 3 sides; therefore, you need to move forward 3 times by the same unit but the turtle should change its direction 2 times by 120 degrees.

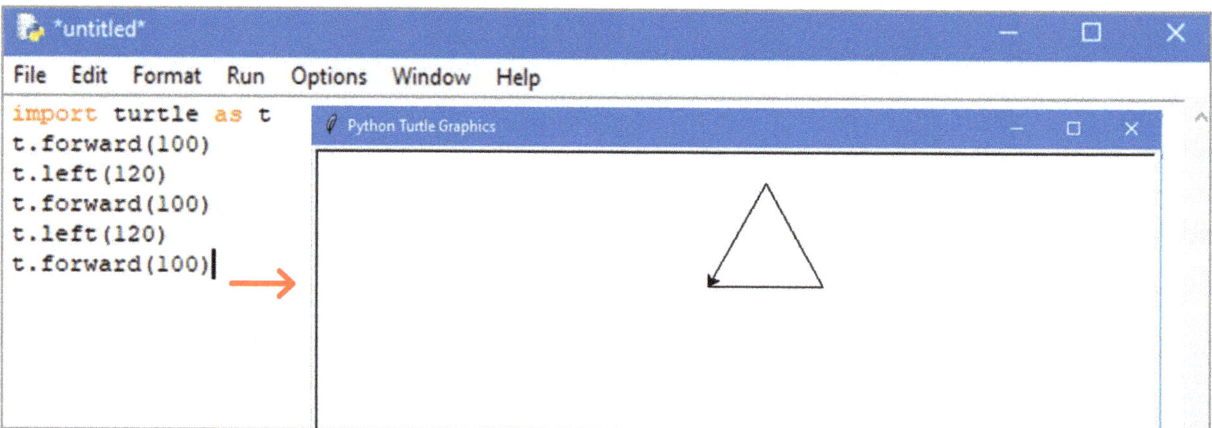

DRAW A CIRCLE

t.circle(r) statement will help you to draw a circle with radius 'r'.

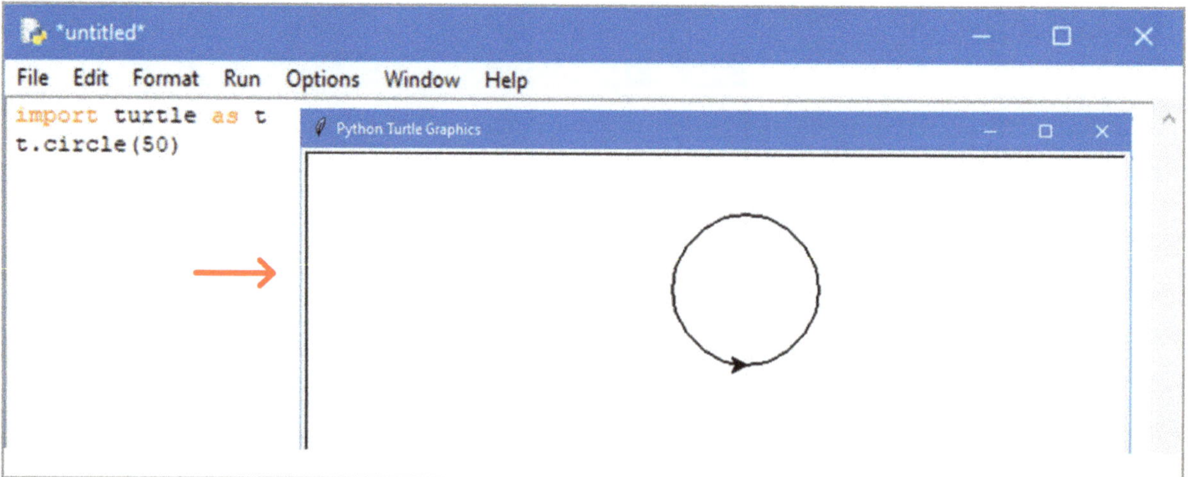

CHANGING THE SCREEN COLOUR

By default the turtle always opens a screen with a white background. However, you can change the colour of the screen at any time using the following command:

t.bgcolor ("colour")

Colour can be red, green, blue, yellow, magenta, etc.

Brain feed: Putting the colour in " " is very essential, otherwise it would show an error.

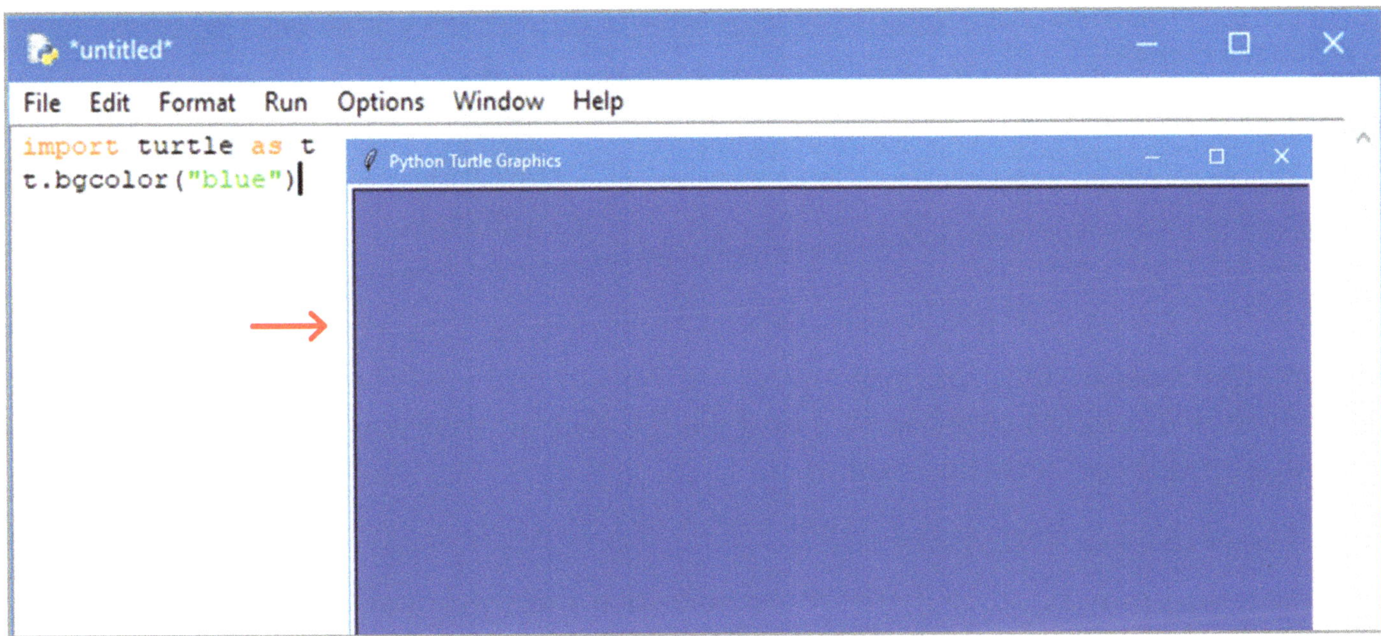

CHANGING THE TURTLE AND PEN COLOR

When you first open a new screen, the turtle starts as a black figure and draws with black colour.

As per your requirements, you change the colour of turtle and pen with the help of following commands:

CHANGING THE PEN COLOUR

t. pencolor ("colour"). This effects the outline or the ink colour.

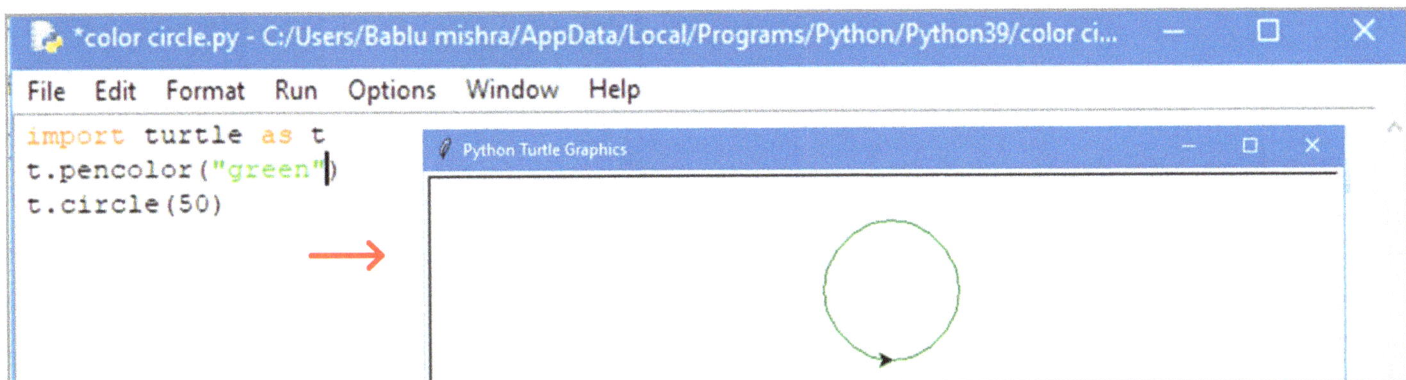

CHANGING THE TURTLE COLOUR

t. fillcolor ("colour"). This effects the fill colour of the drawing.

Here, we have drawn a triangle with outline as red and filled it with green colour.

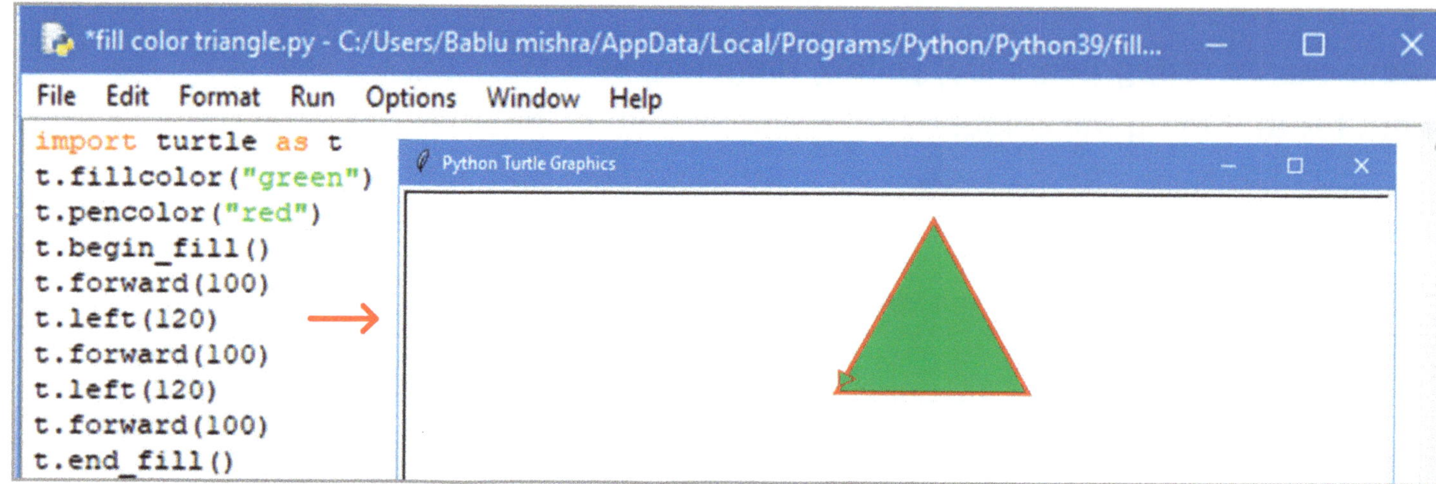

When you use t.begin_fill(), you are telling the Python that you are going to draw a closed shape which will need to be filled in. t.end_fill () indicates that you are done with creating your shape and it can now be filled in.

CHANGING THE PEN SIZE

Sometimes, you may need to increase or decrease the thickness of the pen. You can do this using the following command: t. pensize (thickness)

You can keep changing the value of thickness to change the thickness of the outline of any figure.

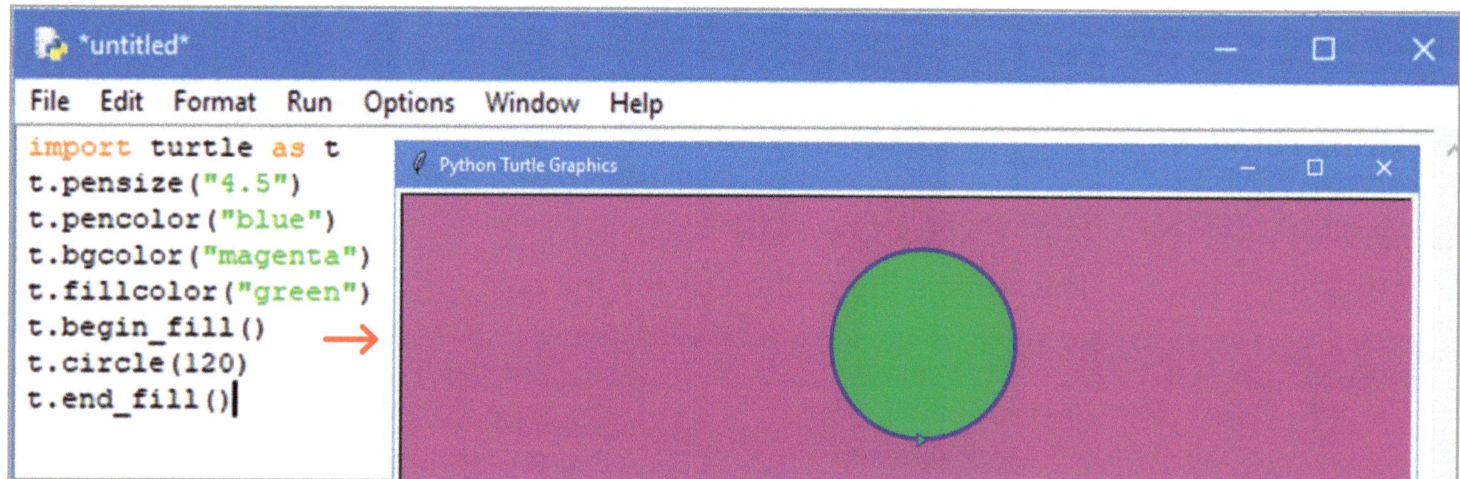

CHANGING THE TURTLE SHAPE

The initial shape of the turtle is not the same, but a triangular figure. However, you can change the way the turtle looks. You can have a look at some of them by typing in the following commands:

t. shape ("turtle")

t. shape ("arrow")

t. shape ("circle")

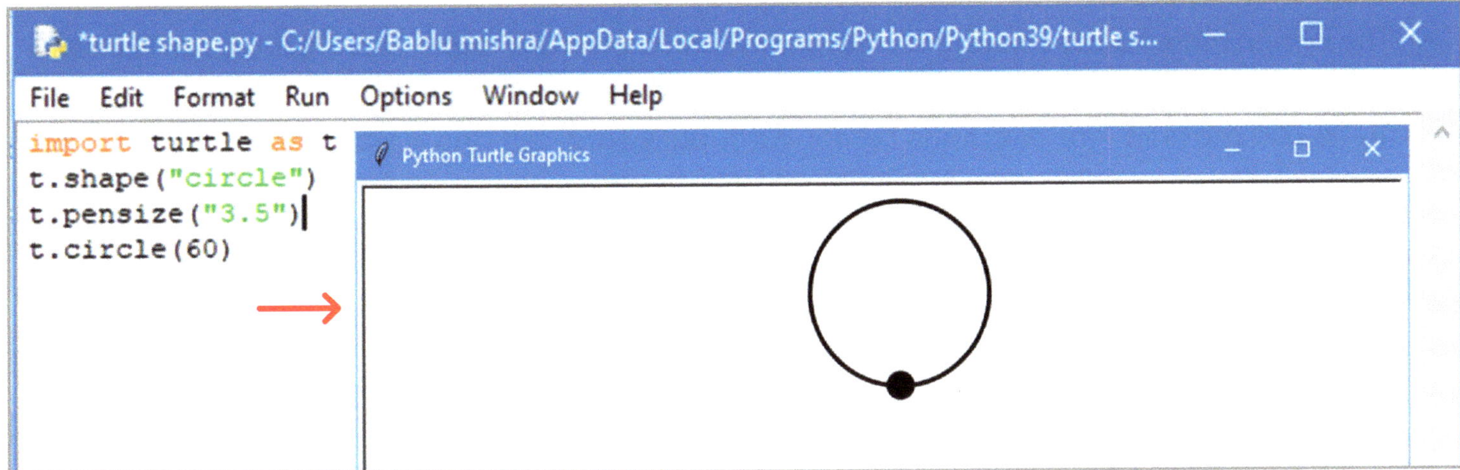

CHANGING THE PEN SPEED

The turtle generally moves at a moderate pace. If you want to decrease or increase the speed to make your turtle move slower or faster, then you can do so by typing the following command: t. turtle (speed)

The speed can be any number ranging from 0 (the slowest speed) to 10 (the highest speed). You can play around with your code to see how fast or slow the turtle will go.

t. home ()

The t. home () function will move the turtle to its original coordinates (0, 0) and set its direction to 0 degree. Calling home () is the same as calling t. goto (0, 0).

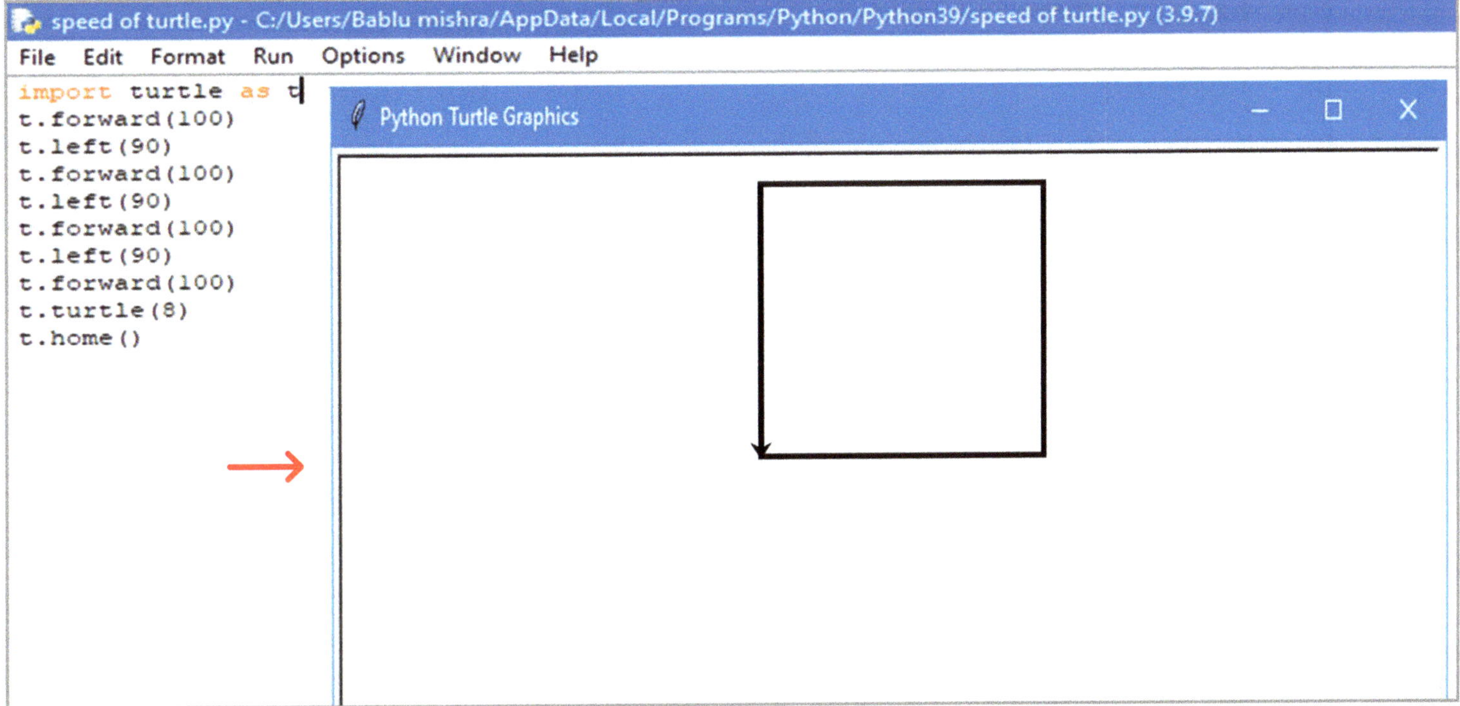

LET'S HAVE A LOOK

- In the computer world, a library is a set of important functions and methods that makes programming easier.
- The Python turtle library contains all the methods and functions to create shapes and animation.
- Python Programming Language helps us to draw and create various types of shapes and images.
- Turtle can move in four directions *i.e.* forward, backward, left and right.
- We can't run our coding as a program until it is saved.

BRAIN TEASER

1. Multiple Choice Questions:

Tick (✓) the correct answer:

a. A ______________ is a set of important functions and methods that makes programming easier.

i. Program	☐	ii. Code	☐
iii. Library	☐	iv. Book	☐

b. ______________ library of Python has functions to draw different shapes.

i. Pandas	☐	ii. Numpy	☐
iii. Turtle	☐	iv. None of these	☐

c. Which command/(s) helps to move the turtle in forward direction?

i. T.forward(100)	☐	ii. T.fd(100)	☐
iii. T.bk(100)	☐	iv. Both (i) and (ii)	☐

d. By default, turtle always opens a screen with ______________ background.

i. White	☐	ii. Black	☐
iii. Green	☐	iv. Orange	☐

e. Which command changes the colour of the pen?

i. t.bgcolor ("color")	☐	ii. t.pencolor ("colour")	☐
iii. t.end_fill ()	☐	iv. t.fillcolor ("color")	☐

2. Write the uses of the following commands:

a. t.circle(r) ______________________________

b. t.bgcolor(colour) ______________________________

c. t.fillcolor(colour) ______

d. t.pencolor(colour) ______

e. t.begin_fill(), ______

f. t.end_fill() ______

g. t.pensize(thickness) ______

h. t.shape("turtle") ______

i. t.shape("arrow") ______

j. t.shape("circle") ______

k. t.turtle(speed) ______

l. t.home() ______

3. Answer the following questions:

a. Write a program to draw a geometrical figure that has 5 sides and each angle is 72°. What is this image known as?

______

b. Write a program to draw a circle with outline thickness of 6 and colour as green. Fill the circle with red colour.

______

c. Write a program to draw a hexagon that has 6 sides and has each angle as 60°.

______

d. Find the output of the following codes. Take out the printouts of those shapes and paste here in the empty space.

i.

```
File   Edit   Format   Run   Options   Window   Help
import turtle as t
t.forward(100)
t.left(90)
t.backward(50)
t.forward(100)
t.right(120)
```

ii.

```
File   Edit   Format   Run   Options   Window   Help
import turtle as t
t.forward(160)
t.left(80)
t.backward(120)
t.forward(160)
```

iii.

```
File   Edit   Format   Run   Options   Window   Help
import turtle as t
t.forward(100)
t.right(90)
t.forward(100)
t.home()
```

iv.

```
File   Edit   Format   Run   Options   Window   Help
import turtle as t
t.left(80)

t.forward(60)
t.left(90)
t.forward(60)
t.left(90)
t.forward(60)
t.left(90)
t.forward(60)
t.left(90)

t.left(40)

t.forward(100)
t.left(60)
t.forward(100)
t.left(60)
t.forward(100)
t.left(60)
t.forward(100)
t.left(60)

t.left(50)

t.forward(120)
t.left(70)
t.forward(120)
t.left(70)
t.forward(120)
t.left(70)
t.forward(120)
t.left(70)
```

LAB ACTIVITY

Look at the drawing made in Python program. Can you guess the coding for this program and create the same in your computer?

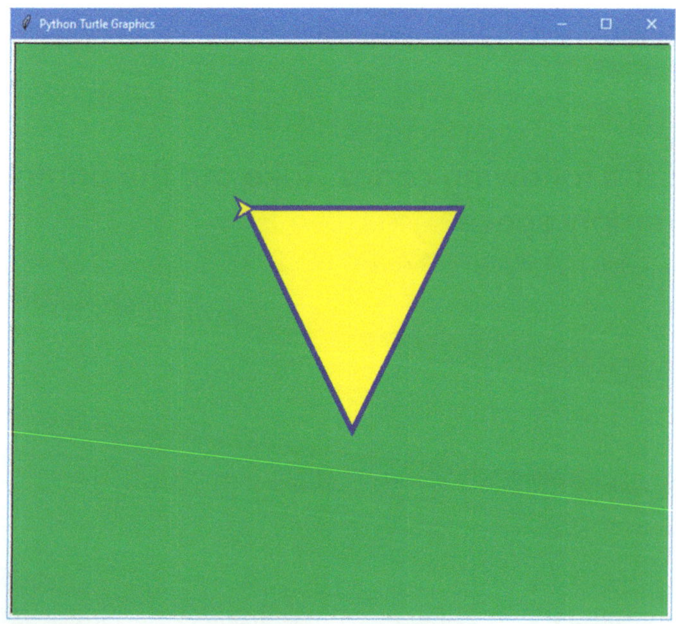

GAMING WITH KODU

We all love playing games on our mobile phone or computer system. Do you ever think how these games are created? Who are the creators of these games and what elements do they use to create an experience for the player?

What is Game Design?

Game design can be considered to be the planning arm of the entire process for making a video game. No video game gets made without a plan, and video game design is, more or less, the process of making that plan. The field is somewhat a hybridization of creativity and technical skills that combine into a cohesive, fleshed out idea that people can work with using concrete and actionable tasks.

Game design is one-part creativity with deciding the atmosphere, story, and aesthetics of the video game, and one-part technical know-how deciding game mechanics, balancing, and so forth. It is a robust field of study that involves just as much knowing how and why to do a certain thing as it is using your imagination to create novel possibilities.

However, no matter which side you talk about, game design is about creating the initial plan, knowing the tools and techniques to create that plan, and how that will dictate how the full game comes together as one experience. This is a concept that surpasses many other aspects of video game development, such as even what game engines to use.

There are a number of ways you can approach to game design, but often an informal approach is the most suitable method to begin with.

Step 1: Developing a game idea.

Create new game ideas or explore from already existing games like pacemaker, candy crush, maze, airplane troops, etc.

Once you've achieved that, you might add another layer of complexity, and then another.

Step 2: Testing

Testing should be done in between the game creation process. Making alterations, and then testing to ensure they have worked as you intended should be done as you progress, not at the end of the process.

Getting other users test your games for you is another solid step in this process. Other users will have different approaches to game design, and will have their own solutions to problems you encounter that you may not have considered previously.

Step 3: Refinement

With each new version you can more easily see where improvements have been made, and how successful your updates have been. You can revert to previous attempts if you have to, and try different approaches.

What is Kodu?

Kodu Game Lab is a 3D game development environment that is designed to teach kids basic programming principles. Kodu allows creators to build the world's terrain, populate it with characters and props, and then program their behaviors and games rules in a bespoke visual programming language.

The core of Kodu Game Lab is it's intuitive interface.

Programs for the Kodu Game Lab characters are created as sequence of numbered rows. Each row has a WHEN part and a DO part. When the WHEN part side is true, then the action on the DO side is done. For example:

In this case when the character sees an apple the character will move towards it.

STARTING KODU

1. Click the Kodu Game Lab icon on the desktop.

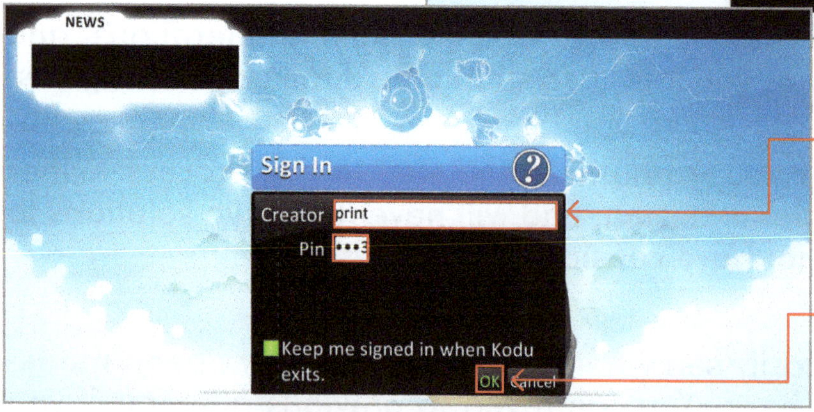

2. Enter the Creator and Pin.

3. Select Keep me signed in when Kodu exits if you are working on your personal computer and click OK or Cancel.

Let's create our first game called pothole city. In this game, if the player falls in the pot hole the game ends.

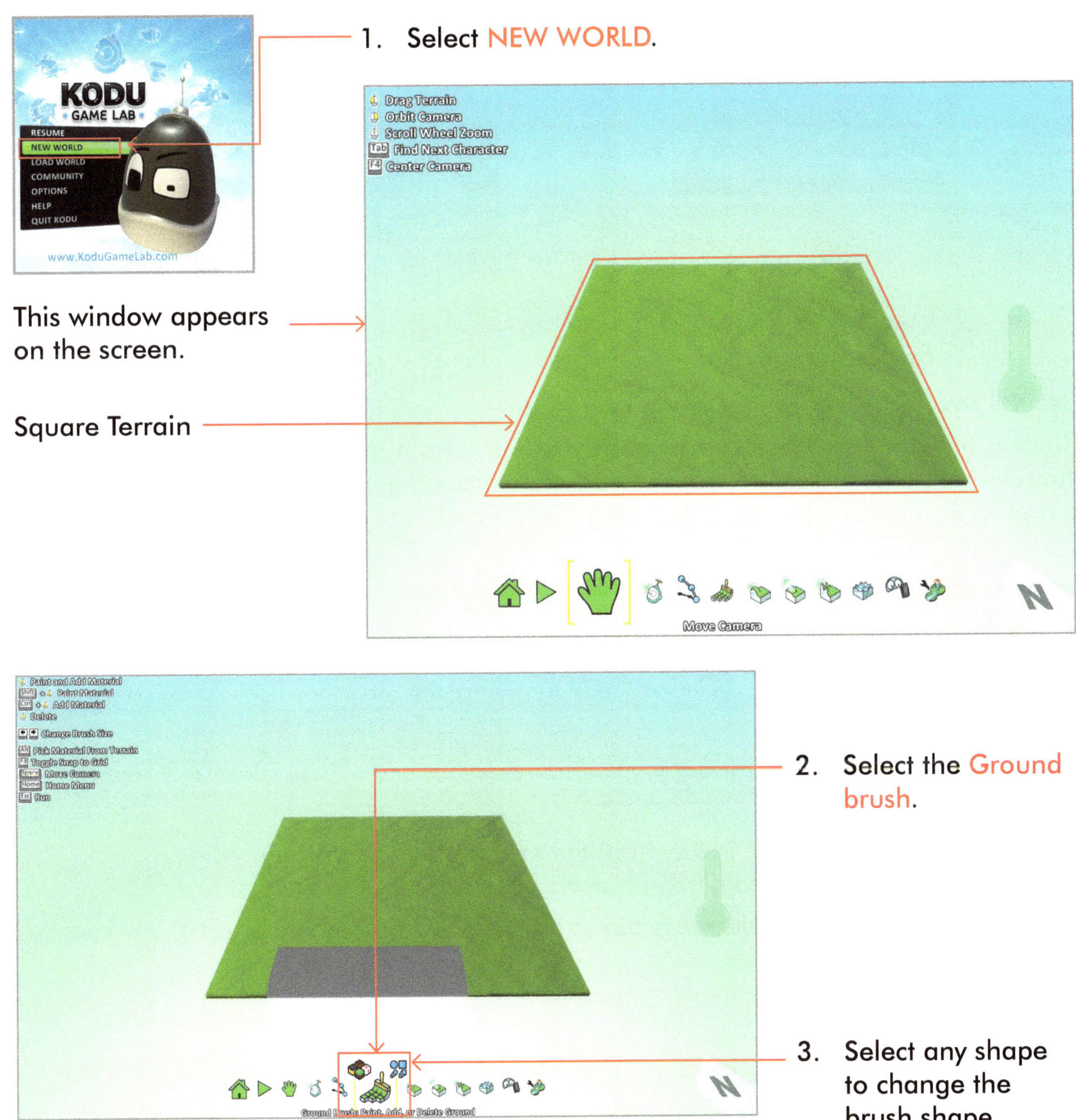

The size of the brush can be changed by using the left arrow or right arrow of the keyboard. Right arrow helps to increase and left arrow helps to decrease the size of the ground brush.

If you want to change the Ground Brush shape, you can select from Square, Round, Linear Square Brush, Linear Round Brush, or the Magic Brush.

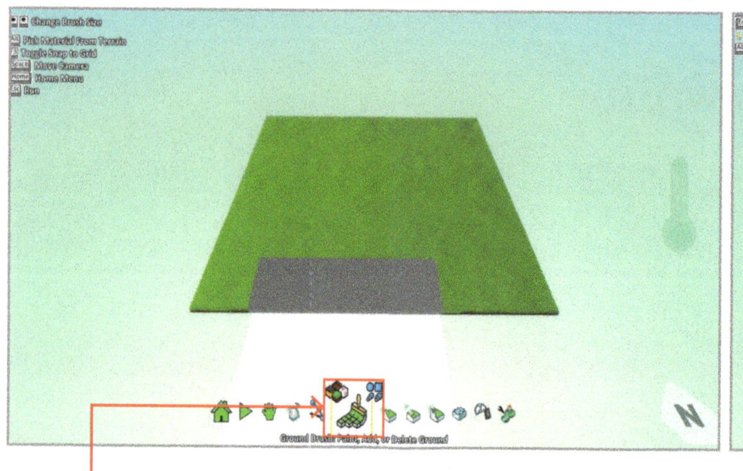

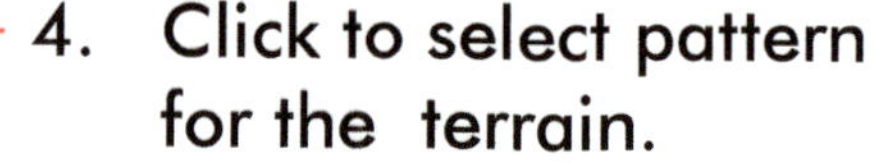

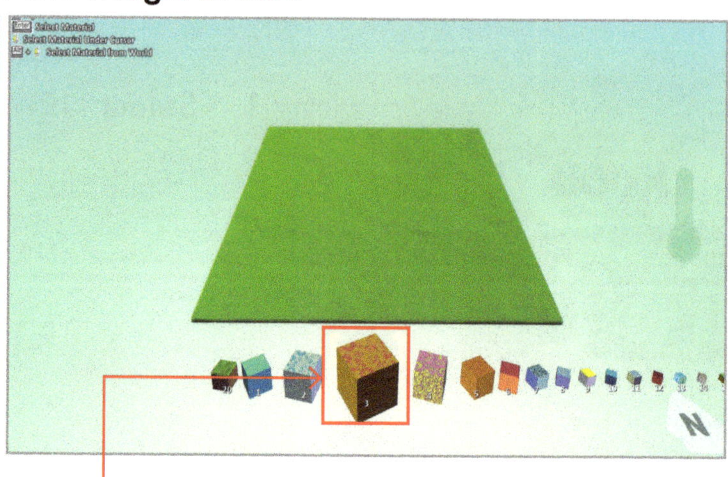

4. Click to select pattern for the terrain.

5. Change the pattern to paint the terrain.

Use the scroll wheel of the mouse to decrease the magnification.

Holding the Ctrl Key doesn't replace the existing terrain and draws a new terrain with the selected pattern. If Shift Key is pressed while dragging the mouse the existing terrain is replaced with the selected pattern and it won't add any new piece of terrain.

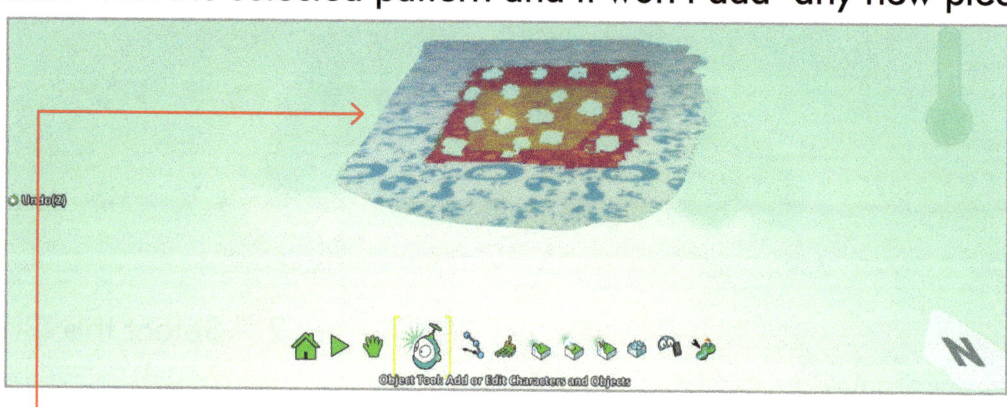

6. Hold the Ctrl Key from the keyboard while dragging the mouse and different layers of terrain around the first layer.

Once the terrain is drawn, decrease the size of brush with the help of an arrow keys.

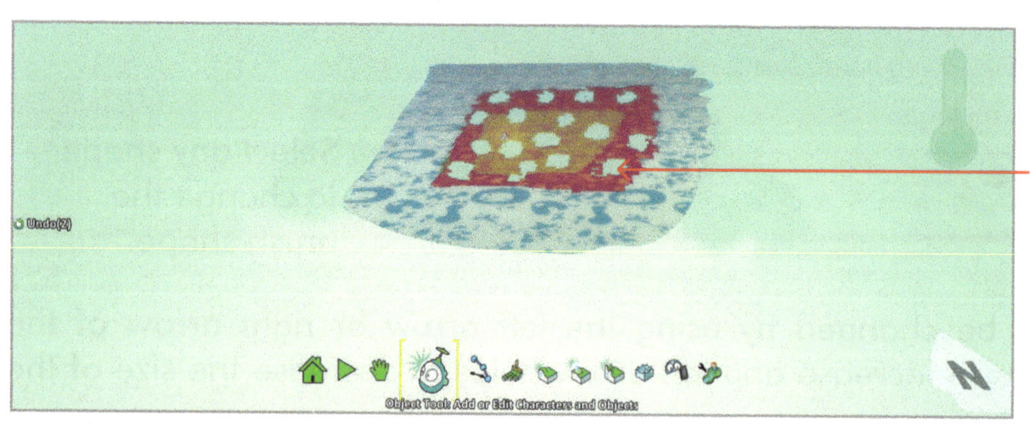

7. Right-click on the terrain to delete terrain and create the pot holes.

Now, we are done with the terrain. Let's add the player and start playing the game.

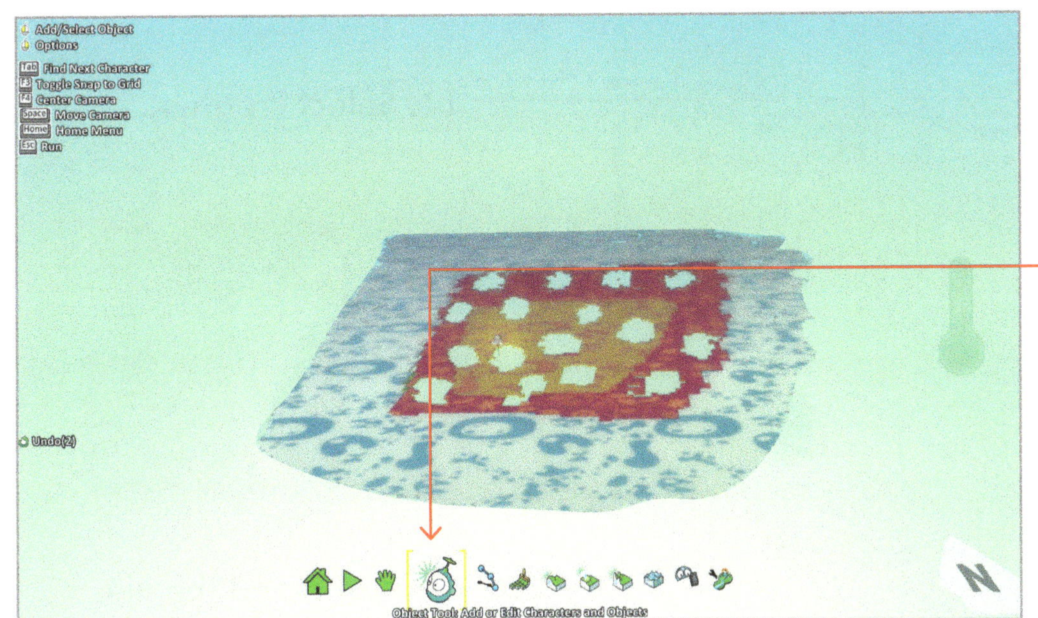

8. Select the Object Tool and add the player.

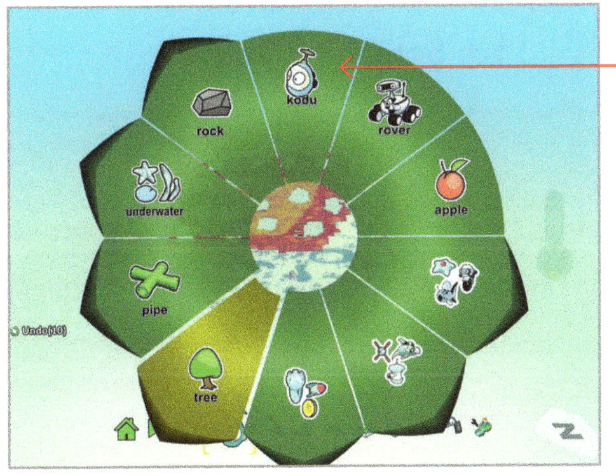

9. Select Kodu.

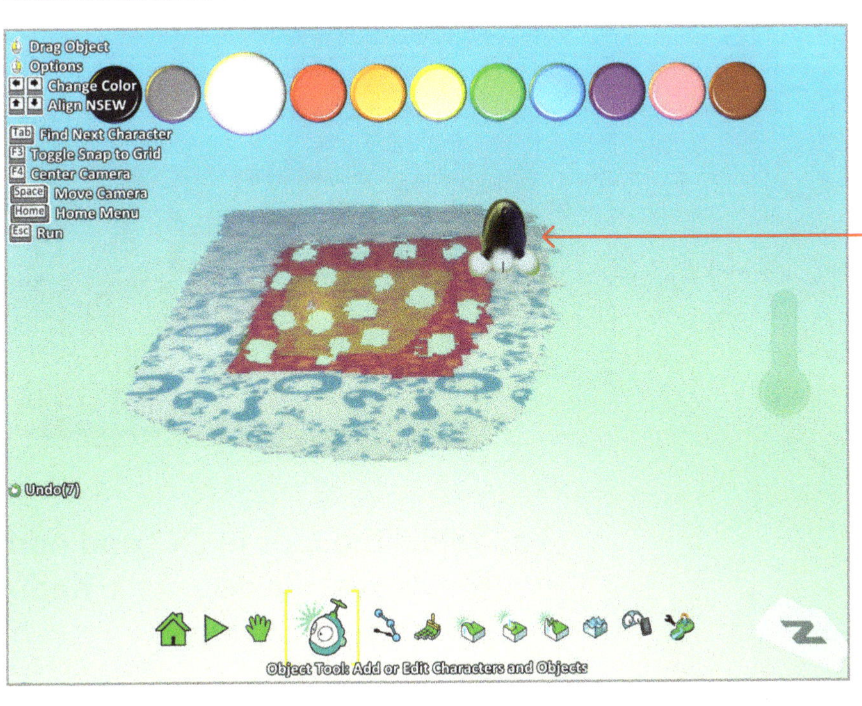

10. Right-click on Kodu to program it.

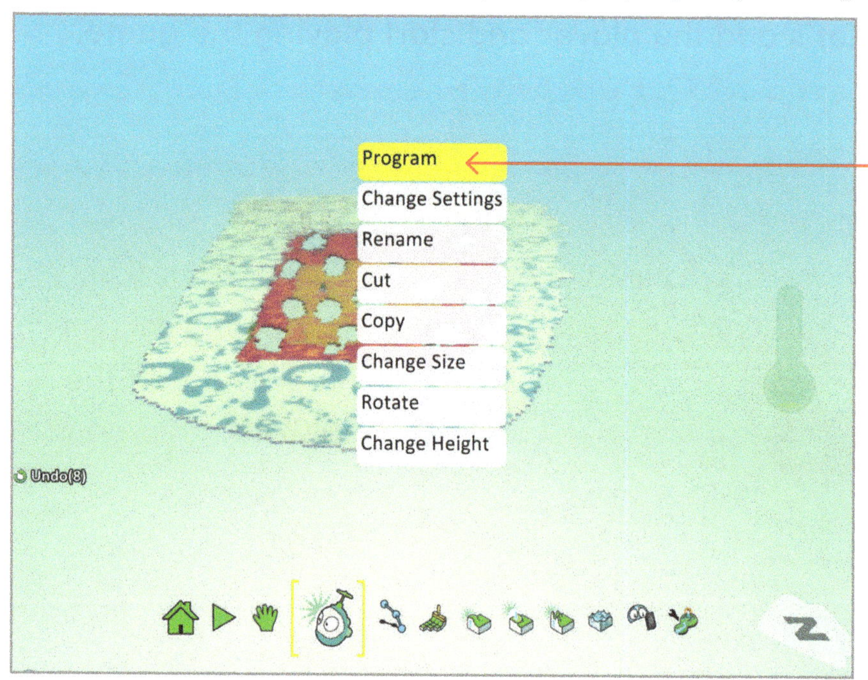

11. Select Program.

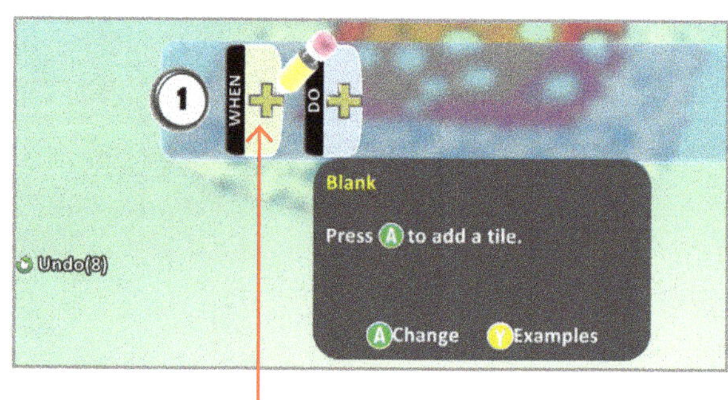

12. Click + and add the tile.

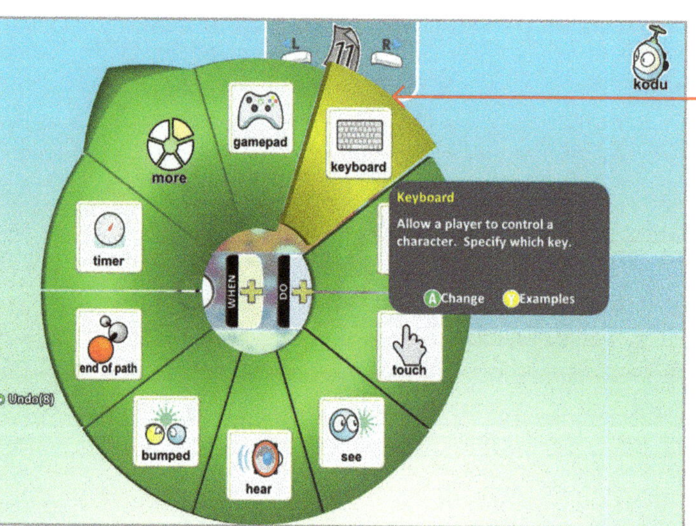

13. Select keyboard.

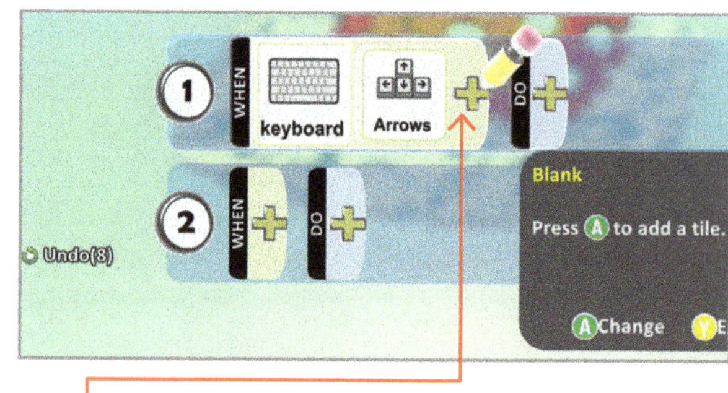

14. Click + and add the tile.

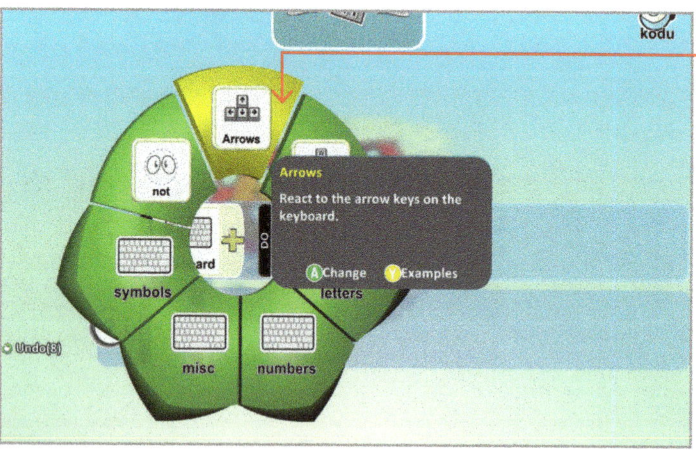

15. Select Arrows.

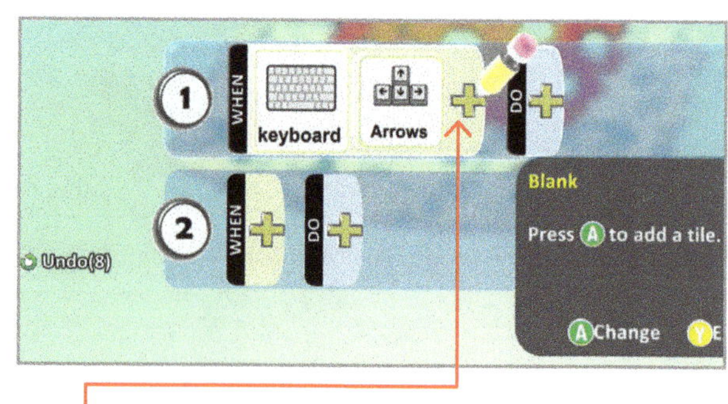

16. Select the tiles in DO and add the move tile to move Kodu with the arrow keys.

Remember

Always press the Esc key to come to the previous screen.

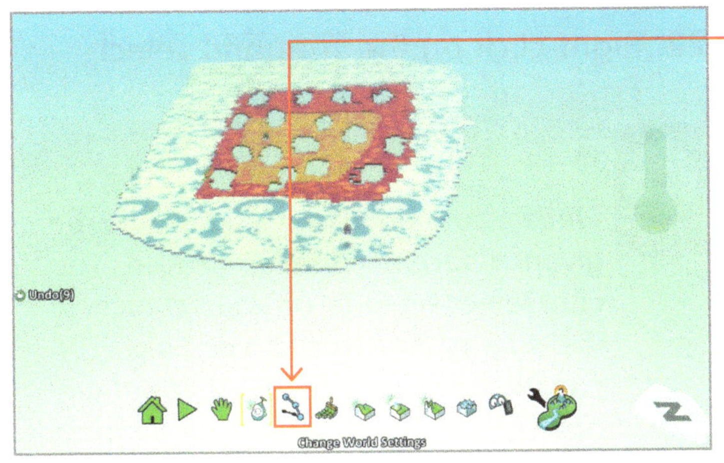

17. Click on Change World Settings.

With the above tiles Kodu would start moving if the arrow keys from the keyboard are pressed.

But Kodu will not fall if it steps into the pothole as there is a transparent glass wall around all the boundaries. We need to disable the glass wall.

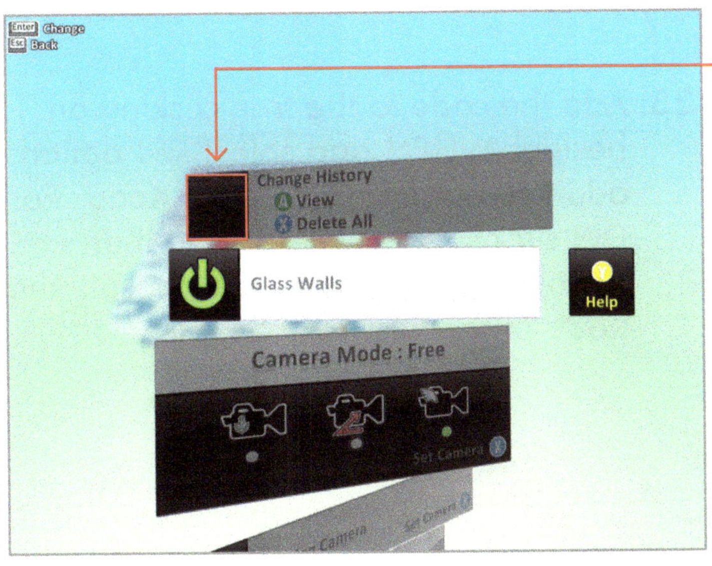

18. Click Glass Walls so that green colour may be removed.

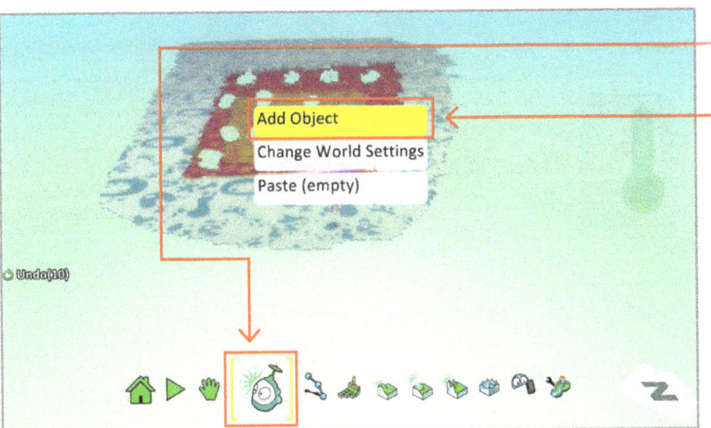

19. Click on Object Tools.

20. Right-click and select Add Object.

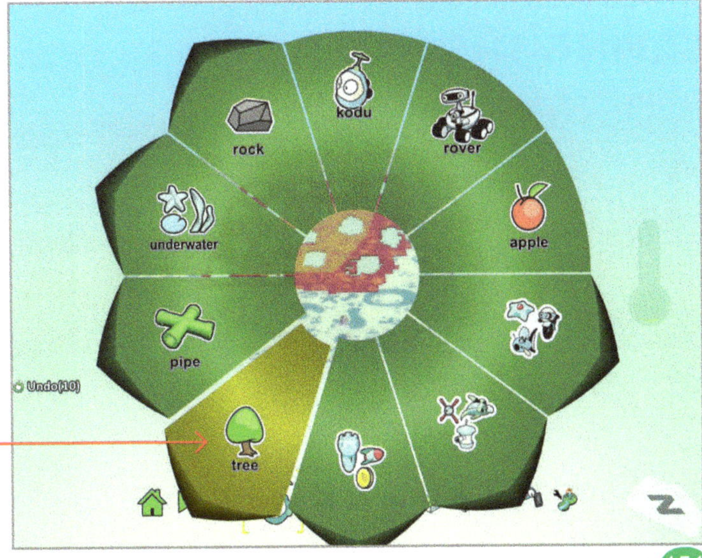

21. Select a Tree.

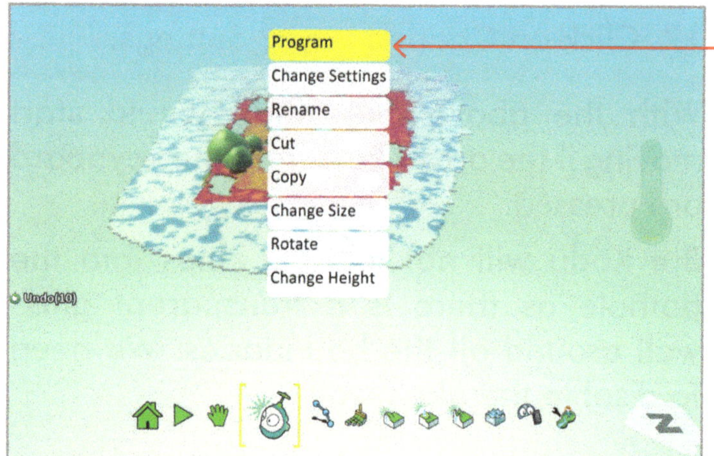

22. Right-click on the Tree and select Program.

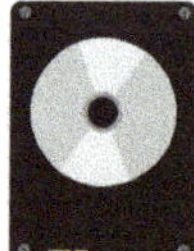

Remember

Once you select tree you would be given different varieties of tree, you can select anyone of your choice. If the size of the tree is very big, you can increase/decrease the size of any object by right-clicking on the object and selecting Change Size.

23. Add the code to the tree clicking on + besides WHEN and select see option, add not option, and select Kodu. For DO click + select game and then end option so that when tree doesn't see Kodu program ends.

24. Click on Play game and test the game.

When the Kodu falls into any of the Pot holes and tree is not able to see it, the program ends.

Remember

Press the Esc key to come to the previous screen.

SAVING THE GAME

1. Click on Home menu.

2. Select Save my world.

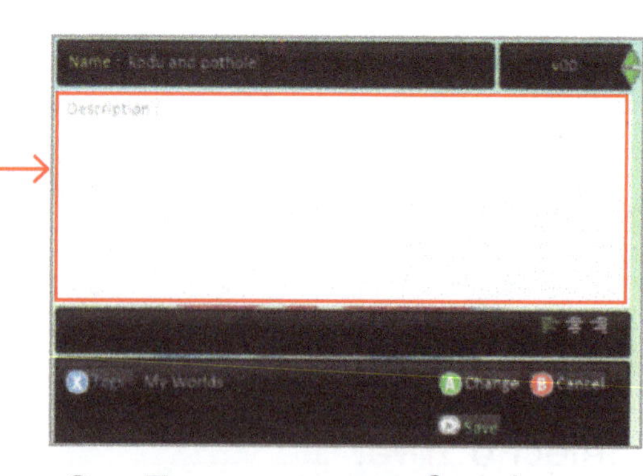

3. Type a name for the game and click save.